ARTFUL NOISE

MUSIC IN AMERICAN LIFE

A list of books in the series appears at the end of this book.

ARTFUL NOISE

PERCUSSION LITERATURE in the TWENTIETH CENTURY

THOMAS SIWE

UNIVERSITY OF ILLINOIS PRESS
Urbana, Chicago, and Springfield

3 4 5 6 7 C P 7 6 5 4 3
∞ This book is printed on acid-free paper.

Library of Congress Cataloging-in-Publication Data
Names: Siwe, Thomas, author.
Title: Artful noise: percussion literature in the twentieth century / Thomas Siwe.
Description: Urbana: University of Illinois Press, 2020. | Series: Music in American life | Includes bibliographical references and index. |
Identifiers: LCCN 2020005314 (print) | LCCN 2020005315 (ebook) | ISBN 9780252043130 (cloth) | ISBN 9780252085000 (paperback) | ISBN 9780252052019 (ebook)
Subjects: LCSH: Percussion ensembles—20th century—History and criticism. | Percussion music—20th century—History and criticism.
Classification: LCC ML1030 .S58 2020 (print) | LCC ML1030 (ebook) | DDC 786.809/04—dc23
LC record available at https://lccn.loc.gov/2020005314
LC ebook record available at https://lccn.loc.gov/2020005315

CONTENTS

PREFACE

It was the fall of 1953 and I had just begun my music studies at the University of Illinois, the state's flagship university located in Champaign-Urbana. It was my good fortune to be enrolled in a pioneering program of study led by Paul Price, a legendary percussion pedagogue. As the first of its kind and leading to a bachelor of music degree in performance, this program was designed expressly for the percussionist whose goal was to become a professional player. The basic curriculum was the same as that for other instrumentalists with the addition of a course entitled "Percussion Ensemble." All of the other instrumental groups (strings, brass, woodwinds) included a similar chamber ensemble requirement. For the percussionist, however, this was the first-ever accredited course dedicated to the performance of what was, at the time, a nascent body of musical works written solely for percussion instruments.

Price was a taskmaster and I, along with his other percussion students, put in many long hours of practice. Since the school had limited practice facilities, Price allowed students to use his office for this purpose during the evening hours. Late one night, I was practicing and took a break. Price kept a small wooden file box on his desk that contained a listing of original works written for percussion ensemble, including titles, publisher (if any), and instrumentation. There were roughly thirty cards in the file and I copied them in order to begin my own file of percussion works. Fifty years later, my file had grown to nearly fifteen thousand titles including both percussion solos and ensembles.

The amazing story of this unprecedented development of literature for a single family of musical instruments is detailed for the reader in this book. It begins early in the twentieth century, a period of stunning technological advances.

Following a career as a performer, I had the opportunity to return to my alma mater in 1969 to assume the directorship of the program that Paul Price had established in 1950. A new course had been added in my absence. "Percussion Literature" was an advanced offering that focused on works for both solo percussion and percussion ensemble and for which there was no textbook. My students met once a week to listen to tape recordings of important percussion pieces. Thanks to the music school's substantial library of scores and my own personal collection, the class was often able to listen to works while following a score. "Percussion Literature" was primarily for students who most likely upon graduation would direct their own percussion programs. Knowing the details of each work and the resources required and having the ability to analyze its structure with an understanding of the composer's intent would be paramount to those students' success.

Beginning with the 1920s, composers created unique and sometimes experimental works featuring percussion. In the ensuing decades, new genres emerged as composers discovered new ways to realize their musical art. As a teacher of percussion literature, I believed that it was important to present each work in its historical context and, if possible, to place it within these evolving genres. Possessing some knowledge of a composer's background and the culture that he or she referenced when creating a new work would be helpful when preparing for a performance. Consequently, I included sufficient biographical information about each composer without duplicating what the students would be presented with in their music history courses. Musical terms and foreign words used to describe percussion instruments and techniques were also part of the course's content.

The works presented in my percussion literature course excluded those written for pedagogical reasons, for example, technical etudes and exercises; novelty works; and arrangements of popular and classical music. I also excluded ethnic percussion ensembles such as the Indonesian gamelan and Korean Samul nori. The music that I focused on was first heard in the works of Igor Stravinsky, Béla Bartók, Darius Milhaud, and others who found new ways to orchestrate percussion within their symphonies, concertos, and chamber music. There was a thread that connected their innovations to the explosion of new works for percussion instruments that followed. As the twentieth century progressed, important compositional styles evolved: serialism, chance music, and works that bridged different art forms such as theater and dance. I felt that organizing my course within these new genres would help students to better understand the music they were studying.

The twentieth century realized the production of various musical styles that have subsequently been codified and accepted by music historians. The need to have this information compiled and synthesized in a readily accessible source became apparent over the course of my teaching career. This book examines percussion literature's evolution: how it came to be and the styles that composers embraced as they produced a large body of music for percussion instruments alone within this time period. I have selected percussion solo and ensemble works that I believe best exemplify each genre. A short list of other works that relate in some manner to those selected and examined has been added to the end of each chapter for the reader's consideration.

I hope that this history of percussion music, from its origins to the end of the twentieth century, will encourage percussionists to explore further the many works written during this time period in addition to the examples I use. I realize that for many only the most recent, au courant works are considered exciting and worthwhile programming for one's recital or concert. However, the percussion music created during the twentieth century includes many musical gems. Like your grandmother's jewelry, older percussion works may seem out of style, but are nonetheless valuable and are indeed critical to understanding the music of the present day.

ACKNOWLEDGMENTS

I want to extend my heartfelt thanks to the people who have helped make this book possible: Dr. Kathleen Kastner for her expert critique and constructive suggestions; Dr. Christopher Shultis for his invaluable advice and for finding and correcting numerous errors; Dr. Michael Siletti who went over the bibliography with meticulous precision; Marilyn Campbell whose suggestions and corrections helped finalize the text; Laurie Matheson, director, and her supportive staff at the University of Illinois Press; and Dr. Joan Fortschneider, my chief grammarian and wife, to whom this book is dedicated.

A special acknowledgment to the directors and staff members, past and present, of the University of Illinois Music and Performing Arts Library for years of steadfast support.

ARTFUL NOISE

INTRODUCTION

A substantial body of musical literature for solo and ensemble percussion was created in the twentieth century. By century's end, the database of the Percussive Arts Society listed over fourteen thousand works for solo percussion and percussion ensemble. Why were so many twentieth-century composers inspired to create works solely for percussion? This book will attempt to answer that question by selecting and carefully examining as many solo and ensemble works for percussion as possible. It will cover representative works by important composers who, over the century, helped create this new body of musical literature and it will demonstrate how events, both private and public, influenced their writings. The focus will be on the musical work itself, what resources it required, its construction, and how it relates to the styles that evolved during the time period in which it was created. Historical and biographical information will be added to help understand the composer's intent.

During the 1900s, many well-known composers produced significant works for percussion instruments alone. The collective volume of their creative efforts is enormous. Consequently, it was necessary to select both the artists and works that best exemplified the recognized musical styles and trends that appeared throughout the twentieth century, for example, serialism, indeterminacy, chance music, electronic music, mixed media, and others. I hope an examination by genre will help the reader to better understand the explosion of creativity that produced such a unique and remarkable repertoire for instruments of percussion, instruments that in the previous century were relegated to the back of the orchestra.

It seems that no single label can be attached to the art, architecture, or music created during the 1900s. In his book *The Rest Is Noise*, Alex Ross writes: "In the twentieth century, . . . musical life disintegrated into a teeming mass of cultures and subcultures, each with its own canon and jargon. Some genres have attained more popularity than others; none has true mass appeal."[1] Why didn't a new music style dominate the twentieth century? What made twentieth-century composers take such different artistic paths? Perhaps some of the answers can be found in the events that occurred at the beginning of the century.

"Between 1900 and 1922 rumblings in all the arts began to surface, but musical activity continued relatively undisturbed."[2] As the twentieth century began, the concert music most likely heard in both Europe and the Americas was of the Classical and Romantic genres. This music, along with French Impressionism, held sway with both concert organizers and listeners. In fact, a body of work by composers that included Haydn, Mozart, Beethoven, Ravel, and Debussy became a large part of what was called the "standard repertoire," repertoire that continued to dominate both orchestra and chamber music programming until the end of the century.

Still, there were "rumblings" in the musical arts, caused by a number of composers who rebelled against the past, questioning the very aesthetics of earlier musical styles. They began dissecting the parameters of music composition, examining the very foundations of musical construction. They were more interested in exploring new forms than in composing music of deep emotional content. For them, the new and different was their raison d'être; traditional compositional concepts and forms were passé. "After 1922 the musical world could no longer ignore or dismiss the artistic revolution that was unfolding."[3]

The decades before the First World War saw a number of European artists, poets, and musicians rebel against the traditional approaches to their art and against a middle-class audience, the bourgeoisie. Renowned turn-of-the-century composers such as Claude Debussy (1862–1918), Richard Strauss (1864–1949), and Richard Wagner (1813–1883) had pushed traditional harmony and rhythm to their limits with unresolved chords and elusive cadences. "Simultaneously with the dissolution of functional tonality in the late 19th and early 20th centuries came the dissolution of conventional rhythmic organization in the works of some composers."[4] These composers felt they had no new roads to explore. For them the fin-de-siècle era was dead by 1905, ending a period of Romantic extremism that had been the dominant musical style. A solution for some composers was to look back at an earlier period and to write in a neoclassical style. For others it was a time to try something new, to reexamine the various parameters of music and to experiment in ways that set them apart from their contemporaries. New works created by what some writers called "futurists" or "experimentalists" often confused and antagonized the listening public. The listeners felt deceived. The break with past tradition was too radical and the music did not fulfill their expectations. "At the end of World War I, a gap had opened between the concert hall and living composers who conceived of music as an exploration of the contemporary world. That gap did not close with the passing of time."[5]

Chapter 1

ORIGINS

Experiments within Tradition

It is difficult to find just one event, new composition, provocative painting, or cultural movement that directly led to the radical changes in the arts at the onset of the twentieth century. We can, however, look back at a cluster of historical events that still reverberate in today's world, ones that significantly influenced artists and composers during the first quarter of the twentieth century.

In 1916, a group of artists and poets banded together and declared their discontent with bourgeois society. They met at the Cabaret Voltaire in Zurich, Switzerland, where they adopted the nonsensical name "Dada" as their moniker. To bring attention to the group, the Dadaists, as they were called, issued a manifesto in 1920 stating that the group's intent was to reject the "established modes of artistic rendering"[1] and, with great fanfare, embraced "nothing" as a new standard for the arts. They proceeded to "take past and present and make fun of everything in it by parody, pastiche, ridicule, and desecration."[2] The Dadaist poet Tristan Tzara (1896–1963) invented "chance poems" in 1919. His approach was as follows: "A newspaper article is cut up into separate words. These are shaken in a bag, and then copied in the order in which they are removed from it."[3] (Later in the century, composer John Cage would use similar "chance methods" as an approach to composing.) It was in 1913 that the French artist and Dadaist Marcel Duchamp (1887–1968) mounted a bicycle wheel upside down on a stool. The following year he chose the first "readymade," a bottle-rack from a local hotel, exhibiting both bike and rack as "objets d'art." From 1915 to 1923, Duchamp worked on a unique multidimensional work titled *The Bride Stripped Bare by Her Bachelors, Even* (*The*

Large Glass). Of significance to percussionists were Duchamp's directions indicating that this particular work could be realized as a musical composition. "Duchamp states that the composition may be performed on a player piano, mechanical organ or any other new instruments for which the virtuoso intermediary is suppressed."[4] (Using chance operations, a multiple-percussion realization with instruments made from glass was performed by Donald Knaack on February 5, 1976, in Buffalo, New York.)

Another group of artists who, like the Dadaists, rejected the artistic standards of the time called themselves Futurists. Founded in 1909 by the Italian poet Fillippo Tommaso Marinetti (1876–1944), the Futurist movement embraced whatever was new, dangerous, and exciting, for example, automobiles, airplanes, film, and radio. Skillful propagandists, they staged provocative multimedia performances to provoke and challenge a complacent middle-class listening audience. Futurists often mounted performances that included simultaneous acts, events that incorporated incidental music, avant-garde poetry, and dance along with a display of Futurist paintings. The goal was to create controversy and bring attention to their cause. "To shock and outrage was much a part of the modernist movement in the visual arts"[5] and in music. These public events were a precursor of the so-called "happenings," multi-artistic events that became popular for a short period of time in the 1960s and 1970s.

One member of the Futurist group, Luigi Russolo (1885–1947), a painter turned musician, conceived and built several sound-producing instruments he called "*intonarumori*." These mechanical instruments were capable of producing a variety of sounds that Russolo categorized into six families, including one for percussion sounds. Unfortunately, the instruments did not survive the ravages of World War II. In photographs, we see instruments that appear to be large wooden cabinets with cylindrical horns mounted in front to aid sound projection. Without significant amplification, the instruments were reported to be difficult to hear. In one photo, a rear view shows a mounted cymbal inside the cabinet. In other photos, the players are pictured standing behind each machine with their hands on levers that purportedly controlled pitch and volume. Orchestra music written by Russolo, Francesco Balilla Pratella (1880–1955), and other Futurist composers incorporated the intonarumori into their scores using graphic notation (mainly lines of various heights, thicknesses, and lengths) to indicate pitch, volume, and duration. Starting in 1914, Futurist concerts were given in halls throughout Europe; these events aroused the interest of the musical establishment. "Russolo's concerts in the early 1920s still caused fierce controversy, but impressed several outstanding composers, including Maurice Ravel, Arthur Honegger, Darius Milhaud, and the prophet of future Avant-gardes, Varèse."[6]

Image I.I. Luigi Russolo and Ugo Piatti in their workshop in Milan. Photograph from Luigi Russolo, *L'arte dei rumori* (Milan: Edizioni futuriste di "Poesia," 1916).

Even before the Dadaists and Futurists, one composer caught the attention of fellow composers as well as the public with his provocative compositions for the dance. The Russian-born composer Igor Stravinsky's (1882–1971) three works for ballet, *L'Oiseau de feu* (*The Firebird,* 1910), *Pètrouchka* (1911), and *Le Sacre du printemps* (*The Rite of Spring,* 1912) gained international acclaim with the last work causing the audience to riot at its Paris premiere. Its notoriety did not escape the attention of composers. "The reception of Stravinsky's *Rite of Spring* in Paris had given not only new cachet to such reaction in the musical world but also a model to emulate."[7] To the public, the work seemed violent. It rejected traditional tonal structure, relying instead on shifting rhythmic and metrical patterns to provide forward motion. Heavily percussive, it marked a pivotal point in twentieth-century music. Aaron Copland writes, "The key work of this period is, by common consent, Stravinsky's ballet of pagan Russia, *The Rites* [*sic*] *of Spring,* composed for Sergei Diaghilev's Ballet Russes in 1913. This is not the composer's most perfect work, but it is certainly his most strikingly original composition."[8]

Born in Russia, near St. Petersburg, Stravinsky became interested in music at an early age (his father was a singer). Though he studied law, his passion for music eventually led him to a career as a composer. At the University of Heidelberg, he became friends with the son of the noted Russian composer

Nikolai Rimsky-Korsakov (1844–1908) and became a regular guest of the family household. Stravinsky "began taking regular lessons in orchestration"[9] from Rimsky-Korsakov who tutored him free of charge. He considered Rimsky-Korsakov both teacher and mentor and the influence of the composer of *Scheherazade* is evident in Stravinsky's skillful orchestrations, including his writing for percussion. "A signal change in Stravinsky's fortunes came when the famous impresario Diaghilev commissioned him to write a work for the Paris season of his dance company, the Ballets Russes."[10] The result was the production of Stravinsky's first ballet, titled *The Firebird*. His association with Diaghilev, though strained at times, continued until the ballet master's death in 1929.

Though Stravinsky's percussion scoring in *Le Sacre du printemps* included some innovative features, it continued to use timpani and other percussion instruments in the fashion of the time, namely to outline the beat (albeit with a great deal of force), to add color to a passage (tambourine and antique cymbals), and to provide punctuation to musical phrases (bass drum and timpani). With its fast tempi, mixed meters, sudden tempo changes, loud dissonant chords, and polytonal passages, *Sacre* challenged both player and listener.

The instrumentation for *Le Sacre du printemps* requires an unusually large wind and brass section including four oboes, four bassoons, and eight horns. The percussion section calls for six players, plus two timpanists. Five kettledrums, including a piccolo timpano for a high B-natural, are required. Instructions in the score direct the second timpanist to assist in tuning the drums so that the principal player can "follow the beat." Today, many professional timpanists have designed individual approaches to the part, enabling a single player to cover most of what Stravinsky wrote. Musically this is helpful since a number of dramatic gestures over four drums are best played in a soloistic manner. The timpani part also indicates that the drums are to be played with snare drumsticks (wooden sticks) in specified passages. (Fig. 1.3)

The section-percussion parts cover the following: triangle, guiro, tam-tam, bass drum, tambourine, and cymbals antique (*crotales*). Though orchestrated primarily in the traditional manner, Stravinsky does explore some unusual approaches for this group of instruments. At one point he notates the triangle to be played fortissimo, striking it with a wooden stick. (Fig. 1.1) For the guiro he carefully notates the stroke direction, specifying both up and down strokes (Fig. 1.2) and for the tam-tam, which in most works of the times was used sparingly, if at all, Stravinsky creates long ostinato patterns. Performing the tam-tam part requires great sensitivity and control so as to allow the steady rhythmic line to be heard on the beat, not before or after it. A startling effect is created when the tam-tam is forcefully scraped with a metal triangle beater along its edge. (Fig. 1.3) The bass drum is to be played with a normal beater and with snare drumsticks when indicated. At one point in the "Danse de la terre" ("Dance of the Earth"), the bass drum articulates a three-against-four rhythmic scheme in conjunction with the timpani. Rapid crescendi and sharp accents make the part demanding. (Fig. 1.4) Stravinsky scores the tambourine in traditional manner, uniting it with the English horn to evoke the exotic East in the section titled "Action Rituelle des Ancêtres" ("Procession of the Wise Elders"). Cymbals antique, played forte, add to the cacophony in the "Dance of the Adolescents." (Fig. 1.1)

To summarize, when scoring *Le Sacre du printemps,* Stravinsky used timpani, bass drum, and tam-tam to enhance the powerful rhythmic drive of this famous composition. He also demonstrated his ear for new and unusual color effects such as the tam-tam glissando and the use of wood on the triangle. Overall, Stravinsky's use of percussion in his three ballets was a small, but noteworthy, step in the evolution of scoring the orchestra's battery section. Of the utmost importance was Stravinsky's contribution to helping make the percussionist an equal partner with other instrumentalists, as demonstrated in his dramatic chamber work *Histoire du soldat* (*A Soldier's Tale*).

In 1917, historical events in Russia dramatically changed Stravinsky's life. In that year, revolutions occurred that toppled the autocratic rule of the Russian tsar and brought the Bolsheviks into power, causing Stravinsky to exile himself and his family to Switzerland. Cut off from his source of income, including the royalties from his ballets and other music, he joined with two Swiss friends, the author C. F. Ramuz (1878–1947) and the conductor Ernest Ansermet (1883–1969) to design a work that needed only minimum forces, one that would be able to travel from town to town and not require a large theater or incur huge production costs. With the financial help of the Swiss industrialist Werner Reinhart, Stravinsky wrote *Histoire du soldat* for chamber septet and three actors. The title page indicates that the work is to be read, played, and danced (*lue, jouée et dansée*). With a text by Ramuz, *Histoire* tells the classic Faustian tale of good versus evil. A soldier, on leave from the war, meets the Devil, who trades a book that foretells the future for the soldier's old violin (his soul). The soldier becomes rich, but soon realizes that wealth does not bring happiness. His efforts to buy back his violin fail and the story ends with the "Triumphal March of the Devil," represented musically by the drums.

Histoire du soldat is scored for violin, double bass, clarinet, bassoon, cornet, trombone, and an array of percussion instruments "to be played by one player."[11] In preparing the percussion part, Stravinsky purchased a number of drums and cymbals and worked out both the setup of the instruments as well as the sticking (indicated in the score by stems up and down). A bass drum, four drums, a cymbal (attached upside down to the bass drum), a triangle, and a tambourine together create a small multiple-percussion setup. A picture of Stravinsky in his studio with some of his percussion equipment can be found in James Blades's *Percussion Instruments and Their History*. Stravinsky also indicated that certain notes were to be played with a specific mallet or stick. With all this attention to detail, one would assume that the percussion part would be easily read and there would be no question as to what, when, and how to execute the notes. Unfortunately, the various printings of the manuscript contain numerous notational errors, especially in the drum part. The translation into various languages of the instrument nomenclature, the mallet and stick selection, and the composer's directions make for a great deal of uncertainty as one prepares to play the part.

A number of prominent percussionists have made efforts to correct the errors and to ascertain, with varying degrees of success, how best to interpret the part. Famed composer/percussionist William Kraft (b. 1923) approached Stravinsky during a 1961 recording session of *Histoire*. He asked why the field drum (the deepest-sounding snare drum) was notated on the top line of the staff. Stravinsky's reply was "Because it is on the right."[12] The result of Kraft's discussion with the composer revealed that the disposition of the drums was not an ascending or descending scale; it was "not bass-tenor-alto-soprano, but bass-soprano-alto-tenor."[13] To contemporize the percussion notation, Kraft renotated the part in 1963 to reflect his findings. Kraft writes: "It is of the utmost importance to know that Stravinsky worked out the percussion part . . . by acquiring the instruments and playing them himself."[14]

In "A Journey to the Source," Morris Lang, a former New York Philharmonic percussionist, examined a number of questions regarding other discrepancies found in the *Histoire*'s percussion part. Lang visited Winterthur, Switzerland, and, with the permission of the Reinhart family, was able to examine the original manuscript housed there. His findings answered a number of questions. Lang confirmed the layout of the drums in relation to their positions as notated on the staff lines. He also lamented the many inconsistencies found in the printed parts and noted that the alternating stems only indicated alternate sticking. Stravinsky notated the drum part to reflect his own hands-on experimentation. A diagram in the score drawn by the composer shows the bass drum positioned on the player's left with the snare and field drums to the right. Many players assumed that all the drums should be placed from the lowest to the highest (left to right) and that the notation reflected this arrangement, that is, low drum on the lowest staff line, high drum on the top line. As it turned out, we now know that this was not the case. In 1987, the publisher Chester Music released a new edition of *Histoire*, with a completely renotated percussion part edited by the percussionist/historian James Blades (1901–1999). In addition to correcting printing errors, this version arranged the drums sequentially from low to high, reflecting common practice by century's end.

The incidental music that Stravinsky wrote for *Histoire* is often played as an instrumental suite, one that includes marches, chorales, and three short dances—"Tango," "Waltz," and "Ragtime." The suite begins with "The Soldier's March." The narrator sets the scene: a soldier is on his journey home for a ten-day leave traveling "down a hot and dusty road." Stravinsky writes a solo vamp for field drum and bass drum (Fig. 1.5) to accompany the narration, which is cut short if the work is played as a suite without stage action. Later in the "March," Stravinsky adds a tambourine (today easily mounted and struck with stick) to the bass and field drums, creating a jaunty figure of three beats against the string bass's constant two. (Fig. 1.6) "As always in Stravinsky, the level of rhythmic complexity is quite high."[15] The "Royal March" follows, adding a snare drum to the mix of drums. Here Stravinsky notates edge and center of the bass drum, creating a high-to-low sound in imitation of the string bass. (Fig. 1.7) Also, he notates a six-stroke roll. "Yes, it is six strokes—to be played on the large drum with the snares on."[16] (Fig. 1.8) In the first of the three dances, "Tango," he calls for bass drum, snare drum (sans snares), and suspended cymbal to accompany a haunting melody played by the violin. (The non-snared drum is the middle pitch of the three drums.) Traditionally, the cymbal is attached to the bass drum. Some percussionists use a separate suspended cymbal here rather than the mounted one to maximize the instrument's resonance. Stravinsky does not indicate exact durations for the cymbal, using instead the usual idiomatic cymbal notation. (Fig. 1.9) For the "Ragtime" movement, Stravinsky calls for non-snared drum, tambourine, and triangle. The opening bars written for drum, tambourine, and triangle must have presented logistical problems in early performances of the work. Today, percussionists can use commercial mounting devices so that both triangle and tambourine are easily played with beaters appropriate to each instrument. (Fig. 1.10) Later in the movement, Stravinsky precisely notates dynamics for the large and small snare drums. (Fig. 1.11) The most difficult and most soloistic writing is found in the final "Marche Triomphale du Diable" ("Triumphal March of the Devil"). Here the composer utilizes all the drums plus a cymbal. As the "Marche" progresses, the nonpercussion instruments drop out except for the violin, which soon ends, and a final fourteen-bar multidrum solo brings down the curtain. (Fig. 1.12) Prior to this final passage, Stravinsky's last dynamic indication for the drums is piano, but the effect is that of a crescendo as the sound of the drums takes center stage and the writing becomes more complicated with the addition of sixteenth-note triplets.

For most of the twentieth century, Stravinsky was the dominant new music figure in the western world. "As the outstanding composer of Diaghilev's ballets, Stravinsky became a world figure."[17] Throughout his career, he continually sought new ways of expressing himself through music. After immigrating to the United States, he began to lecture and write about music. His work *Histoire du soldat* "had a decisive influence on younger composers in France, America, and Germany."[18] For the percussionist, Stravinsky's contributions were significant: his early ballets brought attention to the orchestra's percussion section; his chamber work *Histoire* demanded a high level of skill. In it, he created a percussion part that asked the player to perform with both skill and musicianship on an array of instruments. Unusual for the time, the work was important to the evolution of today's literature for solo percussion. Béla Bartók, another composer of this generation, contributed to this process as well.

In 1917, Béla Bartók (1881–1945) began composing the music for *The Miraculous Mandarin*, a pantomime-ballet with narrator. The story, by the Hungarian author and screenwriter Melchior Lengyel (1880–1974), tells the tale of a young girl enlisted by a gang of hoodlums to entice unsuspecting men into their lair so as to assault and rob them. One of the intended victims is a wealthy Chinese mandarin (an elite official) who repeatedly frustrates the attackers' efforts. At one point in the ballet, the would-be robbers try to hang the mandarin, accompanied by glissandi celli, piano, and timpani. The prurient nature of the libretto provoked official censorship and delayed the work's premiere until nine years after its completion. It finally premiered on November 27, 1926, in Cologne. Bartók used the delay to revise both music and text. Even then, the performance caused a scandal and the work was subsequently banned: "the *Mandarin* proved too heady a wine for the censors."[19]

The scoring for timpani and percussion is not unusual for the era in which it was written. For the timpanist, four drums are required. When scoring for timpani, Bartók keeps the timpani writing within the range of an octave so that the player can use two sets of middle-range drums to comprise a set of four. At this point in time, many orchestras owned only two pedal drums (machine timpani) and a few hand-tuned kettles. In this work, machine-action timpani are imperative. The extended glissando timpani passages create an ominous sound in support of the stage action. (Fig. 1.13) Bartók continued to explore this technique in his 1936 work, *Music for Strings, Percussion, and Celesta* and in his *Sonata for Two Pianos and Percussion*.

The Miraculous Mandarin percussion section requires four players. It calls for a suspended cymbal to be played with both the thin and heavy ends of a drumstick, marked *col legno* (*c.l.*), and a pair of cymbals played two ways, crashed (*ordinaire*) and rubbed (*frottè*). Also needed are high and low drums (with and without snares), triangle, xylophone, tam-tam, and a bass drum to be played with both the usual mallet and a wooden drumstick. In this early work, Bartók began to explore the possibility of creating subtle timbre and pitch variables from standard orchestral percussion instruments, what we now call "extended techniques." Specific directions on how to play the crash cymbals, and what end of the stick the player must use to strike the suspended cymbal, timpani glissandi, and others all demonstrate this sensitivity. Bartók continued to expand this repertoire of extended techniques for percussion in the first of his three piano concertos.

Bartók completed his first piano concerto in 1926. It was premiered in Frankfurt the following year. Instructions in the score designate the percussion instruments (including timpani) to be placed, if possible, directly behind the piano. The reason becomes evident in the work's second movement, which requires an intricate interplay between piano soloist and percussionists. (Fig. 1.14) *Piano Concerto No. 1* requires timpani and three percussionists. In notating the percussion part, Bartók created a unique numerical system that described how, where, and with what to strike each instrument. The following translation is taken from the Boosey & Hawkes's score.

> The percussion is for 3 performers (tympany not included). Where two parts are joined by "{" the two instruments concerned must be played by one performer. The effect and manner of playing are by figures as follows:
>
> 1. In the centre (of the drumhead) with tympany sticks;
> 2. In the centre (of the drumhead) with the point of the side-drum sticks;
> 3. Round the rim (of the drumhead or the hanging cymbal) with the point of the side-drum sticks;
> 4. Round the rim (of the hanging cymbal) with the tympany sticks;
> 5. Round the rim (of the hanging cymbal) with the handle of the side-drum sticks;
> 6. In the (raised) centre of the hanging cymbal with the handle of the side-drum sticks;
> 7. On the rim (of the hanging cymbal) with the handle of one of the side-drum sticks while the other is fastened to the leather hanger of the cymbal so that the point of the stick touches the cymbal;
> 8. /\ With 2 side-drum sticks, beginning quite at the rim (of the side-drum) gradually getting over to the centre of the drum head and then back again to the rim;
> 9. Quite at the rim (of the cymbal) with two tympany sticks.

This elaborate set of instructions demonstrates, again, the care Bartók took when orchestrating for percussion. He carefully notates the subtle differences in timbre between edge and center, hard and soft sticks, on both drums and suspended cymbal. He employs a wide range of dynamics with an ear to balancing these timbral nuances; every note is carefully marked. On the instruction list, number 7 directs the player to fasten a snare drumstick above the suspended cymbal in such a manner as to create a "sizzle" cymbal effect. Instruction number 8 requires the player to start a roll at the very edge of the drumhead, then move to the center and back again to the edge, creating a natural crescendo-diminuendo along with a subtle change in color. Bartók continued to use some of these extended techniques in his future works, but discontinued the complicated numerical notation system.

For percussionists, Bartók's most important contribution to the evolution of their literature has to be the *Sonata for Two Pianos and Percussion*. "Its almost unprecedented dynamism establishes the *Sonata* as one of Bartók's most significant works."[20] Commissioned by the Basel section of the International Society for Contemporary Music (ISCM), its first performance took place in Basel, Switzerland, on the 16th of January 1938. Bartók and his wife, pianist Ditta Pásztory, were joined by percussionists Fritz Schiesser and Philipp Rühlig in what has been described as a successful first performance.

The published score includes a setup plan for staging the work. If the pianos are configured as shown, the plan works with a few exceptions; the pair of cymbals needs to be nearer to Player I and the triangles and suspended cymbals can be located more conveniently. Player I is responsible for the timpani part, which calls for three drums. Again, Bartók keeps the range of the kettles within an octave (F—f) with a few high F-sharps. (Some timpanists like to add a fourth drum to help with the frequent tuning changes.) In addition to the timpani, Player I is also responsible for several passages on the other percussion instruments with the exception of the bass drum and the xylophone. These two instruments are exclusive to Player II's part. Other percussion instruments required include: two side drums (with and without snares), a tam-tam, two suspended cymbals, and two triangles. Nothing exotic, the instrumentation was standard equipment for orchestras of the time. A note in the score mentions that a third player "may be employed for the Xylophone" if needed. The keyboard percussion skills of many of the drummers at that time were limited and this may be the reason for the note, but "experience has proved that two skilled players are sufficient,"[21] then and now.

There are a number of extended techniques found in the *Sonata*'s percussion parts as Bartók continues to investigate timbre variations that can be heard by striking the surface areas of the percussion instruments in various locations and by using a variety of mallets and sticks. For example, the score calls for the suspended cymbal to be played on the extreme edge with a wooden stick, with a heavy wooden stick on the dome, with soft mallets, and "with the fingernail, or the blade of a pocket knife on the very edge." Notations in the triangle part indicate the use of a wooden stick, marked *col legno* (*c.l.*), as well as the normal metal triangle beater and, in one passage, "a heavy metal beater (short and rather thick)." In addition, there are extended passages for the two snare drums that explore the edge and center head sounds of both, primarily at the very softest intensity level. The printed percussion parts are well crafted with the nonpitched percussion printed on single lines. Notes written below the line are to be played at the edge of the drumhead; notes on the line are played in the center of the instrument. This notational approach is superior to the numerical one used in the piano concerto.

The *Sonata* begins with a pianissimo timpano roll on a low F sharp leading to an ominous seven-note figure played in octaves by Piano I. "The opening bar gives the impression of descent, as it were, into a (deep) well."[22] From the opening assai lento in 9/8 time with its F sharp tonal center, Bartok slowly builds both intensity and forward motion that is interrupted twice by sudden and startling *sforzandi* played by Piano I in unison with the suspended cymbal, to be struck on the dome. At the allegro molto that follows, a solo bar of timpani (F sharp and C) announces the main theme with its tonal center of C. Though the primary meter is 9/8, the main theme is, in reality, a bar of 4/4. The tension caused by this juxtaposition of duple and triple rhythms is unsettling. Bartók continues to use this ploy as the pianos and timpani carry on in triple time with the two side drums and xylophone playing rhythmic phrases that echo the main theme.

The first movement of the *Sonata* is considerable in length, almost the same duration as movements II and III combined. As the pianos develop the main and secondary themes of the first movement, the timpani and percussion play an integral part providing metrical and dramatic emphases. Bartók uses both for color and thematic imitation with occasional short solo riffs. "The battery in this movement is chiefly one of emphasis, of underlining, only rarely is attention focused upon it."[23] Bartók starts many phrases with a single percussive "crack" with the pianos quickly responding. A long fugal section begins at the Vivo section with a phrase more rhythmic than melodic. It reaches its climax at the Vivacissimo when both pianos and side drums lock into the triple meter in stretto-like fashion. From here to the end, Bartók drives the music forward aided by the timpani, whose diminished fifth emphasizes the movement's two main tonal centers. Finally, all is resolved on the very last C major chord. With its rapid interplay between the four players and its many tempo changes, the *Sonata*'s first movement proves to be both one of the most demanding and truly satisfying chamber music experiences.

If the first movement of the *Sonata* lacks extended passages of thematic importance for the battery, the final two movements provide ample material for the percussionists to "assume a soloistic function."[24] The second movement begins with four bars of solo percussion played by two side drums, one with snares marked *con corda* (*c.c.*) and one without marked *senza corda* (*s.c.*), accompanied by the suspended cymbal. (Fig. 1.15) The tempo is slow (Lento, ma non troppo); the dynamic level very soft. The feeling Bartók creates in this passage is somber; the pace slow, dirge-like. Piano I joins this soft percussive texture with a chromatic, chantlike melody imitated by Piano II at bar 9. The movement builds to a climax at bar 19 and slowly returns to the original dynamic levels ending in bar 27. This opening section requires great skill and sensitivity by all players, especially Percussion II. The pianississimo roll in the first bar for snare drum demands the ultimate in technical control, similar to that at the beginning of Maurice Ravel's *Bolero*. As the movement progresses, the texture becomes more atmospheric with resonant chromatic runs and glissandi passages by Piano I ending in a dramatic fashion with four staccato dissonant piano chords and a five-note xylophone solo.

In contrast to both the first and second movements, the *Sonata*'s final movement is joyful and dancelike and, surprisingly, in the key of C major. A fast 2/4 tempo marked allegro non troppo begins with rapid tremolos by both pianos introducing the xylophone that states the main theme. (Fig. 1.16) For the timpanist and percussionist, this movement requires quickness and agility as Bartók writes continuous pitch changes for the kettledrums and Percussion II scurries from instrument to instrument. The two main themes of this movement's development section involve all four players with melodic snippets passed rapidly from instrument to instrument. The movement ending is an extended coda with resonant piano sounds fading out over a snare drum ostinato.

For the historian Halsey Stevens, "the *Sonata* remains a unique work, not only in Bartók's catalogue, but in the entire field of music. The outraged cries it once aroused have long since subsided, and it has been admitted to the small group of genuine masterpieces produced in this [the twentieth] century."[25] Bartók had difficulty finding success in the United States after emigrating from his native Hungary before the start of World War II. He died of leukemia in New York City on September 26, 1945. By 1949, he finally began to receive the notice he deserved—"his works were more performed by American orchestras than those of any twentieth-century composer except [Richard] Strauss and [Sergei] Prokofiev."[26]

Whereas Stravinsky emphasized the dramatic, bombastic qualities of percussion sounds and Bartok probed their subtle nuances, Darius Milhaud (1892–1974) explored the sounds of American jazz and the instruments and techniques used by early drum-set players. He is credited with "being amongst the first to incorporate elements of true jazz into 'high-art' music."[27] Born in Aix-en Provence, France, Milhaud revealed his musical talents at an early age. As a child, he improvised on the family piano and in 1909, with the encouragement and support of his family, entered the Paris Conservatory at age seventeen where he studied violin, piano, and composition. As a student, Milhaud demonstrated his talent for writing, composing numerous pieces in a modernistic mode for a variety of instrumental and vocal combinations. He was a member of the French Les Six, which was more a group of composer friends than a school of composition. Milhaud was an eclectic composer who found musical inspiration in almost every sound he heard as well as in the prose and poetry of his day. During the First World War, he was stationed in Rio de Janeiro, Brazil, as a secretary to the French dramatist and diplomat Paul Claudel (1868–1955). In a 1914 collaboration with Claudel, he wrote music for a proposed ballet, the orchestration of which included a large percussion section requiring twenty instruments, including wood and metal castanets, whistles, mouth siren, and a wind machine. Notably, the scoring avoids ethnic Brazilian percussion instruments. In one section of the work, the percussion instruments play alone for thirty-three measures (plus an added vamp) to accommodate dance and stage movements. The work, titled *L'Homme et son désir* (Man and His Desire) was premiered June 26, 1921. Milhaud commented: "I was anxious about the passages for unaccompanied percussion, but they did not provoke any hostile demonstration."[28]

Following the Great War, Europeans became fascinated with the jazz music of African Americans. "Primitivism, as exemplifying a Western perception of cultural 'otherness,' is a most important artistic concept of this period, with clear application to Milhaud's *La Création du monde*."[29] Milhaud writes of a 1920s trip to Great Britain where he saw and heard Billy Arnold's band at the Hammersmith Palace. "It was during this visit to London that I first began to take an interest in jazz,"[30] he writes. During trips to New York City in 1918 and 1922, Milhaud visited the nightclubs of Harlem where, by all accounts, he fell in love with the sounds and rhythms heard there. As a result of these experiences, Milhaud wrote, "More than ever I was resolved to use jazz for a chamber work."[31]

In 1923, Milhaud completed *La Création du monde* (The Creation of the World), a ballet in six parts for chamber orchestra and dance: he arranged a more popular version, *Suite de concert,* in 1926. "The scenario for *La Création* focuses on the African myths of creation."[32] The chamber orchestra for the *Suite* requires a woodwind quintet (doubling flutes and clarinets), two trumpets, trombone, piano, timpani, two violins soli, cello, and bass. Most important to this mix was the addition of the quintessential jazz instruments, the saxophone (E flat) and a drum set. The drum set included bass drum with pedal and attached cymbal (*grosse caisse à pied avec cymb.*); a snare drum (*caisse claire*); two other drums (*caisse roulante* and *tambourin*), which serve as middle and low tom-toms; and a suspended cymbal. The usual wood block (*bloc de bois*) and cowbell (*bloc de métal*) are required as well as a tambourine that is both struck with the fist (*le poing*) and rolled using a thumb-roll technique (*le pouce*). Performance directions regarding the cymbal attached to the bass drum merit explanation. The score calls for "gross caisse à pèdale avec cymbale décrochable." "Milhaud is referring to a special apparatus, popular in early jazz, that consisted of a small metal arm which was attached to the stem of the foot pedal."[33] A small metal ball was fixed on the end of the flexible metal arm that would strike the inside surface of a cymbal attached to the bass drum. When only the sound of the bass drum was desired, the drummer could reach down and move the arm (*décrochez la cymb.*) so as not to hit the cymbal. This device was later superseded by the low-boy cymbal mechanism and eventually the high-hat. There is no improvisation for the percussionist; the drum part is fully notated (Fig. 1.17) and very challenging in spots.

Between 1929 and 1930, Milhaud composed a concerto for solo percussionist and chamber orchestra. *The Concerto pour batterie et petit orchestre* (Concerto for Percussion and Small Orchestra, opus 109), "was commissioned and first performed by Theo Coutelier at the Palais des Beaux Arts in Brussels in 1930 as part of the Pro Arte Orchestra concert series with the composer conducting."[34] Versions with piano or band accompaniment exist, as well as a version that seems to imply the use of two players. The *Concerto* displays little of the jazz influence found in his 1923 work, *Création.* In this work, "Milhaud sought to distinguish areas of sound using 'polytonality' and spatial representation."[35] He wanted a "rugged (*rude*) and dramatic" interpretation, not a "jazzy one" and forbade the addition of a cadenza. The percussion part requires a drum kit with added toys, comparable to the one used in the *Création,* plus four kettledrums. This large array of instruments could easily keep an orchestra's percussion section busy. Played by one percussionist, it becomes a tour de force. In addition to the four timpani, the soloist's requirements include a triangle, suspended cymbal, cowbell, wood block, a pair of crash cymbals, castanets, slapstick (*fouet*), ratchet (*crecelle*), tambourine, tam-tam, and three graduated drums without snares, designated as *caisse claire, caisse roulante,* and *tambourin provençal.*

The *Concerto* is in two sections, fast (*vif*) and slow (*modéré*) and runs a total of approximately seven and a half minutes. At the percussionist's first entrance, the timpani present a strong rhythmic and melodic phrase in imitation of the primary theme first heard in the orchestra. (Fig. 1.18) The rhythmic movement is vigorous and the sound loud. The five-measure phrase ends with a fortissimo quarter note played by the pedal bass drum with attached cymbal. In the slow section, the mood is somber and the dynamic level soft. Milhaud writes a five-note figure that requires a sensitive touch as it moves softly over twelve different surfaces comprised of woods, skins, and metals. (Fig. 1.19) A hypnotic ostinato is played pianissimo both on the timpani and the tom-toms. (Fig. 1.20) Two loud, brief interjections of the primary theme interrupt the tranquility of the Modéré section just before the work concludes, ending softly on a final timpano A natural.

Many composers of the early twentieth century explored and expanded the use of percussion, particularly in their symphonic works. The Germans Richard Strauss and Gustav Mahler (1860–1911), the Russians Sergei Prokofiev (1891–1953) and Dmitri Shostakovich (1906–1975), the French Maurice Ravel (1875–1937) and Claude Debussy were all great composers who used percussion creatively. They wrote extensive and sometimes innovative percussion parts for many of their orchestral works, but none had the impact on future percussion solo and ensemble literature in the twentieth century as did Stravinsky, Bartók, and Milhaud. This trio of composers experimented within the traditions of their time and found new and fascinating ways for percussionists to make music. Their efforts helped other contemporary composers focus on the musical potential of the battery, eventually leading to the beginnings of a solo and ensemble repertoire for percussion.

Fig. 1.1 Stravinsky, *Le Sacre du printemps* ("Dance of the Adolescents," reh. no. 29)

Fig. 1.2 Stravinsky, *Le Sacre du printemps* ("Procession of the Wise Elders," reh. no. 70)

Fig. 1.3 Stravinsky, *Le Sacre du printemps* ("Mystic Circles of the Young Girls," reh. no. 103)

Fig. 1.4 Stravinsky, *Le Sacre du printemps* ("Dance of the Earth," reh. no. 72)

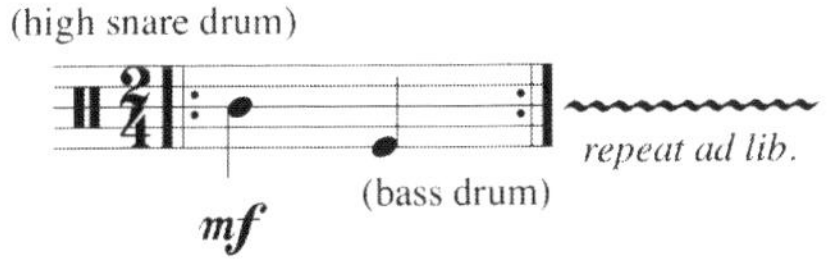

Fig. 1.5 Stravinsky, *Histoire du soldat* ("The Soldier's March," meas. 91)

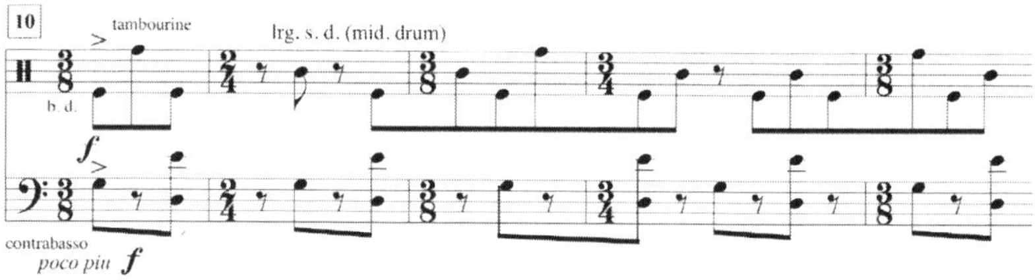

Fig. 1.6 Stravinsky, *Histoire du soldat* ("The Soldier's March," reh. no. 10)

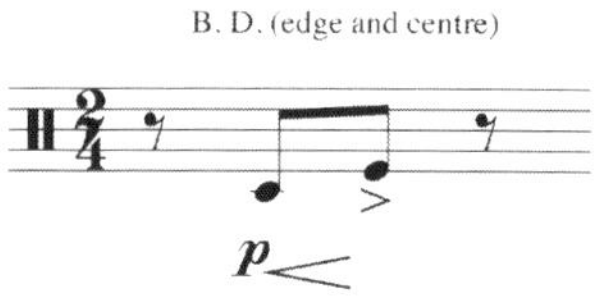

Fig. 1.7 Stravinsky, *Histoire du soldat* ("March Royale," meas. 11)

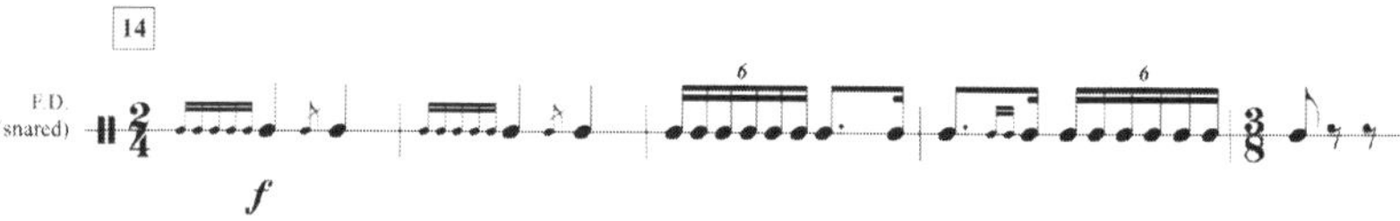

Fig. 1.8 Stravinsky, *Histoire du soldat* ("March Royale," reh. no. 14)

Fig. 1.9 Stravinsky, *Histoire du soldat* ("Tango," reh. no. 1)

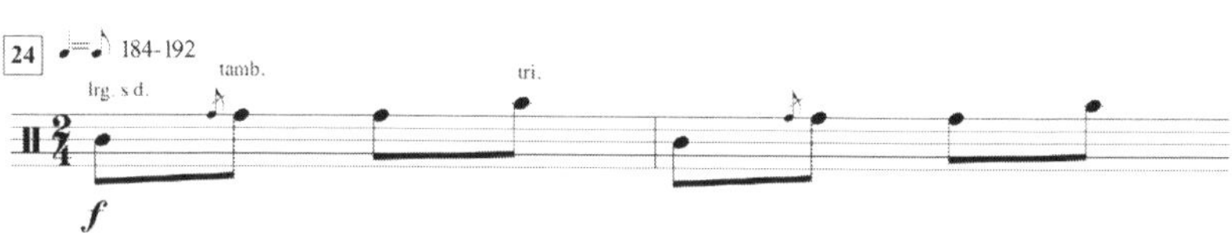

Fig. 1.10 Stravinsky, *Histoire du soldat* ("Ragtime," reh. no. 24)

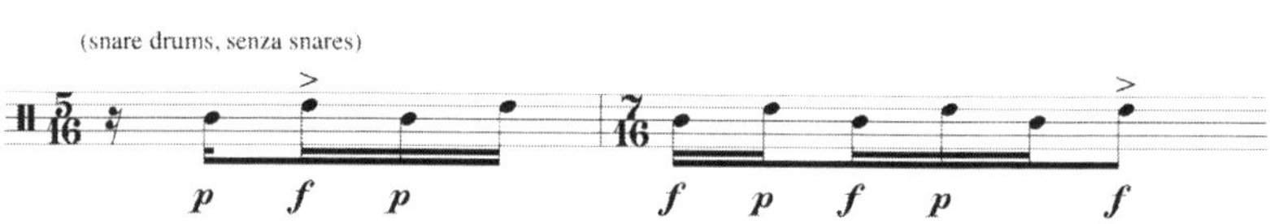

Fig. 1.11 Stravinsky, *Histoire du soldat* (Ragtime," meas. 65)

Fig. 1.12 Stravinsky, *Histoire du soldat* ("Triumphal March of the Devil," meas. 108)

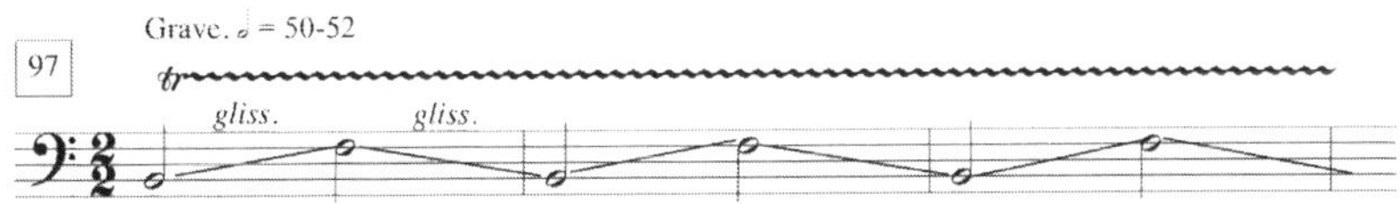

Fig. 1.13 Bartók, *The Miraculous Mandarin* (timpani, reh. no. 97)

Fig. 1.14 Bartók, *Piano Concerto No. 1* (Mvt. II, meas. 1–4)

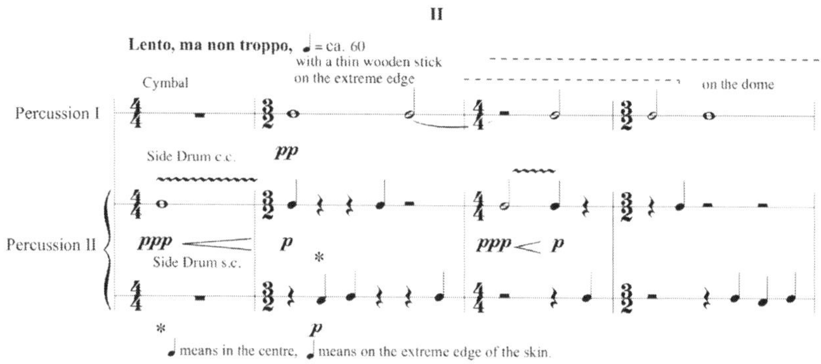

Fig. 1.15 Bartók, *Sonata for Two Pianos and Percussion* (Mvt. II, meas. 1–4)

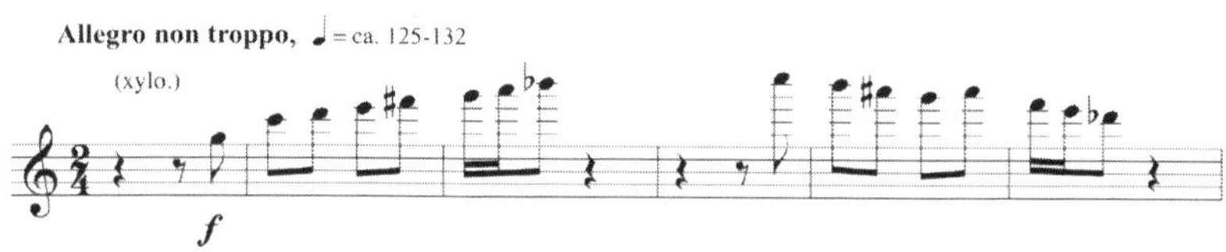

Fig. 1.16 Bartók, *Sonata for Two Pianos and Percussion* (Mvt. III, meas. 4–9)

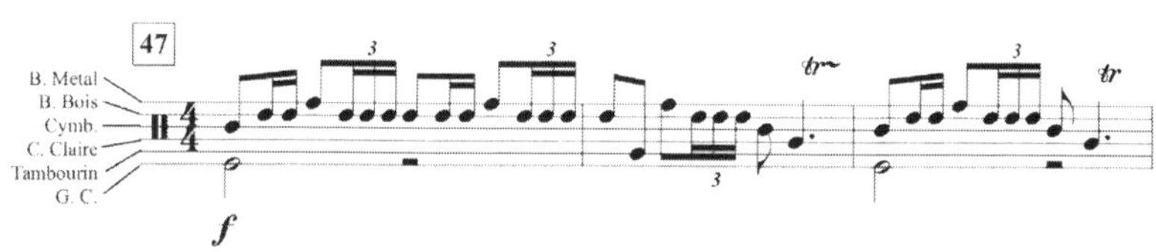

Fig. 1.17 Milhaud, *La Création du monde* (reh. no. 47)

Fig. 1.18 Milhaud, *Concerto pour batterie et petit orchestre* (reh. no. 5)

Fig. 1.19 Milhaud, *Concerto pour batterie et petit orchestre* (reh. no. 92)

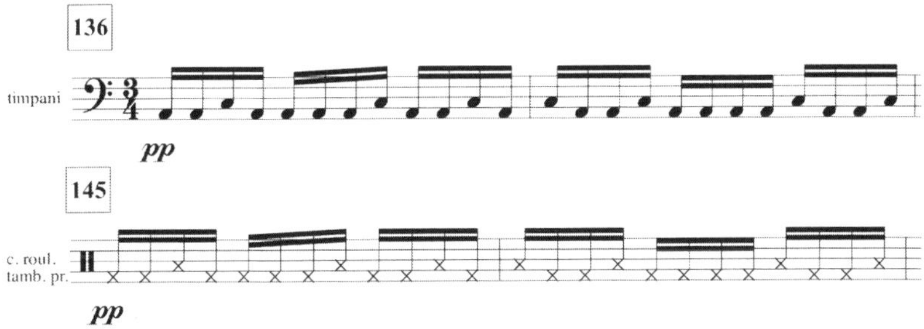

Fig. 1.20 Milhaud, *Concerto pour batterie et petit orchestre* (meas. 136–137 and 145–146)

Chapter 2

AN EMERGING LITERATURE FOR PERCUSSION ENSEMBLE

From the following 1910 program note written by the composer Arnold Schoenberg, one senses that change was in the air during the first decades of the twentieth century: "I feel the heat of rebellion rising in even the slightest souls."[1] Many, but not all, composers were reevaluating the various parameters of music composition, including harmony, rhythm, and timbre. "While some composers clung to tonal inheritance, content to articulate their musical thoughts through revisions of Western tradition, others saw this as a turning point for their musical style."[2] Exploring the characteristics of rhythm and timbre, a few adventurous composers found ways to create music using only instruments designated as percussion. In the 1920s, several works for ensembles of percussion instruments were written as part of larger compositions—symphonic, choral, and operatic. In 1925, composer George Antheil attempted (without success) to combine mechanical pianos and percussion as accompaniment to an early experimental film. By the 1930s, a few iconic works for ensembles of percussion instruments were written, creating paradigms for other composers to follow. Between 1930 and the entrance of the United States into World War II, there emerged a small body of solo and ensemble works that would help emancipate percussion from its traditional role in the decades that followed. "The passage of a single generation, 1930–60, has seen come into being a concert literature scored exclusively for percussion ensemble."[3]

We have already noted that Milhaud, in his 1921 ballet *Man and His Desire,* included an ensemble section scored for twenty different percussion instruments. Within the same decade, the Russian composer Alexander Tcherepnin (1899–1977) composed his first symphony. It included a scherzo movement scored for an ensemble of ten percussionists. Premiered in Paris on October 29, 1927, Tcherepnin's *Symphony No. 1* nearly caused a riot: "police being summoned to the Paris Théâtre du Châtelet to quell an audience aroused by the work's scherzo for unpitched percussion and string instruments tapped with the bow as if they were wooden drums."[4] Only three minutes in duration, the percussion movement is built on a simple eight-bar phrase first stated by two snare drums, bass drum, and tambourine. (Fig. 2.1) Castanets, triangle, cymbals, and wood blocks complete the orchestration. Tcherepnin wrote: "No one, at the time, noticed that the rhythms that I used in the scherzo were merely reductions, to their purely rhythmic value, of the themes of the symphony's first movement, which precedes the scherzo."[5] Tcherepnin was a prolific composer, with eleven symphonies and numerous other works including a *Sonatina for Timpani and Piano* (1939). "At the time of his death, he was working on two symphonies, one for percussion alone."[6]

Another work from the 1920s included a large choir of percussion instruments positioned not within a symphony, but within an opera. The entr'acte from the opera *The Nose,* by Russian composer Dimitri Shostakovich, unnerved the audience at its premiere. Begun in 1927, *The Nose* was first performed in 1929 in a concert version with a full production given the following year in Leningrad. Based on a story by Nikolai Gogol (1809–1852) in which the protagonist's nose takes on a life of its own, the premiere was deemed a success with sixteen performances despite its unusual story line. Not all those in attendance at the premiere were enthusiastic. One listener wrote: "When the *entr'acte* with fourteen percussion instruments started, the stunned audience started rushing out of the hall. . . . I too, fearing damage to my ear drums, also ran out."[7] The published score for the entr'acte calls for ten percussionists and requires the following instruments: bass drum, tam-tam, three suspended cymbals, tambourine, snare drum, tom-tom, castanets, and triangle. The entr'acte's primary rhythmic theme is first stated by the bass drum. (Fig. 2.2) The cymbals answer in augmentation followed by a repeat of the original motive by the tambourine. The tempo is fast and the dynamics loud. Interestingly, the composer passes rhythmic fragments rapidly between instruments and for the first time we see percussion sounds moving from high to low. The beginning meter is in 2/4, changing to 6/8 and finally to 3/4. The entr'acte is 200 bars long, climaxing in a long crescendo. Throughout the opera, Shostakovich's demands on the percussion section are considerable. The writing is challenging, especially for the xylophone. In addition to those instruments used in the entr'acte, the work calls for glockenspiel, ratchet, and flexatone, plus several special effects—four pitched alarm bells, police whistle, pistol shot, and a hammer. The premiere of *The Nose* received negative reviews and, given the politics of the time, the work wasn't heard in Russia again until the 1970s.

Another adventurous composer, the talented American pianist, writer, composer, and inventor George Antheil (1900–1959) made his reputation as the "bad boy of music." Antheil's 1925 work, *Ballet mécanique*, though unique to his oeuvre, was to define his compositional career. Originally titled *Message to Mars*, it brought unwanted notoriety to Antheil, mostly due to an ill-conceived performance held in New York's Carnegie Hall on April 10, 1927. Antheil commented on the effect that performance had on his career in his 1945 biography, *Bad Boy of Music*: "it is frankly my nightmare."[8]

Ballet mécanique was conceived as a work for sixteen mechanical pianos (pianolas), percussion, and film. In the early 1920s, Antheil sought out the American cinematographer Dudley Murphy (1897–1968), "who agreed to make the movie provided the French artist Fernand Léger would collaborate."[9] After the music was written and the pianola rolls were produced, they found that the music was twice as long as the film and the coordination of the multiple pianolas from a central electrical system was problematic. "Both film and music became known separately."[10] Years later, the two works, film and music, were finally performed together on October 18, 1935, at the Museum of Modern Art in New York City with the music arranged for one pianola. Antheil produced many different versions of *Ballet mécanique*. Early performances of the work for one self-playing piano were held in Paris at the Maison Pleyel during the years 1925 and 1926. The "first real performance (with eight pianos, xylophones, and percussion) of the *Ballet Mécanique* was on July 16, 1926 at the [Paris] home of Mrs. Christian Gross, wife of an American diplomat."[11]

The popular 1953 revision of the *Ballet mécanique* is scored for glockenspiel, small and large airplane propeller sounds, gong (tam-tam), suspended cymbal, wood block, triangle, military drum, tambourine, small and large electric bells, tenor drum, bass drum, two xylophones, and four pianos. In three sections (reflecting the original version's three movements), the musical material consists of short melodic themes that are easily recognizable, including the one that opens the work. (Fig. 2.3) The timpani are used melodically, vigorously emphasizing one of the principal themes. (Fig. 2.4) Highly rhythmic, each theme is continuously repeated with minor variations often combined together to form a thick, cacophonous texture. Organized into what Antheil calls "time blocks," each section contains variations of the opening themes. The pianos, the keyboard percussion instruments, and the timpani are used to articulate the thematic material with the other percussion sounds used as texture or underlying drones. According to Antheil, the airplane propeller sound acts as "sort of an organ point."[12]

Antheil obviously wrote the *Ballet* to make a statement about the increasing importance and presence of machines in the early twentieth century, a theme much akin to the Futurist manifestos described in the introduction. The airplane motors, electric doorbells, and the rhythmically driving, fast tempo of much of the work makes it stand out from other contemporary works of this time. Rhythm is central to the work's success. Extended passages at a loud dynamic level create little contrast. The "lack of extensive dynamic nuances emphasizes the importance of the rhythmic texture of the work."[13] *Ballet mécanique* did not find its way into the emerging percussion ensemble literature that was too soon follow due, in part, to its reputation after the Carnegie Hall fiasco and also because Antheil's compositional output took a different direction from that point on. The work is really a tour-de-force for piano, not percussion, even though the xylophone parts are virtuosic. Compounding the problem, neither score nor parts became readily available until the publication of the revised version. Antheil had no desire to follow the success of *Ballet mécanique* with other works similar in style. In his biography he writes about his creation: "I was not successful *en toto*, but it was a 'try' towards a new musical conception, extending, I think, into the future."[14]

With the expanding use of percussion instruments in many of the orchestra and chamber works after the turn of the century, it was inevitable that composers would realize the expressive possibilities of this family of instruments and begin to write works for solo percussion and percussion ensemble. During the 1930s, many composers began to do just that. From 1930 to the end of the decade, at least thirty-two works for solo percussion and percussion ensemble were composed, many written to accompany the new "modern" dance form championed by the American dancer Martha Graham (1894–1991). On the West Coast of America, composers/dance accompanists Lou Harrison and John Cage created unique percussion pieces, expanding our percussion palette of sounds with items they found in Asian gift shops and local junkyards. Spanish-born violinist and composer Amadeo Roldán mined the Afro-Cuban rhythms of Havana's cabarets, producing two seminal percussion ensembles, works designed to be played in the concert hall. Other composers, like the American John Becker, the Cuban Jose Ardévol, and France's Henri Tomasi wrote concert works for percussion with forms anchored in the classical tradition.

If any single figure in the history of music could be designated the father of percussion ensemble music, it would be the French American composer Edgard Varèse (1883–1965). Born in France and raised in Italy, Varèse was, from an early age, rebellious in nature, a character trait that, along with his early studies in science and mathematics, strongly influenced his approach to composing music later in life. His first encounter with percussion instruments was as a young student in Italy. "Edgard attended music classes at the Turin Conservatory and even sat in for a time in the percussion section of the school's orchestra."[15] Varèse returned to France in 1904 where he studied music at the Paris Conservatoire and the Schola Cantorum: conducting with Vincent d'Indy (1851–1931) and composition and counterpoint with Albert Roussel (1869–1937). He remembered, "By the time I was twenty, I had an enormous amount of music written."[16] We know little about these early works by Varèse, or if they reflect his later approach to writing for percussion, as they were reportedly destroyed in a Berlin warehouse fire, circa 1918. Prior to World War I, the youthful Varèse had established himself as both a conductor and composer in Paris and in Berlin. Later in life, Varèse remarked that he had written works for choruses he had conducted in Berlin using "special percussion instruments that I had collected myself, which singers often played themselves."[17] We do know that Varèse attended concerts given by the Futurists and that he was aware of both their notoriety and their musical efforts. He heard the so-called *intonarumori* constructed by Russolo and even endorsed a later keyboard version of Russolo's noise-producing instruments. But Varèse rejected the Futurists' aesthetic and its *arte dei rumori* (the art of noise) as inimical to art. Schooled in the sciences as a young man, Varèse's approach to music would be nothing like that of the Futurists. "Varèse's esthetic position was vastly different from that of his contemporaries, and he stands apart as one of the most original figures of twentieth-century music."[18]

"Varèse emigrated to America in the midst of the Great War."[19] He had, like many of the émigrés of the time, fled the disruption war caused to the European art scene. It was his hope to find work in the United States as a conductor and, perhaps, to find an audience sympathetic to his musical creations. Upon his arrival in New York, Varèse realized some success both as a conductor and as an organizer of support groups for like-minded composers. In 1921, inspired by his newly found country, Varèse completed his mammoth symphonic work, *Amériques*, a work he had begun in 1918. "With 27 woodwinds, 29 brasses, and the largest percussion battery of the time, Varèse stretched the post-Romantic orchestra to the breaking point, weaving a towering tapestry from unimaginable sonic strands."[20] Unique to *Amériques* is Varèse's use of a large percussion ensemble element within the score that serves the function of a separate yet equal orchestra section along with winds, brass, and strings. This approach to orchestration was far ahead of its time: "This is the single most decisively original element in Varèse's music, setting it apart from his predecessors and elder contemporaries."[21] The score requires not only many of the standard percussion instruments, but also a cyclone whistle, steamboat whistle, crow call, string drum (lion's roar), and, for the first time, Varèse's signature sound, a siren. Regarding the use of a siren, Varèse's wife, Louise, writes: "He now elevated one to the rank of musical instrument in the score he was working on, to which he was to give the title *Amériques: Americas, New Worlds*."[22] The siren and the other unique sonic sources are integrated and used in the percussion section in the same manner as and equal to the other, more traditional, percussion sounds. (Fig. 2.5) Instruments normally used in theaters as sound effects to simulate nature or to evoke a busy metropolis are notated with the detail of articulation composers usually reserved for more traditional instruments. What were formerly sound effects became legitimized and part of Varèse's timbral palette. (Note, in Figure 2.5, Varèse notates rolls with both the traditional tremolo line as well as with three hash marks, ensuring that the rolls be played unmeasured, not as eighth, sixteenth, or thirty-second notes.) At rehearsal number 12 he calls for a suspended cymbal to be played with a bow "[This might be the very first indication of the use of bass bow on a cymbal in the literature!]"[23] Varèse's homage to his new homeland, *Amériques,* premiered on April 9, 1926, with Leopold Stokowski (1882–1977) conducting the Philadelphia Orchestra.

The decade of the 1920s was the most creative, productive period of Varèse's career. He completed five new works, all of which included parts for percussion instruments. He also organized an association, the International Composers Guild (ICG), designed to bring contemporary music to the listening public. "By its nature the ICG was a breeding ground of ideas; it was a stage, a meeting place, a listening place, and an inspiration for its composer members."[24] By 1927, when the ICG ceased its activities, its record of accomplishments included 18 concerts, the performance of 126 new compositions, 55 world premieres, and several American premieres. "Most of all, however, the ICG could boast of having programmed a large number of historically significant compositions."[25]

At a March 4, 1923, ICG concert, Varèse conducted *Hyperprism,* a brief four-minute work for nine winds and brass players and nine percussionists. According to Varèse's wife, *Hyperprism* "caused a very big commotion."[26] The critics were not kind—"The shock of *Hyperprism*—its unmoored forms, its unbridled showmanship, its sheer noise, was liberating or appalling. Many first listeners laughed."[27] Dedicated to the Mexican poet José Juan Tablada (1871–1945) and his wife, Nena, *Hyperprism* requires a multitude of percussion equipment (seventeen unique percussion sounds) including a siren and a lion's roar (the latter Varèse preferred calling a string drum). "As it would have been impossible to find sixteen professional percussion players willing to give the amount of time required, Varèse appealed to Margaret Heaton, at that time head of the Dalcroze School of Eurhythmics, with the result that her entire school collaborated, each member taking on one or two instruments."[28] As in *Amériques*, Varèse wrote detailed performance instructions, for example, *frotter rudement membrane avec le pouce* (thumb on tambourine), *agitez l'una contre l'autre* (crash cymbals rolled), *très seré* (closed roll). Varèse followed *Hyperprism* with another wind and percussion work, *Intégrales*, which the ICG premiered in New York City on March 1, 1925, with Leopold Stokowski conducting. Scored for eleven winds and brass with four multiple-percussion parts, *Intégrales* proved to be one of Varèse's most popular and lasting chamber works.

Despite the success Varèse found in his new homeland, he had hoped for more. Plagued by the lack of funds and struggling to get his symphonic works performed more than once, Varèse decided to return to France. In 1928, he moved back to Paris, "hoping to find greater creative freedom and success in the new and yet familiar surroundings."[29] Unfortunately, his hopes were never realized. By 1931, he was, however, able to complete a small work for percussion instruments alone, *Ionisation*, which rose to iconic status by the end of the century. Though *Ionisation* was not the first work written for percussion alone, it was by far the most influential due, in part, to the prestige of its composer, but more so to the power and integrity of its construction. "No one could hear *Ionisation* and not recognize its strength as a work of art, nor the lasting and legitimizing effect it had for composers of percussion music."[30]

Edgard Varèse's *Ionisation* was completed in Paris on November 13, 1931. This landmark composition, written for thirteen players utilizing forty percussion instruments, was "the work that he was most satisfied with and proud of" according to his wife, Louise.[31] Varèse himself wrote his friend and colleague Carlos Salzedo the following: "*Ionisation*, the title of my piece for percussion, has turned out well—cryptic, synthesized, powerful, and terse. And, as for structure: stunning mechanics. What I like most about myself is my modesty."[32] *Ionisation* was given its premiere on March 6, 1933, in New York's Carnegie Hall with the pianist, composer, and lexicographer Nicolas Slonimsky (1894–1995) conducting.

The construction of *Ionisation* has been the focus of a number of analyses since its writing. Included in an early publication of the score was an analysis by Slonimsky, who believed the work was "written in a sonata form, with the first subject given out by the *tambour militaire*."[33] Two other authors, the percussionist/composer Jean Charles François and composer Chou Wen-chung, Varèse's former student and collaborator, examined *Ionisation* and concluded that Varèse's compositional approach was unique (as opposed to thematic in the traditional sense as Slonimsky believed), based primarily on the parameter of timbre.[34] "Because of Varèse, timbre became one of the primary elements of much twentieth-century music, no longer secondary to pitch and rhythm."[35]

Fortunately, Varèse gave us insight into his approach to composition throughout his career both in his writings and in numerous lectures. He defined music as "organized sound." In a 1959 lecture given at Princeton University, Varèse conceived musical organization (form) as the result of a process similar to the formation of crystals in science. With regard to rhythm, he said: "Rhythm is too often confused with metrics. Cadence or the regular succession of beats and accents has little to do with the rhythm of a composition. Rhythm is the element in music that gives life to the work and holds it together. It is the element of stability, the generator of form."[36] Varèse used common time signatures not to imply rhythmic hierarchy, but to facilitate performance. "In *Ionisation*, for example, the predominant 4/4 meter of the notation merely serves as a scaffold to contain what is happening."[37]

Varèse grouped the percussion instruments in *Ionisation* to create different structures, each with a recognizable musical texture. The time signature is mostly common time, with the tempo indicated as quarter note = 69 [originally 80]. In the beginning, sustained sounds of ringing metals, lion's roar, drumrolls, and growling sirens serve as a canvas that Varèse dots with rhythmic fragments played on drums, maracas, triangle, and tambourine. (Fig. 2.6) A polyphonic section follows, dominated by a military drum cadence in duple time with the bass drum and cymbals grouped in three. (Fig. 2.7) This material later evolves into and is incorporated with other textures in a manner unique to Varèse—perhaps similar to Schoenberg's additive rather than developmental form. At rehearsal number 7, massed drums suddenly present a strong triplet figure, with accented muffled *cencerro* (Latin-style cowbell), followed by a section with fragmented groups of five sixteenth-notes that include loud "rim shots," providing a powerful, percussive surprise as the interest changes from linear to vertical. These sudden, fortissimo eruptions are found in many of Varèse's works. (Fig. 2.8) He saves the pitched instruments—piano, glockenspiel, and chimes—for a final sonic apotheosis. Avoiding a sense of tonality, Varèse notates the keyboard instruments utilizing all twelve tones. He also alters the tempo for this final section from quarter note = 69 to quarter note = 52 for purposes of clarity. *Ionisation* ends as quietly as it begins with the sounds slowly fading into a residue of ringing metals immersed in a muffled drumroll.

As stated earlier, *Ionisation,* so important to the evolution of percussion ensemble music, may not have been the first work written for an orchestra of percussion instruments. It appears that the creation of two short studies by a young Cuban composer, Amadeo Roldán (1900–1939), preceded *Ionisation* by a few months. The island nation of Cuba and its capital city, Havana, have a long tradition of support for both classical and indigenous music. In 1919, the violinist/composer Amadeo Roldán immigrated to the island, becoming first violinist for one of the city's two symphony orchestras. He wrote a number of works, both symphonic and chamber, drawing on Cuba's African musical heritage for inspiration. "It was Roldán who introduced large numbers of native percussion instruments and the African-style counter-rhythms and accented offbeats into symphonic scores."[38] In 1930, he composed a set of six brief *Ritmicas* for winds and percussion; numbers five and six are for percussion alone. Less than five minutes in total duration, those two *Ritmicas* contain some challenging rhythmic figures. Each require eleven players and a large battery of instruments including: four sets of claves sounding from high to low designated *muy aguda, aguda, grave,* and *muy grave*; a guiro (serrated gourd); cencerros; maracas; a *quijada del burro* (jawbone of an ass); bongos; timbales; timpani; *bombo* (low drum); and a *marimbula* (a resonant wooden box with mounted strips of metal, sounding like a pizzicato double bass). A list of instructions in the score describes how some of the instruments are to be played, along with an explanation of any unusual notation. In the *Ritmicas,* Roldán calls for the guiro to be struck as well as scraped, and the bongos to be played on the edge, in the center, and at a normal position as well as rubbed. The direction for playing the maracas includes grasping the maraca heads in hand or wrapping them in handkerchiefs to create a muted (*sordino*) effect. Other directions are also given that demonstrate Roldán's knowledge of native performance techniques: "For the first time, the notation of the rhythms by Cuban folk instruments was executed with precision."[39]

Ritmica No. V is based on the *son clave* (3–2 version) and begins with the rhythm passed from player to player ending in a sforzando at bar 11. In bar 51, there is a tempo change. A faster *montuno* beat begins and the 3 of the 3–2 clave rhythm becomes a driving ostinato figure played on the marimbula. Other players are slowly added until the work climaxes with an ending sonic roar. *Ritmica No. VI* is more dancelike, built around the clave theme as well. Of the two studies, it contains the more difficult rhythmic patterns including stressed groups of threes, fours, and fives across bar lines (Fig. 2.9)—rhythms that Roldán must have heard played in the clubs of Havana and which are still heard in today's popular Latin music. After the premiere, Roldán's two percussion *Ritmicas* found their way into the percussion ensemble canon early on. On March 10, 1931, a performance of Roldán's *Ritmicas* was given at the New School for Social Research in New York City under the auspices of the Pan-American Association of Composers (PAAC) with Adolph Weiss (1891–1971) conducting.

The Cuban José Ardévol (1911–1981) wrote three percussion works: *Estudio en forma de Preludio y Fuga* (Study in Form of Prelude and Fugue) (1933); *Suite* (1934); and *Prelude à 11* (1942). All three works included use of the piano as a percussion instrument. The *Prelude and Fugue* study is approximately eight minutes in duration and calls for thirty-seven players and a vast arsenal of both traditional and ethnic percussion instruments, some thirty-two in all. According to the manuscript, Ardévol began the work on the 30th of May and completed it on June 3, 1933, a period of only five days. Unlike Roldán's *Ritmicas*, it does not exploit indigenous Cuban music even though it calls for claves, maracas, and a few other indigenous instruments. Rather it looks to the European traditionalists by using classic forms (prelude and fugue), while embracing the aesthetic of the Futurists in designing a radical work primarily for nonpitched percussion instruments. "His *Estudio* demonstrates that he was open to the ultramodern, universalist aims of certain U.S. composers in the 1930s."[40] The *Prelude* (marked lento) opens with a crescendo of police whistles, sirens, and tremolo piano clusters (played with the fists) and culminates in a thunderous crash of drums, tam-tams, and other percussion sounds. The movement is brief, less than three minutes. It is without any recognizable line, getting its forward motion by a contrast of dynamics and by the development of a few small rhythmic cells. It ends as it begins. The *Fugue* movement begins in 6/8 meter with a single tenor drum stating a six-bar subject. (Fig. 2.10) The exposition continues with a high timpano and one African drum restating the subject, while the tenor drum plays a countersubject in 2/4 meter. This polymetric structure, 2/4–6/8, continues throughout the work ending with a coda in 5/8. The fugue subject is highly syncopated and easily recognizable. Ardévol manipulates this subject through augmentation, diminution, and retrograde processes. He notates stretto-like sections where fragments of the subject are presented in rapid succession. With such a large instrumental force, the highly contrapuntal texture is often dense and the volume of sound overwhelming. (If the work was premiered in Cuba, I cannot find any record of it.) The score is currently housed in the Philadelphia Free Library as part of the library's Edwin A. Fleischer Collection. It eventually received a number of performances after World War II.

When Varèse terminated the International Composers Guild's activities in 1927 (he believed the guild had accomplished its goals), he lent his name and reputation to a new organization, the PAAC. The Mexican composer Carlos Chávez, "who had participated in the Guild (ICG) approached [Varèse] with the idea of a similar organization for American composers."[41] The PAAC existed from 1928 to 1934 and sponsored numerous concerts in both the Americas and Europe. Chávez became the PAAC's Mexican representative and Roldán became the president of the West Indies section.

Carlos Chávez (1899–1978) was born in a suburb of Mexico City, a metropolis that would benefit greatly from his life's work as a conductor, composer, and arts administrator. Chávez was a skilled pianist, and his training as a composer came mostly through the study and analysis of the Classical and Romantic literature. A ballet, *El Fuego Nuevo,* composed in 1921, included a large percussion section and garnered national attention. At the age of twenty-nine, Chávez was named director of Mexico's National Conservatory and, in the same year, was asked to become musical director of the newly formed Orquesta Sinfonia de Mexico. Under his leadership, both organizations prospered and continue today. He not only wrote music, but also authored the 1937 book *Toward a New Music,* in which he anticipated the advent of electronic music. Throughout his career, Chávez contributed articles on music and art to one of Mexico City's newspapers, *El universal.* Through his writings, compositions, and conducting, he brought attention to the culture and art of the Mexican people. In 1958, he was appointed to the Charles Eliot Norton Chair of Poetics at Harvard University.

From an early age, Chávez was fascinated by Mexico's native music, imagining how the music of ancient Mexico would sound. In museums, he discovered ancient flutes, ocarinas, and drums and, when commissioned to write a work to accompany an exhibit of Mexican art, he composed the chamber work *Xochipilli.* Written at the request of Nelson Rockefeller, *Xochipilli* (the name given to the Aztec god of music and dance) was premiered at New York City's Museum of Modern Art on May 16, 1940, in conjunction with the exhibit "Twenty Centuries of Mexican Art." Its style and unique instrumentation were conscious efforts on the part of Chávez to evoke the lost music of native Mexicans. Written for indigenous percussion and wind instruments, the score lists contemporary replacements, but it is clear that Chávez preferred the former. The percussion requirements include large and small two-toned log drums (*teponaxtle*), rasping stick (*omichicahuaztli*), two small Indian drums, various rattles, and two large single-headed drums (*huehuetl*). Along with the piccolo, flute, and E-flat clarinet, Chávez added a part for conch shell that enters near the work's finale, bringing *Xochipilli* to an exciting conclusion.

His most popular work for percussion, *Toccata for Percussion Instruments,* was written in 1942. It has been suggested that this sextet was written at the request of John Cage, but Cage's group was unable to perform the work. The *Toccata* required traditional orchestral percussion techniques (specifically the snare drum roll) putting it out of reach for the dancers and composers who primarily comprised Cage's ensemble. The work was premiered in Mexico City on October 31, 1947, by the percussion section of the National Conservatory of Mexico Orchestra, Eduardo Hernández Moncada (1899–1995), conductor, and proved a success even before its publication in 1954. That year, *Chicago Daily News* music critic Roger Dettmer noted the popularity of the *Toccata*: "Not one, or two, but three new recordings suddenly of this fascinating, sophisticated-primitive piece for tom-toms, gourds, rattles and a dozen other percussive oddments."[42] The *Toccata*'s popularity continued for decades, topping the Percussive Arts Society's list of most often performed percussion ensembles for many years.

The overall form of the *Toccata* is in three movements: fast-slow-fast. Chávez uses standard compositional devices of imitation and repetition. Small rhythmic themes are presented and passed between the membranophones, creating recognizable melodic contours. "Stratification and independence of the instrumental parts results in a predominantly contrapuntal texture."[43] A short melody with a strong cadence emerges from the interplay of the drums, whose pitch areas range from high (tambor indio) to low (bombo). The timpanist (three drums) and a percussionist, who is responsible for an array of three membranophones (Indian, side, and tenor drums), reinforce the melody. (Fig. 2.11) At rehearsal number 19, a sudden fortissimo roll played by the military drum begins, then diminishes quickly to a pianissimo. The other five players enter sequentially with drumrolls at a soft dynamic level. A great crescendo follows and the drums then fade away leading to a pianissimo roll on the suspended cymbal that begins the second movement. This simple, yet attractive, compositional device has been imitated by composers of percussion music ever since.

The second movement provides great contrast to the first. Scored for metal instruments plus a xylophone, it proceeds at a slow, hypnotic, clocklike pace. Orchestra bells, tubular chimes, and xylophone offer melodic potential, but Chávez uses them primarily for their timbre (color). A unison section ends the movement without relieving the sense of tension that permeates the entire movement.

A solo timpani passage over three drums begins the final allegro. Its marchlike melody, in duple time, is derived from a ternary version heard in the first movement. This reprise of the material from the opening movement provides a sense of continuity for the listener. The glockenspiel heralds a change of tempo that leads to an intense, hocketlike episode between drums and timpani. Claves and a snare drum help keep things together. The music shifts abruptly with a climactic *vivo* section led by the Indian drum. The work ends with a reprise of the opening timpani march that slowly fades away.

Chávez composed another percussion sextet, *Tambuco,* in 1964, and a solo timpani work, *Partita for Solo Timpani,* in 1973. *Tambuco* was commissioned by Clare Boothe Luce and premiered on October 11, 1965, with the Los Angeles Percussion Ensemble, William Kraft, conductor. "Chávez coined the one-word title as an imitation of percussion sounds."[44] The work calls for two unusual instruments—a chromatic set of Swiss brass bells and a large water gourd, floated upside-down on the surface of a bowl of water and struck with a mallet to produce a low, resonant sound. (Bowls carved from monkey wood make a good gourd substitute.) *Tambuco* features contrasting sections of pitched versus nonpitched percussion. Keyboard percussion instruments (marimba, glockenspiel, xylophone, and vibraphone) join brass bells and a celesta forming one group. Against these pitched instruments, a battery of cymbals, triangles, rattles, raspers, claves, and drums play small rhythmic figures. Chávez writes: "The music of this work develops in a constant process of consequent evolution."[45] He avoids any serial techniques and deviates from the conventional contrapuntal procedures and classical developments. These two postwar works, *Tambuco* and *Partita,* never attracted the listening audience that found the more traditionally composed *Toccata* so accessible.

Other works to consider: *Abongo* (1933) by John Becker (1886–1961); *Trio for Two Marimbas and Piano* (1950) by Robert Kreutz (1922–1996).

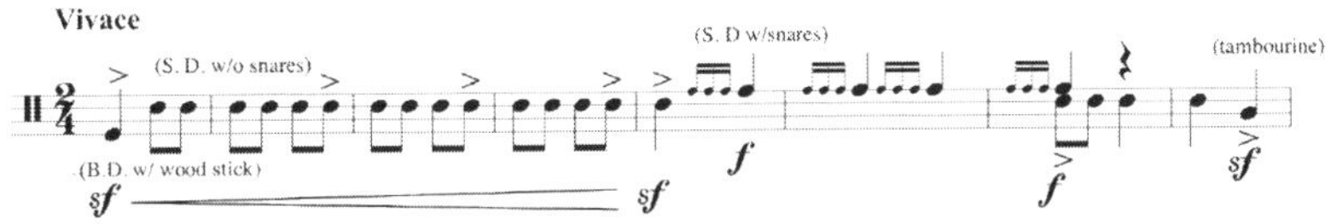

Fig. 2.1 Tcherepnin, *Symphony No. 1* (percussion movement theme)

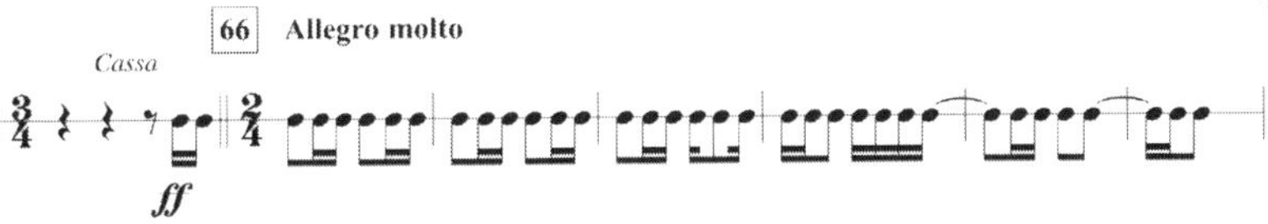

Fig. 2.2 Shostakovich, *The Nose* (entr'acte theme)

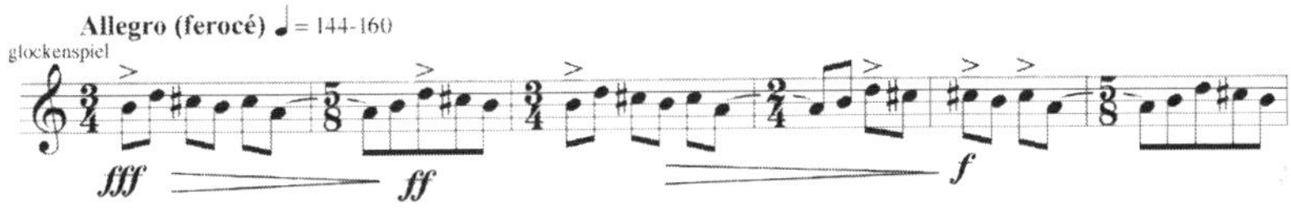

Fig. 2.3 Antheil, *Ballet mécanique* (opening measures)

Fig. 2.4 Antheil, *Ballet mécanique* (reh. no. 78)

Fig. 2.5 Varèse, *Amériques* (12 meas. after reh. no. 6)

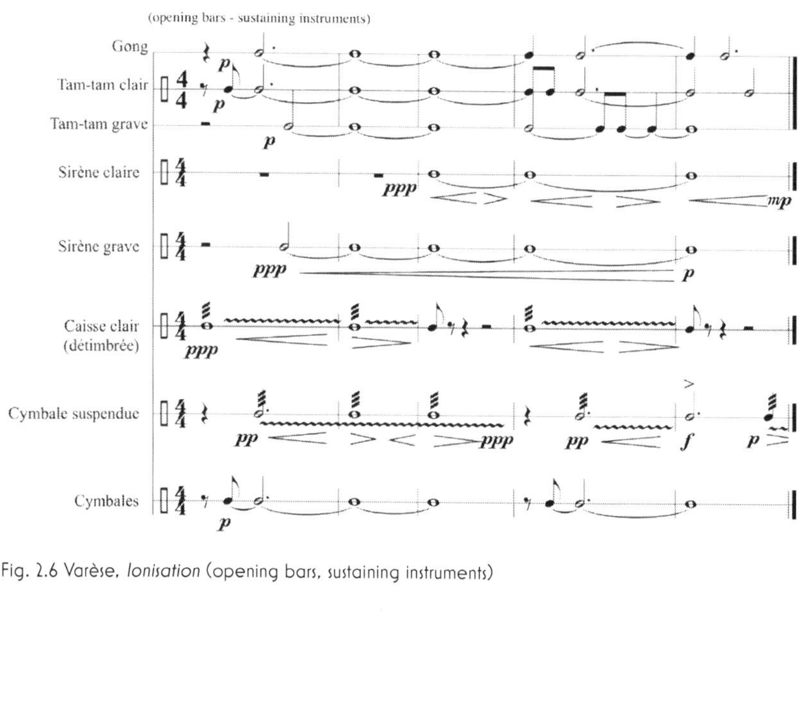

Fig. 2.6 Varèse, *Ionisation* (opening bars, sustaining instruments)

Fig. 2.7 Varèse, *Ionisation* (meas. 8–11, drums and cymbals)

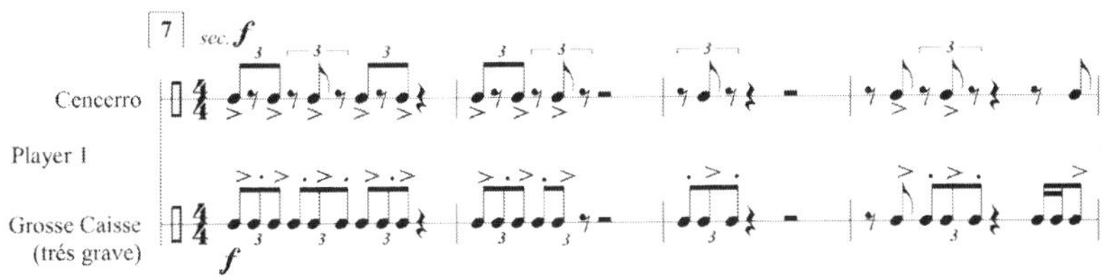

Fig. 2.8 Varèse, *Ionisation* (reh. no. 7, cencerro and bass drum)

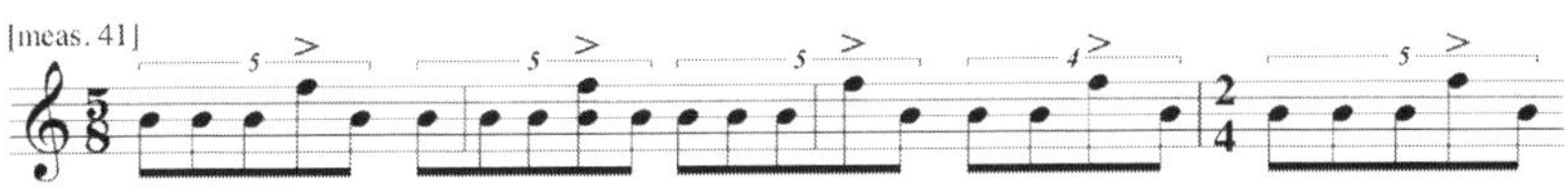

Fig. 2.9 Roldán, *Ritmica VI* (meas. 41, bongos only)

Fig. 2.10 Ardévol, *Fugue* (fugue subject)

Fig. 2.11 Chávez, *Toccata* (reh. no. 20)

Chapter 3

HENRY COWELL AND THE WEST COAST DANCE SCENE

Pounding a piano with fists and forearms, West Coast pianist, composer, and writer Henry Cowell (1897–1965) fascinated the listening public during the roaring twenties. Captured on film early in his career, Cowell appeared to be flailing away at every part of a grand piano within his reach. The California-born iconoclast became a missionary for ultramodern music, his own as well as that of many like-minded composers. His use of tone clusters (played with fists and arms) and his piano pieces that called for scraping the strings brought him notoriety. Not content to exploit just the piano's keyboard, Cowell explored the instrument's interior as well, striking the soundboard and strings with various implements. "Experimenting with the soundboard of the grand piano led him to discoveries in the field of tone-color."[1] After performing a concert of his music in New York City, Cowell "acquired professional management and inaugurated a series of five tours of Europe as composer-pianist (1923–1933) that made him an international figure."[2] Remembered for his radical piano pieces, Cowell also wrote concertos and chamber works that explored the music of other cultures, mostly Asian, assimilating their concepts and sounds and sharing his discoveries with his many students. As a composer, performer, teacher, publisher, concert promoter, and prolific writer of articles, Cowell championed the cause of new music. In celebration of Cowell's sixty-fifth birthday, the composer William Schuman wrote: "For the music of his time Cowell has fought, lectured, organized, written, pleaded, advocated, defended, recorded, published, and, most importantly, composed."[3] Cowell wrote a number of works that featured percussion instruments. One of them, his chamber percussion ensemble work *Ostinato Pianissimo,* became an early twentieth-century classic.

Born March 11, 1897, in Menlo Park, just south of San Francisco, Cowell was an exceptional child. Raised in poverty and home-schooled, he grew up listening to non-Western music (primarily Chinese, Japanese, and Indian) that he heard in the streets of San Francisco. At age five, he studied violin for a brief time until illness (chorea) made it physically painful. Upon recovery, he began taking piano lessons and became quite proficient. By age twenty-two, he was an internationally recognized concert artist. Cowell's activities were not limited to concert performance and composing, however. In 1925, he founded the California-based New Music Society; in 1927, he single-handedly launched a quarterly, *New Music,* a publication that included collections of contemporary works. Over the next twenty-five years, Cowell's publications and recordings brought recognition to many composers who were ignored by the publishing establishment, including Charles Ives (1874–1954) and Carl Ruggles (1876–1971). In 1928, Cowell cofounded, with Edgard Varèse as president, the Pan-American Association of Composers (PAAC), whose charter called for the support of both North and South American composers. Also that year, he began teaching a course in ethnomusicology at the New School in New York.

Despite his lack of formal education, Cowell was able to enroll at the University of California as a special student of the composer Charles Seeger (1886–1979). Under Seeger's tutelage, he codified his ideas about rhythm, harmony, and timbre in his 1930 book, *New Musical Resources.* With the help of the Russian inventor Leon Theremin (1896–1993), Cowell built a machine he called the "rhythmicon," first demonstrated in New York. "The demonstration at The New School took place on January 19, 1932, with the assistance of Clare Reisenberg (better known as Clara Rockmore), the famed Theremin virtuoso."[4] This complicated, yet fragile, unit produced complex cross-rhythms realized at a given pitch that coincided with its rhythmic ratio; for example, rhythms of two against one would produce an octave, three against two a perfect fifth.[5] Cowell featured this device in his symphonic work *Rhythmicana,* as well as in a few other compositions that explored unusual rhythmic schemes.

Cowell's contributions to the percussion solo and ensemble literature include a sextet, *Return,* written in 1938–39, which calls for a pane of glass to be played with a rosined cord. It also contains a part for "wailer" to be realized by a female voice or a siren. It was premiered, along with his 1939 percussion quintet, *Pulse,* at a concert directed by his student John Cage at the Cornish School in Seattle, Washington. Cowell's *Pulse* is written in 7/8 meter with an instrumentation comprised of Asian instruments and junkyard sounds, including three iron pipes and three automobile brake drums. In the 1950s, Cowell produced two works that featured percussion, *Set of Five* and *Concerto for Percussion and Orchestra*. A trio, *Set of Five*, commissioned by the piano/violin duo Anahid and Maro Ajemian, calls for a single percussionist using five gongs placed on a padded surface (to partially mute the sound), a xylophone, an array of Indian tabla drums, a celesta, and a Jalatarang: "musical cups of India, made of porcelain or clay."[6] His 1959 *Concerto for Percussion and Orchestra* featured the percussion section and was premiered in January of 1961 by the Kansas City Philharmonic under the baton of Hans Schweiger (1906–2000).

Ostinato Pianissimo is Cowell's most successful percussion work. Composed in 1934 and dedicated to Nicolas Slonimsky, the score requires seven percussionists and two pianists, with the latter playing "string pianos" (Cowell's term for the grand piano) while muting the strings with one hand to dampen the sound. Percussion instruments include a xylophone, two wood blocks, tambourine (without jingles), guiro (to be tapped with a stick), three tom-toms, three gongs (to be played with both padded and wood sticks), and a set of eight water-tuned rice bowls. Structurally, the work contains a series of eight ostinatos (players 5 and 6 combine to create a single ostinato pattern) of unequal lengths whose repeats are clearly marked in the score with a plus sign. The tempo designated is 60 beats per minute (bpm) to the half note. The dynamic level is pianissimo throughout, with the exception of the concluding bars marked fortissimo. Cowell indicates in the preface to the score that accents are to be brought out sharply, the other notes to be played very softly. His organization of resources in *Ostinato Pianissimo* borrows from musical structures found in Asian music, yet he transforms them into something original. As in the Indonesian gamelan, higher-sounding instruments in *Ostinato Pianissimo* move faster than the lower ones. The low gongs play whole notes, the drums half notes, the blocks/tambourine/guiro quarter notes, and the muted pianos eighth notes. Halfway through the work, the xylophone enters with an accented sixteenth-note pattern moving the piece to its conclusion. (Fig. 3.1) "The overall picture that emerges as a result of Cowell's way of using the instruments—a tapestry of instruments interweaving sounds and colors—is remarkably suggestive of the Javanese gamelan."[7]

Cowell was a pivotal figure in the development of percussion ensemble music. Though his oeuvre was small, his influence was great and it reverberated throughout the century. Students who benefited from his ideas and concepts included Lou Harrison, Johanna Beyer, John Cage, Henry Brant, and many of those who attended his classes at the New School in New York City. His close work with colleagues such as Gerald Strang, William Russell, and Ray Green aided a budding West Coast modern dance movement. Early on, Cowell embraced the musical aesthetics of other cultures, incorporating them into his compositions, leading the way for others to do the same. In many ways, Henry Cowell helped champion the American music of the twentieth century. In his book *Silence*, the composer John Cage remarked: "Henry Cowell was for many years the open sesame for new music in America."[8]

COWELL'S NEW MUSIC

In 1936, the eighteenth edition of Cowell's *New Music: Orchestra Series* was published. It was dedicated to music for percussion and included six scores for percussion ensemble. They appear in the collection as follows: "IV" by J. M. Beyer; *Auto Accident* by Harold G. Davidson; *Three Inventories of Casey Jones* by Ray Green; *Dance Rhythms* by Doris Humphrey; *Three Dance Movements* by William Russell; and *Percussion Music* by Gerald Strang.

The pianist/composer Johanna M. Beyer (1888–1944) was born in Leipzig, Germany, on July 11, 1888, immigrating to the United States in 1923. In New York City, Beyer's musical studies included degrees from Mannes College, and work with composers Ruth Crawford Seeger (1901–1953), Dane Rudhyar (1895–1985), Charles Seeger, and Henry Cowell. Cowell and the Seegers seemed to be the most influential artistically. For a time, Beyer performed secretarial work for Cowell at his New Music enterprise. (Cowell's widow, Sydney, implied in a note to the author that Beyer used Cowell's connections to foster her own compositional efforts. "She was in Mr. Cowell's percussion class when I was but I know little about her, except that she attended to mailing scores for him, along with her own.")[9] Until recently, Beyer's work was relatively unknown. Now most scholars engaged with twentieth-century music are aware of her work.[10] Beyer died on July 11, 1944, the cause listed as amyotrophic lateral sclerosis. She left a modest body of works including piano solos, songs, symphonic movements, chamber music, and percussion ensembles. "One of Beyer's most important contributions is her work for percussion ensemble, constituting some of the earliest examples of this genre."[11] For years, the only source for Beyer's percussion music, with the exception of the fourth movement from a work titled *Percussion,* was the Edwin A. Fleisher Collection located in the Free Library of Philadelphia. Supported in part by the federal WPA music-copying project, the Fleisher Collection was a godsend for many contemporary composers. The collection's holdings were published and disseminated throughout the world, making both performers and ensemble directors aware of this trove of early percussion works. The library's holdings for Beyer include five of the six works she composed for chamber percussion ensemble: *Percussion Suite* (1933), *March* (1939), *Three Movements for Percussion* (1939), *Percussion, Opus No. 14* (1939), and *Waltz for Percussion* (1939).

Beyer's 1933 *Percussion Suite* fails to break new ground, though it does hint at the discipline and creativity demonstrated in her later works. Written for five players, its instrumentation calls for percussion instruments commonly used in orchestras and bands of the time. The septet, *March*, brief at only three minutes, was most likely designed for the dance and not the parade grounds. Its pulse is irregular; the time signature is 4½/4 (nine eighth-notes per measure). Beyer combines sounds to form rhythmic figures that slowly become increasingly dense as the work moves toward its climax. It is a miniature gem! *Three Movements for Percussion* is Beyer's most ambitious of the six works. It is dedicated to John Cage. *Three Movements*, eventually published in 1976, is a palindrome of sorts. Here Beyer utilizes space and repetitiveness to create a composition that anticipates minimalism, a genre popular later in the century. The most available and most often performed of Beyer's percussion music was the fourth movement of a larger work titled *Percussion*. The movement, "IV," is the first work printed in Cowell's 1936 collection of percussion ensembles. "*Percussion* is a five-movement work with unspecified instrumentation scored for nine parts."[12] In movement "IV," the time signature is 7/8, the tempo 144 to the quarter note, and the instrumentation is indeterminate. This is one of a few percussion works written during this time period in which the selection of the instruments is left to the performer. Beyer uses simple accented rhythmic patterns arranged architecturally. The pulse ebbs and flows in conjunction with a rise and fall of the dynamic level. She fills in the last phrase rhythmically with sixteenth notes and tuplets, marked *alargando* [*sic*], ending the work with seven fortissimo eighth notes. The challenge (and the fun) for the performers is in the selection of instruments. The score implies a high-to-low order of sounds and, with the exception of Part 9, all notes are of short duration. (Fig. 3.2) Despite the notated eighth notes, resonances of both long and short duration should be considered when determining the work's instrumentation. Idiomatic percussion writing often ignores precise durations, leaving the selection of percussive timbres, dry to resonant, wide open. When notating percussion, orchestration manuals recommend that composers use "easy-to-read notation"[13] as it is "neither practical nor, in fact, possible to notate exact durations for short-decay instruments. For these reasons, relatively simple rest- and note-values should be used."[14]

Harold G. Davidson (1893–1959) was born in Low Moor, Virginia, on February 20, 1893. He studied at the Cincinnati Conservatory and, upon graduation, taught public school in that state before relocating to California. In 1935, Davidson wrote *Hell's Bells,* a work scored for six percussionists and a trio of pianists, and sent it to Henry Cowell for his consideration. *Hell's Bells* requires two sets of glockenspiel, a five-octave xylo-marimba, a set of tubular chimes, timpani, two tuned gongs, and two tuned cowbells (G flat and C). (Tam-tams could be substituted for the pitched gongs.) The work is whimsical in nature as revealed in Davidson's letter to Cowell in which he stated: "I was merely trying to be funny."[15] Cowell responded with interest and, shortly thereafter, Davidson sent him another work, a piece titled *Auto Accident,* that Cowell published and released in 1936. "The publication of the Davidson piece marked one of the rare times when Cowell published music submitted to him by a composer he had never met."[16]

Auto Accident is definitely tongue-in-cheek, taking us on a programmatic motor trip. It begins with a cheerful street music theme played by the xylophone, which is interrupted several times by ominous timpani glissandi. The first section builds to a climax at which time a player is instructed to break two glass plates with a hammer, each plate resting on a washbowl or crock. The "accident" is followed by the arrival of an ambulance with bells (chimes) ringing and a wailing siren. We then learn that the accident involved casualties as we hear a parody of Chopin's *Funeral March* played on tuned water tumblers with timpani accompaniment. (Fig. 3.3) There are no other known percussion works by Davidson and very little biographical information is available.

"About a mile due west of the [family] farm, about midway between Avalon and the county seat of Chillicothe, there was a little crossroads post office called Cavendish, and Martha Green [mother] listed the birthplace of her youngest son, Ray Green (1908–1997), as Cavendish, Missouri."[17] For a brief period in his career, Green was part of Cowell's West Coast group of composers writing for dance. His mature musical studies included compositional work with composers Ernest Bloch (1880–1959) and Albert Elkus (1884–1962). Green met his wife, the dancer May O'Donnell (1906–2004), when she visited Mills College as a member of the Martha Graham Dance Company. Together they founded the San Francisco Dance Theater and Green became interested in improvisation and dance accompaniment. At one point, he was asked by Henry Cowell "to take over his percussion class at the Ann Mundstock Dance Studio in San Francisco. Green was happy to do this because he was interested in percussion . . . and had already begun to acquire his own personal collection of instruments, including various exotic and Oriental instruments."[18]

Green's early works utilizing percussion instruments include: *Electra: Incidental Music* (1937) for solo flute, timpani, and cymbals, written for a production of *Euripides* at the Greek Theatre in Berkeley; *Suspension* (1942) for piano and percussion, including a large Chinese drum and a pair of tabla designated as "Hindu drums"; *Dance Energies,* written over a period of years (1950–1973), which calls for gongs, cymbals, and drums in a controlled improvisation; *Three Inventories on a Texas Tune* (1934, rev. 1952), which requires a bottle with marbles inside and a train whistle; and *Three Inventories of Casey Jones* (1934, rev. 1952). The last work, in its original form, was part of Cowell's 1936 *New Music: Orchestra Series.*

Three Inventories of Casey Jones premiered in 1938 at the Repertory Playhouse in Seattle at a concert sponsored by the Cornish School with John Cage conducting. The instrumentation calls for five graduated pop bottles (Fig. 3.4), one large bottle with four or five marbles inside, two drums (high and low), two suspended cymbals (high and low), four graduated gongs, and piano. The work opens and closes using only percussion instruments—the writing being more atmospheric than rhythmic. The piano is the main instrument throughout the three short movements that are arranged in the traditional fast-slow-fast tempi. The melody Green uses is reminiscent of an early nineteenth-century American folk tune, "Turkey in the Straw." Most likely, *Three Inventories* was written for the dance.

The dancer Doris Humphrey (1895–1958) and composer Wallingford Riegger (1885–1961) are also represented in Cowell's published collection of percussion music. The Humphrey/Riegger contribution to his 1936 *New Music* series is unique because it includes a single-page work titled *Dance Rhythms.* The abbreviated score states that: "These rhythmic patterns are from a group of dances by Doris Humphrey. Nothing but percussion instruments are used for this particular number, the rhythms being improvised by Miss Humphrey and Charles Weidman."[19] The dancers Charles Weidman (1901–1975) and Humphrey met at the Denishawn School located in Los Angeles and, in 1927, started their own Humphrey-Weidman Company. Both dancers continued on to become leading advocates of the then-new modern dance movement. "At the beginning of 1935, the modern dance was anything but a household word to middle America. Few had heard of it; even fewer had actually seen it."[20] Modern dance troupes began to tour America, performing both in vaudeville venues and on college campuses, wryly referred to as the "gymnasium circuit." By the end of the century, modern dance had become the dominant form of expressive dance.

Dance Rhythms is notated in the manner espoused by Cowell, who had written a number of articles on modern dance in the 1930s and 1940s. Cowell advocated for, and composed, music that was flexible and tailored to the needs of dance, using what he called his "elastic form." The work, as notated by Riegger, calls for two drums and a tambourine to be played by one performer, and a gong, suspended cymbal, three blocks, tom-tom, and bass drum by another. Unusually notated is a part for small drum written in a manner that requires the use of a hand-muffling technique. (Fig. 3.5) Riegger's oeuvre includes a 1954 work for orchestra titled *Dance Rhythms*, one of his most popular compositions. The battery needs are standard with the exception of a part for marimba that requires a three-mallet technique. The work is dedicated to the conductor Thor Johnson (1913–1975). *Dance Rhythms* (1954) was later choreographed by Humphrey and titled *New Dance*.

Of the six composers whose works were included in Cowell's collection of percussion ensembles, William Russell (1905–1992) has been credited with being the most influential in the development of the first truly avant-garde American music, that is, music for percussion ensemble. "Writing almost exclusively for percussion instruments in the 1930s, his early works pre-dated and influenced the percussion music of American experimentalists such as Henry Cowell, John Cage, John Becker, and Lou Harrison."[21] Known primarily as one of the leading authorities on early New Orleans jazz, Russell was a percussionist. For a time, he was a member of a Chinese shadow puppet troupe. He wrote, "I began traveling with the Red Gate Shadow Players in the late '30s, playing Chinese percussion music."[22] The troupe was formed by Pauline Benton (1898–1974), daughter of the president of the University of the Philippines. Benton studied traditional Chinese shadow puppetry in Peking (Beijing) in the 1920s and, along with Russell, formed the Red Gate Shadow Puppets, later the Red Gate Players. The troupe toured widely throughout the United States in the 1930s with Russell providing the music, playing Chinese wood blocks, drums, and Peking opera (glissando) gongs as accompaniment to the actions of the shadow figures.

Born Russell William Wagner in Canton, Missouri, Russell later changed his name to avoid comparison with another composer of note. He studied violin at the Quincy Conservatory of Music in Illinois, furthered his musical studies at Teachers College, Columbia University (New York), and took classes given by Arnold Schoenberg at the University of California, Los Angeles. Russell's compositional output is small, just eight works for percussion ensemble. His interest in jazz and its African roots is apparent in most of them.

During the years 1931 and 1932, Russell composed his *Fugue for Eight Percussion Instruments*. Cowell printed the *Fugue* in an early edition (1932) of his *New Music: Orchestra Series*. It was premiered on March 6, 1933, in Steinway Hall, New York City, as the finale to a concert given by the PAAC that also featured the premiere of Varèse's *Ionisation*. The fugue subject is eight bars in length.

(Fig. 3.6) It is first played by snare drum with the batter head covered with a handkerchief. The eight bars of duple time constitute a written accelerando, beginning with a whole note and ending with eight eighth-notes. The xylophone follows with a restatement of the subject, while the snare drum plays a simple counter-subject phrased in groups of three. The fugue ends with a *tutti* presentation of the subject in retrograde leading to a dominant-tonic cadence. Unusual xylophone techniques include the use of a bass bow to activate the bars and a glissando across the resonator tubes. Russell composed two additional movements, "Prelude" and "Chorale," in 1985 for the North American New Music Festival at the State University of New York at Buffalo.[23]

Russell's *Ogou Badagri* is a ballet based on the voodoo rites of Haiti. He composed the work's prelude in Port-au-Prince in 1932. Unable to attend the island's secret voodoo rites, he purchased some drums and hired local drummers to play the rhythms used in the rituals, wrote them down, and incorporated them into the music. He finished the ballet in 1933, but it was not performed until late in the century. At that time, a special retrospective concert given by the percussion group Essential Music featured a limited presentation of the ballet.

Two of Russell's works that found their way into the percussion ensemble canon following their premieres were a quartet, *Percussion Studies in Cuban Rhythms* (1935), and a trio, *March Suite* (1936, revised in 1984 as a quartet). Both compositions were (and are) available through the Fleisher Collection of the Philadelphia Free Library. The quartet, also titled *Three Cuban Pieces,* calls for a *quijada* (a folk instrument made from the jawbone of an ass) and a marimbula (a lamellophone), an instrument used in the Caribbean area that had roots in Africa. This work was easy to play (schooled percussionists not required), facilitating its assimilation into the early percussion ensemble and dance repertoire. The trio, *March Suite,* is programmatic in nature and comprised of five short movements: "School March," "Wedding March," "Military March," "Hunger March," and "Funeral March." In the "School March," the bass drum slowly moves out of meter as the other two players provide a polyrhythmic ostinato. The "Wedding March" begins with a familiar quote from Mendelssohn's *A Midsummer Night's Dream.* A growling stomach sound in the "Hunger March" is produced by rubbing a rosined thumb across the head of a Haitian drum and in the "Military March," a jaunty tune is played on a slide whistle to percussion accompaniment.

A 1936 jazz-inspired work, *Made in America,* was initially a trio but later revised as a quartet for its 1990 premiere. The work uses tin cans, auto brake drums, auto exhaust pipes, lion's roar, a large suitcase, a drum case (played with a pedal), a five-gallon can, and various New Year's Eve noisemakers. Improvisation, à la "hot jazz," is part of this piece.

Another trio, *Chicago Sketches* (1940), was written especially for John Cage. It was first performed on July 18, 1940, at Mills College, California, featuring Cage, his wife, Xenia, and the composer creating a variety of sounds from both standard percussion instruments and found objects such as a suitcase, a washtub bass, and a rhythm washboard. In an interview before his death in 1990, Russell described the source of his inspiration for each of the four movements.

> The first movement, 3525 S. Dearborn, was the address of Jimmy Yancey's home on the South Side of Chicago—he was an early blues pianist. 222 N. State was the address of a famous Chicago jazz club in the 1920s and '30s—The Three Deuces. Baby Dodds played there. The third movement, 5507 S. Michigan, was an ordinary South Side nightclub, but I heard a very good washboard band playing on the street outside their door. 4726 S. State was a South Side saloon where I first heard Cripple Clarence, a rather eccentric blues pianist.[24]

A quartet for three percussionists and piano titled *Three Dance Movements* was completed in 1933 and published in Cowell's 1936 *New Music: Orchestra Series*. The movements, "Waltz," "March," and "Foxtrot," in no way reflect the traditional forms these titles imply. The "Waltz" is written in 7/4, the "March" in 3/4, and the "Fox Trot" in 5/4 time. Cowell's influence is apparent in the piano writing as Russell explores the piano interior, calling for a table fork to strike the strings and then rapidly move across them, marked pizzicato in the score. Keyboard tone clusters, à la Cowell, are used throughout the work with a four-foot-long board used in the "March" to play a tremolo, created by rocking the board back and forth from black to white keys. The three multiple-percussion parts call for a variety of instruments and techniques. Part II requires both Turkish and Chinese suspended cymbals with notes marked "+" to be muffled and notes marked "o" to be played with a stick with rubber bands around one end. In the final movement, Part I calls for a ginger-ale bottle to be broken with a hammer, a theatrical display noted by the press after the premiere in New York at The New School on November 22, 1933. Part III requires two wood blocks, snare drum, tom-tom, and a bass drum played with a foot pedal. The jazz brush "slide" technique is notated as well as rim and head sounds. (Fig. 3.7) In 1990, Russell completed a fourth movement titled "Tango."

Russell's music is full of rhythmic energy and compositional surprises. He brings to his music both the European stylistic influences of his classical training and the rhythms and sounds of American jazz. Russell's percussion writing reflects knowledge gained through his years as a performer with the Red Gate Shadow Players. It is both idiomatic and exploratory, bringing new sounds and techniques to the medium. "Russell's choice of the percussion ensemble as his genre, assembled in a collage of western and non-western instruments with found objects, qualifies his work as perhaps the first truly avant-garde American music."[25]

The final work printed in Henry Cowell's 1936 percussion collection is titled *Percussion Music* (1935), and was written by the West Coast composer Gerald Strang (1908–1983). As early as age five, Strang began to show interest in music, but it wasn't until after he had completed his undergraduate college studies that he decided to formally pursue a career in music. He began graduate studies in music theory at the University of California at Berkeley, and by the time he "left Berkeley in 1929, he decided that he wanted to compose."[26] When Austrian composer Arnold Schoenberg (1874–1951) began teaching at the University of California, Strang attended his classes, eventually becoming Schoenberg's assistant. "This relationship would continue until Schoenberg's death in 1951."[27] Prior to working with Schoenberg, Strang considered himself "an 'autodidact' in contemporary music."[28] His musical oeuvre reflects his studies with Schoenberg as well as that of his other composition teachers, Charles Koechlin (1867–1950) and Ernst Toch (1887–1964). Strang worked with Henry Cowell coproducing concerts in the Los Angeles area. When Cowell was imprisoned in the fall of 1935, Strang took over his New Music publishing firm, serving as director until Cowell's release in 1940. Throughout his career, Strang held a number of teaching positions, including those at California State University—Long Beach and UCLA. He became an expert in acoustics, overseeing the construction of a number of music buildings. Eventually his compositional efforts became focused on computer-generated works. It appears that his only work for percussion was the 1935 trio listed here. Strang died in Loma Linda, California, in 1983.

Percussion Music was written for three players. Composed in 1935, it continued to be part of the percussion ensemble repertoire throughout the twentieth century, in part due to its availability, moderate level of difficulty, and modest instrumental resources. The composer writes: "The aim of composing *Percussion Music* has been to write pieces possessing a musical value in their own right, yet suitable for dancing, and capable of performance by a small number of reasonably well-equipped and trained dance percussionists."[29] The three parts are graded, with Part One being the most difficult. Instrumental resources needed include five Japanese cup bells (usually mounted in some fashion for ease of playing), five temple blocks, two gongs, a large Chinese drum, maracas, suspended cymbal, anvil (or iron pipe), two wood blocks, and a triangle. The score also lists the necessary mallets and sticks and a detailed explanation of unusual notational symbols. The work's three movements form the classic fast-slow-fast musical structure. With its recognizable rhythmic motives and melodies (Fig. 3.8), *Percussion Music* was able to reach a wider audience than the more experimental works published in this early collection of ensembles. As indicated in the score, it was intended to be music to accompany dance and to be played by dancers without classical percussion technique or in dance companies lacking the resources to hire professional musicians.

LOU HARRISON AND JOHN CAGE

In the 1930s and 1940s, the nascent modern dance movement was just starting to garner attention. It needed music that would set it apart from traditional ballet repertoire. Cowell encouraged dancers to use percussion as an accompaniment to their dances. The strong rhythmic definition provided by many percussion instruments proved to be a good medium for dancers versus more melodic sounds that lacked focus. "Most percussion instruments, [Cowell] said, have the asset (when used for dance) that tones are never perfect enough, that is, not focused on one pitch. The more purely melodic an instrument is, the less rhythmic."[30] Through the efforts of Cowell and his students, percussion music and sounds became part of modern dance's musical resources to be used both on stage and in the studio.

Two of Cowell's students who added significantly to modern dance music's concert repertoire were Lou Harrison and John Cage. Both contributed extensively to the musical needs of modern dance prior to World War II as composers and as accompanists. This duo formed the first standing percussion ensemble. Made up of dancers and composers, the ensemble functioned as accompaniment for dance concerts and also performed chamber music for a listening audience. "For both Harrison and Cage, the attraction of the percussion ensemble was not only aural, but also social. . . . Their percussion music, born from interdisciplinary collaboration in music and dance, eventually achieved an independent validity drawing from both western and world music traditions."[31] The period 1939 through 1942 was important to the development of the modern percussion ensemble and its literature. Through Cowell, Harrison met the composer/percussionist John Cage in 1938. Both were students of Cowell and Schoenberg and both composers worked as dance accompanists. Upon meeting, the two young men joined forces to present a series of concerts for percussion ensemble, with and without dance, in cities along the West Coast. The repertoire generated for these events became staples of the modern percussion ensemble following World War II.

Cowell's world music course greatly influenced both Harrison and Cage. He exhorted them to find and use new timbres. "Cowell not only encouraged novel uses of traditional instruments but also urged them to seek new sound-producing media."[32] Harrison recalls: "All of us were haunting junk shops, automobile dismemberment yards . . . finding everything we could."[33]

The "instruments" Harrison and Cage found in junkyards, antique stores, and knick-knack shops were usually designated as nonpitched, but, in fact, many had specific pitches. The two composers grouped these instruments into sets arranged from high to low tones avoiding major triads and other unwanted intervals. They found that the resonant sounds of automobile brake drums and gongs could be muted by laying them on a flat surface or by suspending them, allowing them to ring freely. Arrays of tin coffee cans and pieces of iron pipe made into sets were placed on mats and were played with a variety of sticks and mallets. Mexican maracas, claves, a jawbone, and a tortoise shell colored the rhythmic pulse of their works. In San Francisco's Chinatown, the duo found imported trinkets such as glass and bamboo wind chimes, Japanese cup bells, Chinese tom-toms, Indonesian cricket callers, and Korean temple blocks. To this mix of timbres, they added the standard snare drum, bass drum, wood blocks, and cymbals. Both Harrison and Cage used this rich resource of conventional and exotic sounds in ways unique to their compositional bias. The percussion ensembles created were crafted to be performed by nonpercussionists. Harrison, Cage, Cage's wife, Xenia, dancer Doris Dennison, pianist Margaret Jansen, and others comprised these early groups. They had no difficulty in learning complex polyrhythms and other irregular groupings, but they lacked the technical finesse of trained percussionists. As a result, Harrison and Cage avoided notating snare drum rolls and other idiomatic percussion articulations. Large and expensive instruments such as timpani, marimbas, and chimes were excluded as well. Together they composed over fifteen works for percussion ensemble within the short span of four years (1939–1942).

Born in Portland, Oregon, on May 14, 1917, Lou Silver Harrison (d. 2003) had been involved with the arts since the age of two-and-a-half when he appeared as the orphan boy "Buster" in a stage production of *Daddy Long Legs.* Raised and schooled mostly in Oregon and California, Harrison studied piano as a child and began writing music by the time he was ten years old. In 1935, he met the composer Henry Cowell, who became a central figure in his musical development. Harrison enrolled in Cowell's course "Music of the Peoples of the World" at San Francisco State University and commenced a life-long exploration of world musics and cultures. "Nearly every aspect of Harrison's work shows Cowell's influence."[34] With Cowell's help, Harrison found employment as a dance accompanist and teacher. From 1936 to 1939, he taught at Mills College outside of San Francisco. He later moved to Los Angeles where he studied with Arnold Schoenberg and, in 1943, he moved to New York City. While there, he earned his living as a music critic and as a copyist, notably recopying a number of works by the American modernist composer Charles Ives. A stress-related illness caused Harrison to abandon city life and return to the Big Sur country of northern California where he spent the remainder of his life composing, teaching, and, with his companion William Colvig (1917–2000), building percussion instruments.

Harrison composed a number of percussion pieces prior to his collaboration with John Cage and continued his interest in this medium for many years thereafter. His 1941 work, *Labrynth* [*sic*] *#3*, was "originally intended . . . as a dance drama."[35] This large, multimovement work calls for eleven players and is almost twenty minutes in duration. It utilizes a vast resource of percussive sounds (thirty-two different classes in all) including everything from button gongs to a bass viol, to be played near the bridge with sticks. That same year, Harrison composed *Canticle No. 3*, a work scored for four percussionists, an ocarina player, and a part for retuned acoustic guitar, easily played by a nonguitarist. The work was premiered on May 7, 1942, at the San Francisco Fairmont Hotel's Holloway Playhouse.

Critics often characterize *Canticle No. 3* as "Eastern" or "Oriental" in atmosphere, although Harrison remarked that it was written at a time when he was most interested in Indian and Mexican music. The work begins with the five-toned ocarina playing an engaging, rhythmically vigorous tune in a pentatonic mode. (Fig. 3.9) This theme serves as a source of both rhythmic and melodic material that Harrison develops throughout the *Canticle*, using standard compositional techniques, namely thematic augmentation, diminution, retrograde, and inversion. In Harrison's book, *Music Primer* (1971), written for his students, he explains his approach to composition. He demonstrates how small groups of melodic notes he calls Melodicles can be permutated along with their rhythmic counterpart called Rhythmicles. This approach to composition is evident throughout *Canticle No. 3*. He groups many of the so-called nonpitched percussion instruments into sets, with relative pitches—high to low—each set with its own distinct timbre. The ostinato figures created are finely delineated as he layers them in contrapuntal fashion. Throughout Harrison's career, he embraced melody, whether writing for pitched instruments or nonpitched percussion. "*Canticle #3* illustrates Harrison's lyrical side particularly effectively, contrasting quiet sections foregrounding the winsome ocarina with fortissimo percussion outbursts."[36] *Canticle #3* became one of Harrison's most popular works, recorded and played by percussion ensembles throughout the world.

The Harrison/Cage partnership was apparently a close one. They united to co-compose a quartet for percussion titled *Double Music* (1941). For this piece, both composers agreed beforehand to the rhythmic and durational parameters. Cage wrote the music to parts one and three; parts two and four were composed by Harrison. Upon completion, the four parts were united without the need for alteration. Cage also assisted Harrison in the preparation of his *Fugue* (1942), a work that demonstrates an inventive approach to the realization of a tonal fugue using nonpitched percussion.[37] Harrison had read Cowell's book *New Musical Resources*, in which Cowell explored the correspondence between proportional pitch (or intervallic) values and rhythmic values. These proportions were obtained by Cowell from the natural overtone series of a single pitch. The correspondence was one between pitch and rhythm; thus, slow a pitch down, it becomes a rhythm. In traditional fugues, there exists a constant polarity between tonic and dominant harmonies. The fugue's subject is normally first written in the tonic key and then answered in the dominant key. To accomplish this tonal transposition using nonpitched instruments, Harrison had to find another way.

Harrison's *Fugue* begins with a two-bar introduction, played by the flexatone acting as a sort of pedal tone. The subject follows, played by a metallophone made from an array of resonant metals, such as iron pipes. (Fig. 3.10) The duration of the four-measure subject is then transposed (augmented) to one and a half times the original length, representing the interval of a fifth (2:3) of a tonal fugue. This answer to the subject is played on a set of meditation bells and completes the fugue's first exposition. Harrison introduces other timbres in the following three sections including automobile brake drums, a wooden box, gongs, triangles, bass drum, claves, maracas, and suspended cymbal. The suspended cymbal type was Turkish to differentiate it from the popular Chinese cymbal used in jazz orchestras of the time. Also unique to the *Fugue* were the bell coils that Harrison salvaged from old clocks and mounted on a resonant box (or old guitar). Completing the instrumentation is a galvanized washtub that provides two sounds, center and edge. The work exhibits the following structure:

MEASURE	SECTION	INSTRUMENTATION
1–33	exposition	Metallophones
34–44	first episode	Woods—Skins—Metals
45–75	exposition repeated	Woods—Skins—Metals
75–98	second episode	Woods—Skins—Metals
99–132	exposition in retrograde	Metallophones

"Many of the sectional breaks in the Fugue are not as clear-cut as is suggested by these measure numbers, and formal divisions are frequently elided."[38] The third and final fugal exposition is presented in retrograde and the work ends as it began with the solo flexatone. Harrison's *Fugue* provided extreme rhythmic and ensemble difficulties (too great for the times) delaying its premiere until after its publication in 1960 when a new generation of percussionists rose to the challenge.

John Cage (1912–1992) was born and raised in Los Angeles, California. The son of an inventor, Cage attended Pomona College, leaving after two years for Europe in hopes of pursuing a career as a writer. There he explored painting, poetry, and music, and, for the first time, began to compose. In 1931, he returned to California to study composition, first with pianist Richard Buhlig (1880–1952) and later with Henry Cowell. He continued his studies in New York City with one of Schoenberg's students, Adolph Weiss (1891–1971), and returned to Los Angeles in 1934, where he enrolled in Schoenberg's classes at UCLA. Though not exactly twelve-tone works, Cage's early compositions reflect Schoenberg's influence regarding musical structure.

In 1937, Cage began working as a dance accompanist at UCLA and, in 1938, with the help of Lou Harrison, joined the faculty of the liberal Cornish School of the Arts in Seattle, Washington. There, Cage replaced the school's outgoing dance accompanist, who left a large cache of percussion instruments that Cage was able to use for accompanying dance classes. While only in residence for two years (1938–1940), Cage "often cited this period as seminal to his later work."[39] During his brief tenure at Cornish, Cage presented three all-percussion concerts at the school with added performances in neighboring Montana, Idaho, and Oregon. He recorded his ensemble's work at the school's broadcast and recording studio "in which he could experiment with electronic sounds."[40] He used its resources to create the first work in his *Imaginary Landscape* series. Out of necessity, he wrote his first piece utilizing a "prepared" piano when the wings of the theater's stage could not accommodate his percussion group. Also during his time at Cornish, he began to codify his approach to composition, specifically the use of a compositional process that he called the "square root" formula. It is logical that Cage, working with dancers, would devise a system of composition based on duration since both dance structures and compositional structures are based on time and rhythm. His square root formula provided him with a structure that determined a priori the overall length of the composition as well as the duration of phrases contained therein. He first used this compositional approach in 1939 when composing the work *First Construction (in Metal)*. In its score notes, Cage states that the square root used is 16 times 16. He divides *First Construction* into 16 large sections (15 sections of 16 measures in length and one 9-measure section, which he labels a coda). Each 15-bar section is organized into 4, 3, 2, 3, and 4 measures, with the 9-bar coda grouped into 2, 3, and 4 measures. The rhythmic ideas used are simple, making the structure audible to the listener. At the opening motive, a sustained sound, written as whole notes in common time, is played by four thundersheets (large sheets of metal used theatrically to imitate the sound of thunder). This wash of sound accompanies a more rhythmic figure composed of eighth notes and quarter notes first played in the bass register of the piano. (Fig. 3.11) (The piano is played with pedal throughout the entire work, adding to its texture.) A motive, comprised of half notes, is heard first as four chords played by orchestral bells, automobile brake drums, and Turkish cymbals. Cage manipulates this motivic material in a variety of ways. He adds to this mixture of piano and percussion sounds a number of other metallic sounds: sleigh bells, twelve graduated oxen bells, Japanese temple gongs, anvils, tam-tam, cowbells, and Chinese cymbals. To vary the purely rhythmic texture, glissandi are created by having an assistant move a metal rod across the piano strings and also by lowering and raising a gong into a tub of water while activating it with yarn mallets. The latter sound is one Cage discovered while working with UCLA's aquatic ballet group. "I found that the swimmers beneath the surface of the water, not being able to hear the sounds, lost their places. Dipping the gongs into the water while still playing them solved the problems of synchronization and brought the sliding tones of the 'water gong' into the percussion orchestra."[41] Cage continued to write percussion works using variations on his square root formula (he was not strict in its usage) including a *Second Construction* (1940) and *Third Construction* (1941). This compositional procedure served him well for many years.

In 1941, at the invitation of the artist László Moholy-Nagy (1895–1946), Cage and his wife moved to Chicago. During his brief stay, Cage taught a class in experimental sound at the Chicago School of Design, worked as dance accompanist for Katherine Manning at the University of Chicago, and formed an ad hoc percussion ensemble that performed a concert at Chicago's prestigious Arts Club. His social connections led to a commission from the Columbia Broadcasting System (CBS) to write music for a radio play by the pacifist poet Kenneth Patchen (1911–1972), titled *The City Wears a Slouch Hat*. "Cage wrote a 250-page score in which various sound effects suggestive of the actual sounds of the city were to be considered not as 'effects' but as music."[42] Engineers at the CBS radio station, WBBM, advised Cage that production of the score would not be possible. In a week's time, Cage rewrote the score, including in it some of the percussion and electronic sounds he had already used in his earlier compositions, plus a number of sound effects: foghorn, baby cry, wind, rain, and so on. The work was written to enhance Patchen's descriptive, evocative prose.

Cage left Chicago in the spring of 1942 for New York City. His hope to continue working there for CBS did not materialize. His dream, similar to that of Varèse's, of a center in which he and other like-minded composers could explore the possibilities of the new electronic technologies, was put on hold. In addition, his percussion instruments were stranded in Chicago due to lack of funds to ship them. To earn a living in New York, Cage returned to dance accompaniment while continuing to write for prepared piano, but soon (as we shall see in a later chapter) his life and musical aesthetic were to change dramatically.

The creation of music for percussion, from the decades before World War I to the compositional hiatus caused by World War II, brings us to a historical juncture. Henry Cowell best summarized the early development of percussion music in a 1940 article in the journal *Modern Music*.[43] He identified four developmental directions, the first of which was the creation of a sophisticated art form that was ready-made, absent of gradual development. It began with the Italian Futurists' manifesto and the acceptance of noise as a musical sound source and, for Cowell, it was exemplified by the compositions of Edgard Varèse. The second direction was the expansion of the percussion section in traditional orchestras and ensembles as demonstrated in the works of Stravinsky, Milhaud, Bartók, and others. The third was the derivation of percussion music from folk traditions exemplified by works of Roldán, Chávez, and Cowell. The fourth and final path was the use of percussion music as a complement to modern dance, which Cowell attributes to Harrison and Cage.

It is difficult to argue against Cowell's evaluation regarding the early development of music for percussion. In Europe, the Futurists and Dadaists evidenced the discontent felt by many artists of the time. Their malaise found a home in the rebellious spirit of the French composer Edgard Varèse, who brought to America his passion for creating a new kind of music. His iconic *Ionisation* was but one work in which this influential composer featured percussion. Varèse's immense symphonic work, *Amériques*, with its huge battery of percussion, including the wail of a siren; the stunning chamber work, *Hyperprism;* and his pioneering composition for tape, winds, and percussion, *Déserts*, presented percussion instruments in a new way. In each of these works, percussion is equal to and as important as the other instrumental families.

The future of percussion was, of course, prophesied in the writings of Stravinsky, Milhaud, and Bartók, whose creative and musical scoring challenged percussionists as musicians. Stravinsky integrated percussion into the fabric of his work as evidenced in his three ballets, *L'Oiseau de feu, Pètrouchka, Le Sacre du printemps*; his choral work, *Les noces;* and the musical stage play, *Histoire du soldat.* His "soldier's tale" made the drummer a soloist, requiring the player to perform on an array of percussion instruments, as did Milhaud in his *Concerto pour batterie et petit orchestre.* Composers Stravinsky and Bartók mined the folk music of Europe and Asia Minor, which provided each with primitive rhythmic and melodic materials that they then transformed into high art. Latin composers, like Roldán and Chávez, found inspiration in the indigenous music of their homelands as well as in their cities' cabarets and nightclubs. Bongos, claves, timbales, conga drums, and other native instruments born in Africa, became exciting new timbral resources for composers who adopted their sophisticated rhythms creating innovative aesthetics. In the United States, modern dance played a seminal role in the creation of the percussion ensemble by providing contemporary composers a forum for the performance of their works. Percussion accompaniment for modern dance classes replaced the traditional piano used by classical ballet and accompanists/composers Cage and Harrison united to bring their exotic percussion music to the people of the West Coast and eventually across America to New York City.

The advent of World War II affected most artistic activities throughout the world. In the war's early years, a few American composers continued to write works for percussion instruments, but eventually all efforts were focused on winning the war. In Europe, the war brought creative arts activities to a complete halt as musicians and other artists immigrated to the United States and elsewhere seeking to escape the conflict.

Other works to consider: John Cage: *Dance Music for Elfrid Ide* (1940), *Amores* (1942), *Credo in US* (1942). Lou Harrison: *First Concerto* (1939), *Bomba* (1939), *Fifth Simfony* (1939), *Canticle No. 1* (1940), *Simfony No. 13* (1941), *The Song of Queztecoatl* (1941), *Suite* (1942).

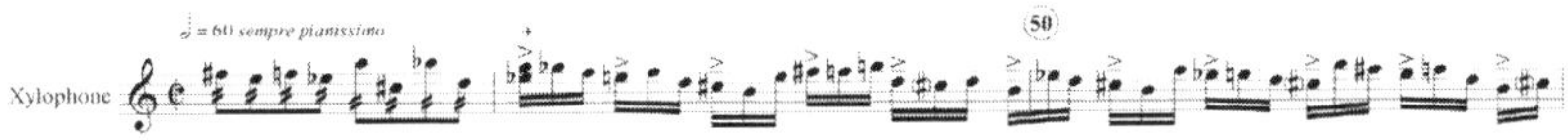

Fig. 3.1 Cowell, *Ostinato Pianissimo* (xylophone excerpt)

Fig. 3.2 Beyer, *Percussion* (Mvt. IV, meas. 1–7). Copyright © Smith Publications, 54 Lent Rd., Sharon, VT 05065. Used by permission.

Fig. 3.3 Davidson, *Auto Accident* (timpani and tuned tumblers excerpt)

Fig. 3.4 Green, *Three Inventories of Casey Jones* (five graduated pop bottles, Mvt. II)

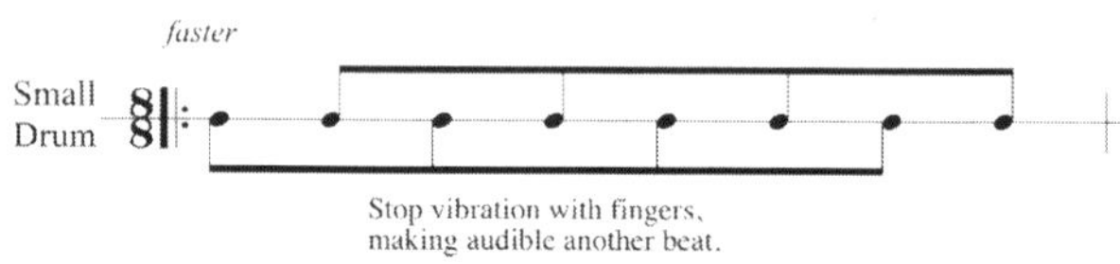

Fig. 3.5 Humphrey/Riegger, *Dance Rhythms* (Part A)

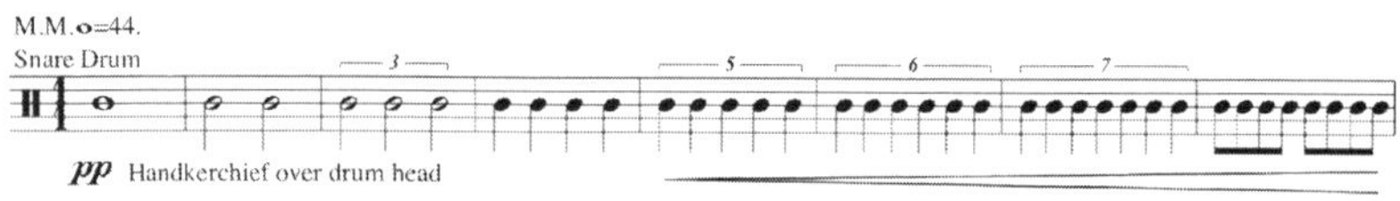

Fig. 3.6 Russell, *Fugue for Eight Percussion Instruments* (fugue subject)

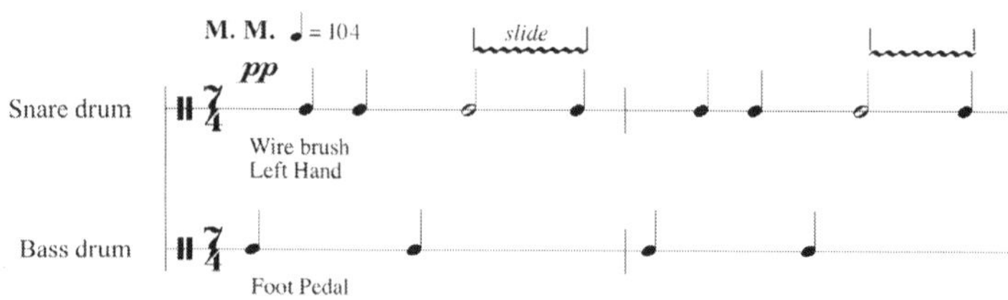

Fig. 3.7 Russell, *Three Dance Movements*, "Waltz" (meas. 1–2)

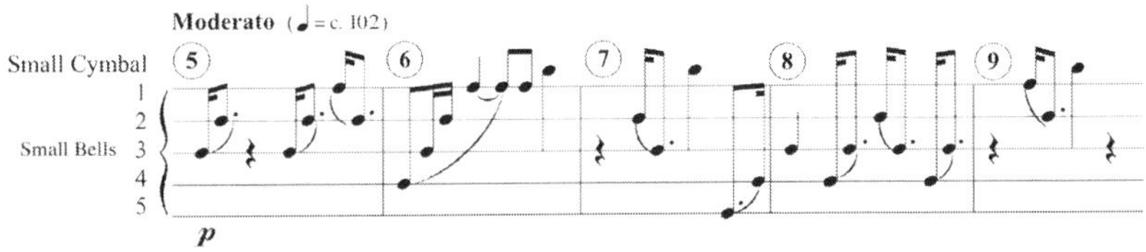

Fig. 3.8 Strang, *Percussion Music* (Mvt. II, meas. 5–9)

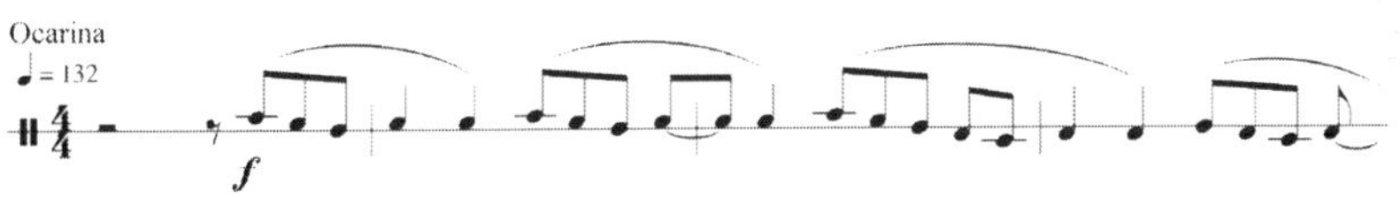

Fig. 3.9 Harrison, *Canticle No. 3* (ocarina, meas. 3–6)

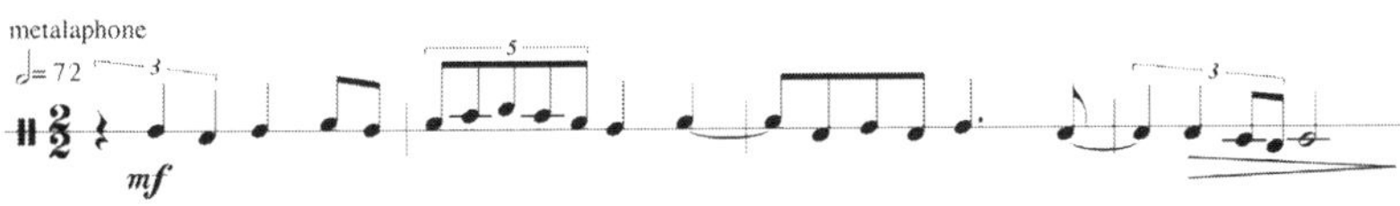

Fig. 3.10 Harrison, *Fugue* (metallophone, meas. 3–6)

Fig. 3.11 Cage, *First Construction (in Metal)* (meas. 1–4)

Chapter 4

POST WORLD WAR II—AMERICA RISING

At the end of World War II, Europe and Asia were in turmoil. The death and destruction wrought by opposing armies left these two continents with problems that would take years to resolve. In Europe, with aid from the United States, the economy slowly started to rebuild and the arts once again began to flourish. Occupied Japan would experience momentous cultural change, embracing Western models of both popular and serious music. In the United States, the war brought an end to the Great Depression and American soldiers, called GIs, returned home to resume their lives. Most of them were young, just out of high school, when drafted into service. When they returned home, they hoped to find work or to continue their schooling and enjoy a more normal life. On June 22, 1944, President Franklin Roosevelt signed into law the Servicemen's Readjustment Act, better known as the GI Bill. It provided millions of returning GIs with a number of benefits, including the financial support necessary to attend college. Without this type of support, most would have been unable to do so.

Prior to World War II, American colleges and universities were bastions of elitism with enrollments of barely a million students nationwide. With curricula geared to the classics, the incoming student body was largely comprised of eighteen-year-olds from well-to-do families being groomed to join the family business upon graduation. Following the war, millions of returning GIs entered colleges, trade schools, and universities, more than doubling previous enrollments. They were mostly from America's working class. These new, older students (many with families) were interested in course offerings and degrees that would lead to a career. As noted by Edward Humes in his book *Over Here*: "Classes filled with guys with no particular interest in Shakespeare or Tolstoy, but who flocked to practical courses that were useful in making a living."[1] Schools, large and small, particularly public universities, responded to the needs of the GIs. On campuses across the nation, students sporting crew cuts and khakis replaced those in white bucks and raccoon coats. Enrollments quickly skyrocketed, dormitories overflowed, and temporary housing was built to accommodate students with families. Small private schools, some newly formed, cashed in on the federal largesse as well. The rapid growth in enrollment resulted in the creation of new departments, new degree programs, and new faculty positions. In college music departments throughout the United States, instrumental specialists, including percussion teachers, were added to faculties for the first time. This was the case at the University of Illinois.

Paul Price (1921–1986) was hired in 1949 as the first full-time percussion specialist at the University of Illinois and remained there until leaving in 1957 for a position at New York's Manhattan School of Music. He had a vision of what a percussion program should be, one not unlike that for violinists and other established instrumentalists. Armed with some early percussion methods books, a small list of percussion ensemble works, and a few published percussion solos, he designed a course of study for a percussion major leading to a bachelor of music degree. The program included a core curriculum—theory, history, and so forth—plus the usual private lessons. In addition, it established a new degree requirement, which was enrollment in what would become the first accredited ensemble course for percussion. His initial effort at establishing a percussion ensemble course was rejected by the school's curriculum committee, which felt that there was insufficient repertoire to justify such a course. Price continued his research, finding additional repertoire (some from the Fleisher Collection of the Philadelphia Free Library), and the new percussion ensemble course became official in the spring of 1951. He was very conscious of the poor image that most other instrumentalists had of "drummers." He was also aware of his role as a pioneer and made every effort to raise the standards of musicianship in his chosen field. He required that his students wear dark blue suits for all percussion recitals and ensemble concerts. He taught them how to walk onto a stage, how to take a bow, and much more. Price limited percussion ensemble repertoire and recital pieces to original works written for percussion instruments; no transcriptions were allowed. Composition faculty colleagues were commissioned to write music for the newly formed ensemble, as were composers from around the country. If students did not like the music

Price recommended, they were challenged to compose their own. Many did, creating a body of usable works for solo percussion and for small percussion groups, trios, quartets, and so on. Price selected many of these for publication in a new company that he founded in 1950, Music for Percussion. It was the first publication house dedicated to music written for both solo and ensemble percussion. Price's pedagogical model was soon copied by other music schools across the nation. The result was that, in a relatively short period of time, composers had access to extant percussion ensembles comprised of trained percussionists who were willing to play their most recent compositions. The impact of Price's vision on percussion pedagogy, on solo and ensemble repertoire, and on the level of performance by percussionists was dramatic and substantial. He continued to champion new music after leaving Illinois, commissioning and premiering percussion ensemble works until his death in 1986.

One of the young percussion students at Illinois who responded to Paul Price's challenge to write percussion music was Michael Colgrass (1932–2019). Born in Chicago, Colgrass was raised in the suburb of Brookfield where, at an early age, he began to play the drums. His primary interest was jazz. By age twelve, he had formed his own band, Three Jacks and a Jill, which performed for local school and community functions. After graduating from high school, he attended LaGrange Township Junior College for a year. At age eighteen, he auditioned for Price and was subsequently accepted at the University of Illinois. "I could read only rhythm at the time and couldn't find C on the treble clef, but I guess they thought I had enough talent to catch up," he recalled.[2] With Price's encouragement, Colgrass wrote his first piece for percussion ensemble, titled *Three Brothers* (1951). Inspired by Woody Herman's 1940s big band chart for four saxophonists, *Four Brothers*, Colgrass crafted a jazz-oriented work that featured solo bongos, snare drum, and timpani with ensemble accompaniment. It was a very successful first effort, one that encouraged Colgrass to pursue a career as both composer and percussionist. Further encouragement came when his quartet *Percussion Music* won the 1952 composition contest sponsored by the National Association of College Wind and Percussion Instructors. The University of Illinois music school's bachelor's degree requirements included two formal recitals. To satisfy this requirement, Colgrass composed three works for his senior recital: a concerto for timpani and brass, a work for seven voices and vibraphone, and a chamber piece for percussion soloist with string quintet. These compositions satisfied the official degree requirements as well as Price's imposed rule that each student perform works demonstrating their skill in three areas of percussion: timpani, keyboard percussion, and multiple percussion (the latter category included any work requiring snare drum technique).

Drafted in 1954, Colgrass joined the Seventh Army Symphony Orchestra stationed in Stuttgart, Germany. Upon completion of his military service, he returned to Illinois in the summer of 1956 to finish his bachelor's degree. Thereafter, he moved to New York City where he continued to compose while supporting himself as a freelance percussionist. In New York, a former member of the NBC Symphony Orchestra and world-famous violist, Emanuel Vardi (1915–2011), heard Colgrass's 1954 work, *Chamber Music for Four Drums and String Quintet*, performed with the composer as soloist. Attracted by the timbre of the four small drums ("timp-toms," a precursor of the Remo RotoToms) as well as Colgrass's virtuosity, Vardi commissioned a duet, *Variations for Four Drums and Viola* (1957), which was recorded for MGM Records. Other works featuring the timp-toms followed: *Fantasy-Variations* (1961) for eight timp-toms and percussion ensemble and *Rhapsodic Fantasy* (1964) for fifteen timp-toms and orchestra. Throughout the 1960s and 1970s, Colgrass continued to compose (operas, songs, and oratorios), concentrating on works for instruments other than percussion. He returned to his first love in 1977 with a composition, titled *Déjà vu*, which won the 1978 Pulitzer Prize for music. *Déjà vu* was commissioned by the New York Philharmonic and featured all four members of the orchestra's percussion section. The composer writes: "In *Déjà vu* I have written a typically classical type of melody to provide the thematic and rhythmic substance of the piece. This theme first appears in a serial form introduced at the beginning of the work by the four soloists, and then later in a purely rhythmical form on non-melodic percussion."[3] The melodic motif runs through the entire work, appearing in different guises (atonal, jazz, romantic) with the four soloists playing simultaneously in a stylistic counterpoint. Colgrass further describes the work as: "Four percussionists playing four separate solos, often in separate tempi, while exploring percussion colors in various styles."[4]

Until century's end, Colgrass continued to write works featuring percussion instruments. Forty years after composing *Variations for Four Drums and Viola*, he wrote *Hammer and Bow* (1997), a chamber work for marimba and violin. Both works evolved from simple motives, a compositional process that Colgrass used throughout his career. This process is most evident in his early work *Chamber Piece for Percussion Quintet* (1954). "I had just studied sonata form with Lukas Foss at Tanglewood and was profoundly affected by its logic and power,"[5] he said. *Chamber Piece* calls for a scale of sixteen membranophones, ascending from the sounds of the low bass drum and timpani to the four high timp-toms. The work opens softly with a staccato, five-note motive played over a bass drumroll. (Fig. 4.1) From this brief motive, others evolve, some more lyrical, as the work develops with sections of contrasting tempi and textures.

In the score, Colgrass takes care to describe not only which instrument to play, but also what mallet or stick one should use for a particular passage. As a composer, his works benefit from his knowledge as a performing percussionist. He carefully notates articulations and dynamic markings for each note, giving instructions on how to achieve both. A staccato sound on resonant tom-toms is made possible by muffling the drum with one hand while playing the written figures with the other. Other technical details demonstrate Colgrass's knowledge of the percussionist's art. *Chamber Piece* ends with a final coda, marked adagio, in which the opening motive reappears in augmentation played softly on the bass drum.

Colgrass brings to his writing an intimate knowledge of the percussion instruments he so creatively exploits. He is keenly aware of their technical and acoustical capabilities as well as their weaknesses. In his work *Déjà vu*, the timpani and pizzicatti orchestra basses are coupled to support both timbre and pitch. The vibraphone is matched by high string harmonics and flute, and the RotoToms are located next to the harp for pitch reinforcement. His writing is both rhythmic and melodic. "To me, drumming is singing,"[6] he claims. Using rhythm, timbre, texture, and the subtlest of dynamic nuances, Colgrass created a body of percussion solo and ensemble works that have withstood the test of time.

During and following World War II, other composers discovered the potential of percussion instruments as a voice for musical expression. After the war, compositions for groups large and small appeared on college percussion ensemble programs. Even popular music groups exploited an ever-expanding palette of percussion sounds with arrangements of both jazz and pop music. In his 1962 master's thesis, Gordon Peters wrote of the impact of new recording techniques and the advent of hi fi and stereo recordings that brought a new awareness of percussion instruments to the listening public.[7]

During the 1950s, one composer whose name appeared frequently on percussion ensemble programs was American Alan Hovhaness (1911–2000). Born Alan Vaness Chakmakjian, he later adopted the surname of his paternal grandfather, Hovaness (adding an additional letter *h* in 1942). Hovhaness began composing music at an early age, penning his first opera at age fourteen. Composition studies with Frederick Converse (1871–1940) at the New England Conservatory of Music constituted his only formal training. He worked as an organist at Saint James Armenian Church in Watertown, Massachusetts, where he was exposed "to the modes and monody of the Armenian liturgy."[8] In the 1940s, a New York City debut brought him to the attention of fellow composers Lou Harrison and John Cage. Publication of his piano music in Henry Cowell's New Music series followed.

Mountains served as inspiration for Hovhaness. His *Symphony No. 50*, written in 1983, was subtitled *Mount St. Helens*, whose violent eruption three years later resonated through his then mountain retreat near Seattle. His piano sonatas and symphonies often carried subtitles such as *Mount Chocorua, Mount Ossippee, To the Holy Mountain*, and *To the Green Mountains*. His very successful *Second Symphony* (1955) was subtitled *Mysterious Mountain*. Mountain views, however, did not inspire him to compose *October Mountain* for percussion sextet. Instead, it was the beauty of the countryside near Tanglewood, Massachusetts, where "on a country road marked 'October Mountain' he parked his car one afternoon and there composed the score for his percussion piece of the same name."[9]

In *October Mountain* (1942), Hovhaness combines archaic and modern styles, creating a work of five short movements featuring pitched percussion (marimba, glockenspiel, and timpani) with percussion accompaniment (tenor drum, bass drum, tam-tam, and gong). Movement I opens with a six-bar introduction in which the marimba plays a short phrase, beginning with a three-note rising figure played *senza misura*, which is answered by the glockenspiel and tam-tam. Two additional phrases lead to a twenty-one-bar stately march featuring the timpani, tenor drum, bass drum, and tam-tam. In the march, five isolated glockenspiel notes outline the opening melodic material. The other four instruments, timpani, tenor drum, bass drum, and tam-tam, play a rhythmic pattern of prescribed lengths. Multiple repetitions of these short, rhythmic lines imitate the isorhythmic controls used in motets of the fourteenth and fifteenth centuries. Hovhaness uses this ancient compositional device to control the drum part rhythms throughout the entire work. He also uses an architectonic, dynamic arch in each of the four outer movements, starting softly and slowly increasing the intensity, with the loudest dynamic marking the center of each movement. Movement III features a marimba and glockenspiel duet. Again Hovhaness references ancient liturgical music by ornamenting each note of a simple melody played by the marimba in a melismatic manner. Uniquely, the glockenspiel is cast here in a contrasting role to the marimba's tuneful material, pitting ancient modality against the dissonance of modern atonality. In movements III and IV, the glockenspiel plays figures incorporating all twelve scale notes. In movement III, the notes are embellished with chromatic flourishes. In movement IV they are presented three times with an ever-increasing intensity, the final presentation marked fortississimo. (Fig. 4.2) *October Mountain* is a well-balanced, tightly constructed work. Hovhaness controls all aspects of the work utilizing both ancient and modern pitch and rhythm controls. It was one of the most-performed percussion ensembles of the twentieth century.

Other works by Hovhaness featuring percussion include two early works for solo percussion and piano (*Invocations to Vahakn* [1945] *and Hakhpati* [1946]); a number of notable chamber works for winds and percussion (*Overture for Flute and 4 Percussion* [1959] and *Mysterious Horse before the Gate* [1963]); and, in 1965, a work for solo xylophone and orchestra titled *Fantasy on Japanese Wood Prints*, which will be discussed in a later chapter.

A large-scale percussion work from the 1950s by Henry Brant (1913–2008), an American composer of Canadian birth, foretold, in a way, the future of university-based percussion ensembles. Calling for a force of sixteen players, skilled at playing both pitched and nonpitched percussion, Brant's *Symphony for Percussion*, completed in 1952, was challenging both for players and conductor. At the time it was premiered, it created monumental logistical problems for rehearsals and performances. By the 1990s, many college percussion programs would have enrollments of sixteen or more students with modern practice space and ample equipment, making it easier to mount such a large work. Also, as mentioned earlier, keyboard percussion technique was considered a specialty early in the century. The new pedagogical approach promoted by Paul Price and other university percussion teachers helped students become proficient at playing snare drum, timpani, and keyboard percussion instruments (the "total percussion concept") rather than simply one or two instruments.

Henry Dreyfuss Brant was born in Montreal, Canada, on September 15, 1913. His father, a professional violinist, encouraged his son's musical aspirations. By age nine, Brant was writing music for found instruments, and at age twelve, he composed a string quartet. As an adult, Brant became a successful Pulitzer Prize–winning composer, earning a living writing for various media: film, radio, jazz bands, and ballet. For years, he taught composition and orchestration at Bennington College in Vermont. His early music studies included attending McGill Conservatorium in Montreal and the Juilliard School of Music in New York City in addition to taking private lessons in composition with composers Wallingford Reigger and George Antheil. Antheil's influence became evident as Brant's musical output reflected the avant-garde ideas of the day. He began writing music for unorthodox combinations of instruments and voices. Upon hearing a performance of Charles Ives's *The Unanswered Question*, with its three antiphonal forces (strings, woodwinds, and solo trumpet), he began focusing on the problem of making clear, multiple-polyphonic lines, determining that spatial separation of the voices was the best solution. "I realized that I had hit a crisis with pieces like my *Symphony for Percussion*, which in places contained more horizontal parts than I know how to make clear."[10] He also embraced jazz and its freedom to improvise. Many of his late works called for extraordinarily large forces. A 1982 work, *Meteor Farm*, is scored for two sopranos, two choruses, three South Indian performers, a West African chorus, jazz band, gamelan, and two percussion ensembles.

Brant's *Symphony for Percussion* was premiered in Urbana, Illinois, on March 13, 1956, with Paul Price conducting as part of the University of Illinois Festival of Contemporary Arts. The work is in four movements titled: "Origins," "Levels," "Currents," and "Upheavals." For the program, Brant wrote:

> In this work my intention was to produce music of symphonic length and proportions, completely limited to the sonorities of a percussion orchestra. I excluded instruments like the piano, which might be thought of as only partly in the category of percussion, but included the celesta, which because of its struck steel bars, is undoubtedly classified as percussion. With these purposes in mind, I scored for an ensemble made up of instrumental family-groups in as complete a way as possible, to some extent resembling the family-group set-up of the symphony orchestra with its high, low, and medium representatives of each tone-quality.

Brant specifies that the work is not programmatic, but one should "imagine, in musical terms, the sense of such phenomena as the origin of the earth."[11]

To prepare for the premiere, Price divided his forces so as to fit player and instruments into one rehearsal space, rehearsing each half separately. The instrumentation was considerable for the time and could have been larger: Price rejected the composer's request to add an organ part and an antiphonal brass choir to the work. Brant divided his instrumentation into three categories: (1) *Instruments of Definite Pitch*: glockenspiel, two standard vibraphones, a rare three-octave C-to-c vibraphone, tubular chimes, three xylophones, celesta, and sixteen kettledrums; (2) *Instruments of Relative Pitch*: sets of four of the following—tom-toms, cowbells, Chinese blocks, fire bells, small dinner bells, suspended cymbals and gongs, a set of eight skillets (described as metal frying pans of various sizes to be hung on the wall of the stage and struck with table knives or rocked back and forth, providing a unique timbral wash as well as a captivating visual display); (Fig. 4.3) (3) *Instruments of Indefinite Pitch*: bass drum, snare drum, maracas, gooseneck lamp (to be scraped with a stick), large scissors, small Jew's harp (laid on a table and snapped), plate-scraper (a flat pottery dish scraped in a circular motion with the top of a sugar bowl), screen-scraper (a window screen scraped in a half-circular motion with a small bowl or small metal coaster), bicycle bell, tone-knife (a well-sounding stainless steel table knife held between thumb and index finger and bounced on a table), saw-bowl (a small ceramic bowl scraped with a fine saw-blade), finger cymbals, and tambourine.

In the first movement, Brant organizes his instruments into five trios that have similar characteristics of pitch, timbre, or sonority. A glockenspiel and two vibraphones become a group of ringing metallophones; three xylophones become a dry wood-sounding group; and three timpanists, with their sixteen kettles, become a group of membranophones. These three groups are comprised of instruments of definite pitch. In addition, Brant scores for two trios from his category *Instruments of Relative Pitch*. Four graduated suspended cymbals, four fire bells, and four gongs make up a set of ringing, metal timbres. A trio of four tom-toms, four Chinese blocks, and four cowbells comprise a set of less resonant, nonmetallic timbres.

The first movement, "Origins," begins dramatically with a trio of timpanists playing interlocking glissando figures using a total of sixteen kettledrums. Keyboard percussion instruments join the drums, adding new melodic material and contrapuntal interest. The celesta introduces a quiet middle section. Here the keyboard percussion writing becomes less bravura and the accompaniment now includes dinner bells, sandpaper blocks, gourd, snare, and bass drums. A transition to the final section brings back the opening material and its instrumentation as the movement comes to a close. Movement II, "Levels," is slower, quieter, and less dramatic than the first movement. The texture is less dense and the emphasis is on a melodic line of limited tessitura. The fifteen timpani are tuned so as to collectively cover an octave, C–c chromatically, and the players are instructed to play their notes cantabile, with a beautiful tone. The third movement, "Currents," is marked "*Leggiero, non agitato*—very neat and clear throughout." Here the emphasis is on rhythm with a dominant, fast-moving syncopated motive first played by the timpani. At rehearsal number 24, fourteen different instruments of indefinite pitch combine to create a contrasting section before the rhythmic motive returns, and the movement ends with its initial material. The fourth and final movement unfolds with the sound and sight of eight skillets followed by a kettledrum cadenza. The movement features both the timpani trio of players and the xylophone group as they trade virtuosic sections of material. The "rocking" skillets return as the piece comes to a close.

Brant's *Symphony for Percussion* is one of the first percussion ensemble works to explore the multimovement symphonic form. He manipulated his instrumental groups much as any composer would the sections of a standard orchestra—brass, woodwinds, percussion, and strings. Creatively scoring for both traditional percussion instruments and "found" instruments (many from his home kitchen) gave Brant a wide palette of sounds and colors with which to work. This successful work reflects the aesthetics of many of the percussion pieces written in the 1950s. Brant continued to compose for many years, exploring his interest in "spatial music." He died at his home in Santa Barbara, California, at the age of ninety-four.

During World War II, many technological advances and new materials useful to the war effort were developed by both sides of the conflict. On the U.S. West Coast, a young drummer by the name of Remo Belli (1927–2016) began experimenting in the mid-1950s with a material called Mylar, developed for the U.S. Air Force by the chemical company DuPont. The result of Remo's experiments was a moisture-resistant drumhead he trademarked under the name Weatherking and the birth of what was to become the world's largest drumhead company. By the 1980s, plastic drumheads would all but replace traditional calfskin heads.

Born September 6, 1923, in Chicago, Illinois, William Kraft began his early musical experiences after his family moved to San Diego, California. At a Mission Beach Ballroom concert, he was inspired after hearing famed Count Basie drummer Jo Jones (1911–1985). He immediately purchased his first set of drums and began his journey as a percussionist. Kraft studied drums with Murray Spivack in Los Angeles while attending UCLA and was drafted into the U.S. Army Air Corps. He spent three years playing drums and piano in an army band in the States and overseas. A band colleague, Saul Davis, recognized Kraft's talent for composition, coaching him on various musical styles. In an email to the author, Kraft remarked: "Those were the best composition lessons I ever had."[12] Upon his release from the service, Kraft moved to New York City where, with the help of the GI Bill, he was able to attend Columbia University as a composition major while taking percussion lessons at the nearby Juilliard School. Upon graduation, Kraft spent a year with the Dallas Symphony Orchestra before joining the Los Angeles Philharmonic where his tenure lasted twenty-five years. In addition to his chair as principal timpanist, Kraft served as the orchestra's assistant conductor and director of the organization's New Music Group.

In recognition of Remo Belli's achievements, Kraft composed a percussion quartet titled *Suite for Weatherkings* (1958). The *Suite* is in three movements: "Fanfare," "Ostinatos," and "Toccata." The *Suite*'s brief, opening "Fanfare" calls for bongos, high and low snare drums, field drum, tenor drum, and bass drum. The high-to-low arrangement of the membranophones offered Kraft the opportunity to manipulate simple melodic motives that, like those in the Chávez *Toccata*, are easily perceived by the listener. Each player enters in turn, from high bongo to the low bass drum, with a soft roll. Together they crescendo to a fortissimo. A short, syncopated motive follows. The movement ends with a loud, sustained crescendo. Movement II, "Ostinatos," has a jazzy dance flavor. The snare drum player lays down a seven-bar brush beat that Kraft turns around for an additional seven bars before repeating. (Fig. 4.4) Above this ostinato, the tambourine enters playing a fourteen-bar solo that includes thumb rolls. At bar 29, the field drum is added, playing the brush ostinato starting on the upbeat and interlocking with the snare drum figure to create a more complex ostinato. Then, at bar 43, the bass drum begins a soloistic rhythmic pattern played by using a rattan stick on one head and a hard timpani mallet on the opposite head. Kraft follows with a short development section, ending the movement with the original brush beat diminishing *al fine*. The final movement is appropriately titled "Toccata" from the Italian "to hit or touch." At a fast tempo, sextuplets and interlocking rhythmic figures are passed between players. Ringing and dry sounds are notated for the frame drum, and the bass drum solo from the middle movement is recalled. *Suite for Weatherkings* was a very popular work, receiving many performances throughout the United States. Kraft later retitled the work *Suite for Percussion,* adding two additional movements, "Andante," which became the second movement, and "Cadence," which completed the now five-movement suite. With an array of ringing, tuned percussion—glockenspiels, vibraphone, and tuned gongs—the "Andante" movement is quieter and more melodic. Kraft notated glockenspiel harmonics to be played by striking the "narrow sides" of the A sharp and C sharp bars with a hard mallet to produce the sound of a tenth, or a diminished twelfth, above the written notes. He ends the movement having the players play tremolos across the instruments using their fingernails. The closing movement begins with a written cadenza for bass drum player using a rattan stick and a hard felt bass drum mallet. Following the cadenza is a section written for "song bells," an early Deagan Company metallophone that had a lower range and a softer sound than the glockenspiel. The movement ends with the ringing sounds of vibraphone and gongs, a driving drum lick, and the raucous sound of a flexatone.

Kraft continued to add numerous works to the percussion repertoire over his long and distinguished career. His mature works include *Des Imagistes* (1974) for percussion sextet and reciter (text by Ezra Pound); *Songs of Flowers, Bells, and Death* (1991) for chorus and percussion orchestra; and *Quintessence* (1985), a concerto for five percussion soloists and concert band commissioned by the U.S. Air Force Band. His most popular concerto, the 1983 *Concerto for Timpani and Orchestra,* will be discussed in a later chapter. (See chapter 11.)

The European recovery following World War II was marked, in part, by the rejection of totalitarianism and the resurgence of liberal ideals. "Liberation from Nazi or Fascist occupation was widely welcomed as an occasion for radical political and social change; an opportunity to turn wartime devastation to revolutionary effect and make a new beginning."[13] For many European composers, new beginnings meant a continuation of traditional musical practices. For others, the prewar work of Schoenberg and his student Anton Webern (1884–1945) was their model. Additionally, young composers began to explore new ways of writing, ones that were more personal and organic, much like the approach of their avatar, Edgard Varèse.

A number of major composers in France, Italy, and Germany were influenced by Webern's organization of sound and timbre and his sparse musical aesthetic. The so-called "post-Webern" school was championed in France by Pierre Boulez (1925–2016) and in Germany by Karlheinz Stockhausen (1928–2007). Both composers studied with the French organist, composer, and teacher Olivier Messiaen (1908–1992), whose works forecast a system of organizing not only pitch, but other musical parameters as well—a precursor of "total serialism." Two postwar camps emerged in the 1950s, the serialists and the non-serialists, creating a compositional divide that lasted until the end of the century. (See chapter 5 on serialism.)

France's recovery from the war was swifter than that of Germany and other European nations. French composers, young and old, began once more to create new music and to have their works played. Their efforts reached the listening public in part through the state-owned radio. "After the liberation of Paris in 1944, musical activities began to revolve around the Radiodiffusion Française."[14] Composer Pierre Schaeffer (1910–1995), the radio station's director, using the technology of the time, produced an early version of electronic music, *musique concrète*, by manipulating prerecorded sounds. (See chapter 7 on electronic music.) Other French composers continued to write much as they had before the war or they followed the lead of Boulez and embraced serialism. Three French composers who eschewed serialism and found their own unique voices were André Jolivet, Marius Constant, and Maurice Ohana.

Inspired upon hearing Edgard Varèse's work *Amériques*, with its large force of percussion instruments, the French composer André Jolivet (1905–1974) became one of his students. "Varèse's impact is evident in Jolivet's experimentation with sound-masses, acoustics, orchestration, and atonal (though non-serial) methods."[15] In 1958, Jolivet wrote a concerto for multiple-percussion soloist and orchestra, *Concerto pour percussion*, that utilized four timpani and a large array of standard orchestral percussion instruments, a much more ambitious work in scope than the earlier percussion concerto of Milhaud. In the 1960s, Jolivet composed *Suite en Concert* for solo flute and percussion quartet, dedicated to the renowned French flutist Jean-Pierre Rampal (1922–2000). In 1968, he wrote a percussion sextet, *Ceremonial,* that paid homage to his mentor, Varèse.

In *Ceremonial,* the influence of Varèse's *Ionisation* is evident in the instrumentation and in the musical materials used to construct the work. Instruments such as high and low sirens, lion's roar (*tambour à corde*), sleigh bells (*grelots*), anvil (*enclume*), slapstick (*fouet*), along with ringing metals and membranophones are the basic colors for both works. To this mix, Jolivet added tuned percussion—sets of tuned cowbells (*cencerros*), fourteen tuned Thai gongs, a set of five tuned African slit drums, plus vibraphone, crotales, tubular chimes, glockenspiel, marimba, timpani, and a *xylorimba* (Fig. 4.5), an instrument that incorporates both the qualities of a marimba (low register) and the xylophone (upper register). Jolivet's writing does not include any extended performance techniques, but he does call for specific mallets and beaters and he carefully notates dynamics.

Ceremonial is episodic in form. It opens with a brief explosion of sound followed by a passage similar to the opening of *Ionisation* with pointillistic drumbeats immersed in a wash of ringing cymbals and tam-tams. In a later segment, Jolivet recalls part of the famous snare drum cadence so evident in Varèse's iconic work. *Ceremonial* ends much as it begins with a sonic blast of drums over ringing metals.

Another French composer, Marius Constant (1925–2004), was born in Bucharest, Romania. He moved to Paris in 1946 on a French government scholarship. Like Jolivet, his musical creativity was not constricted by any compositional dogma. "Constant himself vigorously eschewed the serial movement of the 1950s and 1960s."[16] Constant's body of work demonstrated a wide range of genres, including ballet, orchestra, chamber, and electronic music. In 1963, he founded a new music ensemble, Ars Nova, under the auspices of Radio France and enjoyed a successful career as both composer and conductor. His percussion works include solo pieces and chamber music. In 1969, he composed *14 Stations,* a multiple-percussion solo with accompaniment. It is dedicated to his spiritual mentor, Messiaen, and to the Algerian percussionist Sylvia Gualda (b. 1939). *14 Stations* was patterned after the Roman Catholic liturgy's Stations of the Cross, which depicts events surrounding the crucifixion of Jesus of Nazareth. For each of the fourteen vignettes, a separate percussion setup is needed—these to be distributed across the performance area. The percussion soloist moves from station to station while a sextet of three strings, harpsichord, guitar, and trombone (all amplified) remain seated on a platform. The sounds of the sextet act as a "shroud of sound" over which the soloist is heard. The music is written mostly without meter—the notes inscribed without bar lines, using proportional notation. (Fig. 4.6) Constant often depicts sounds and physical gestures using graphics, a common practice when notating electronic music. The instrumentation includes both standard pitched and nonpitched percussion. Unusual requirements include a two-octave set of tuned wood blocks, Thai gongs, bell plates, lion's roar, and steel drum. Placing a small gong atop a pedal timpano, the composer was able to produce harmonic glissandos by moving the drum's pedal up and down while activating the gong. Constant uses a great variety of instrumental colors in response to the emotional actions depicted at each station from the "Condamnation" to the "Ensevelissement" (entombment). He, like many other composers in the second half of the century, found it necessary to invent new ways to notate both nontraditional sounds and unusual rhythms. This trend continued until computer notation programs became popular with composers in the last decade of the twentieth century.

Maurice Ohana was born in Casablanca on June 12, 1913. He grew up in the North African nation of Morocco where he heard both Spanish and African music. A gifted pianist, he studied in Paris and, following World War II, became a permanent resident. His music is modern, often strident. Like Varèse, he felt that "musical form should be a consequence of musical material, rather than a superimposed scheme."[17] Ohana wrote a number of works that featured percussion, including *Silenciare* (1969) for six percussion and string orchestra, and *Synaxis* (1965) for two pianos, four percussion, and orchestra. The latter work is very dramatic and highly dissonant. "The vibraphone part in *Synaxis* requires metal rulers of specified length to sound non-chromatic chord-clusters equivalent to the black or white notes of the piano."[18] Neither pianos nor percussion are paired in the traditional sense, but rather play a combative role. Both *Silenciare* and *Synaxis* call for large amounts of percussion equipment. In 1961, with the help of Radio France, Ohana worked to establish a massive collection of percussion instruments: "The project was designed to gather together the largest possible collection of percussion instruments from anywhere in the world, these to be stored as a reserve of quality instruments for performers and composers."[19] His most popular percussion work is *Études chorégraphiques* for percussion sextet. It was composed early in his career as a solo work to be performed with dance. A later-published version for four players was also intended for the dance. The final sextet version was written "to fulfill a commission from Les Percussions de Strasbourg, to be staged with choreography by Manuel Parrès for the Ballet Municipal de Strasbourg."[20] Instrumentation for the final version includes crotales, pitched Thai gongs, four pitched Chinese cymbals (both versions), a variety of snared and African drums, plus multiple keyboard percussion instruments. The published quartet version of *Études chorégraphiques* has four movements and its instrumental resources are less demanding. As expected in music written for the dance, Ohana uses a number of different ostinato patterns throughout the work. The second movement, which is slow, opens with a snare drum solo in three-quarter time marked piano. This dirgelike figure is later joined by bass drum and tom-tom, which combine to play groups of five against the metered three. Movement III calls for few instruments, the melodic and rhythmic interest centers on the pitched Chinese cymbal. (Fig. 4.7) The finale is dominated by a loud, rapid moving eighth-note pattern played over a number of different drums.

In a 1987 interview by Christine Paquelet, Ohana speaks to his relationship with percussion.

> I think percussion is something important in my music because it has escaped equal-temperament. Rather than any intellectual acquisition, the percussion has been something that I have known my whole life, and has become an extension of my means of expression. Despite an ear that is trained to hear primarily melody, I wanted also to develop a means of writing pure rhythm, but soon discovered that one can suggest melody in an abstract sense through the use of percussion. This is what I did in *Études chorégraphiques*, particularly in the second movement.[21]

Études chorégraphiques ends with a short seven-bar coda, marked lento. A final drumroll that fades away brings the work to a close. Ohana died in Paris, France, on November 13, 1992.

The years following World War II and the decade of the 1950s saw a resurgence of musical creativity. Percussion works written prior to the 1940s and those newly composed in the 1950s formed a modest repertoire for college percussion ensembles. In the United States, newly hired percussion teachers had both a library of works and interested and talented student performers. In 1951, Indiana University hired Richard Davis Johnson (1921–1983), the first African American percussion professor. In 1954, students at the Eastman School of Music in New York formed a marimba ensemble. Led by percussionist Gordon Peters (b. 1931), the ensemble performed arrangements of classical music and became known as the Marimba Masters, appearing on television nationwide (*The Ed Sullivan Show*, January 12, 1958). That same year, Thomas L. Davis (1931–2011), former member of Dick Shory's (b. 1931) percussion pops orchestra, was hired by the University of Iowa and by the following year had enough students to form a percussion ensemble. In the West, William Kraft, newly appointed to the L.A. Philharmonic, organized the Los Angeles Percussion

Ensemble premiering works by Harrison, Ginastera, and others. In Europe, the Hochschule für Musik located in Würzburg, Germany, hired percussionist/composer Siegfried Fink (1928–2006), whose percussion studio produced players and teachers for many decades. The principal percussionist of Japan's NHK Orchestra, Tomoyuki Okada, taught at Kunitachi University and later at Senzoku College of Music, creating a large program with over one hundred percussion students. Major music schools throughout the world began to recognize the importance of having a full-time percussion faculty member on staff. Consequently, the practice of using adjunct percussion instructors, often members of local symphonies, began to fade. In the decades that followed, music schools large and small became a source of employment for the schooled percussionist.

Other works to consider: *Suite for Marimba* (1950) by Alfred Fissinger (1925–1999); *Trio for Two Marimbas and Piano* (1950) by Robert Kreutz; *Introduction and Allegro* (1951) by Jack McKenzie (1930–2010); *Sonata for Percussion* (1956) by George Andrix (b. 1932); *Trio for Percussion* (1957) by Warren Benson (1924–2005); *Two Structures for Percussion* (1957) by Sydney Hodkinson (b. 1934).

Fig. 4.1 Colgrass, *Percussion Music* (meas. 1–7)

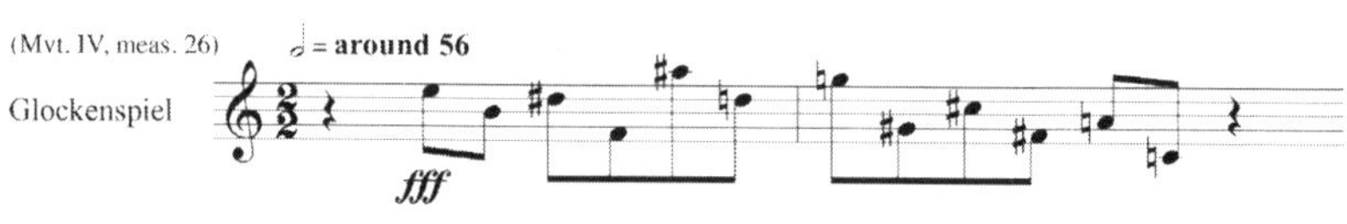

Fig. 4.2 Hovhaness, *October Mountain* (Mvt. IV, meas. 26–27)

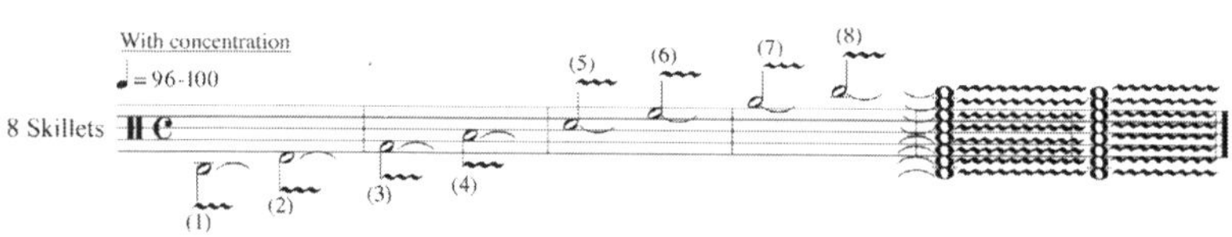

Fig. 4.3 Brant, *Symphony for Percussion* (Mvt. IV, skillets)

Fig. 4.4 Kraft, *Suite* ("Ostinatos," meas. 1–7)

Fig. 4.5 Jolivet, *Ceremonial* (marimba and xylorimba excerpt)

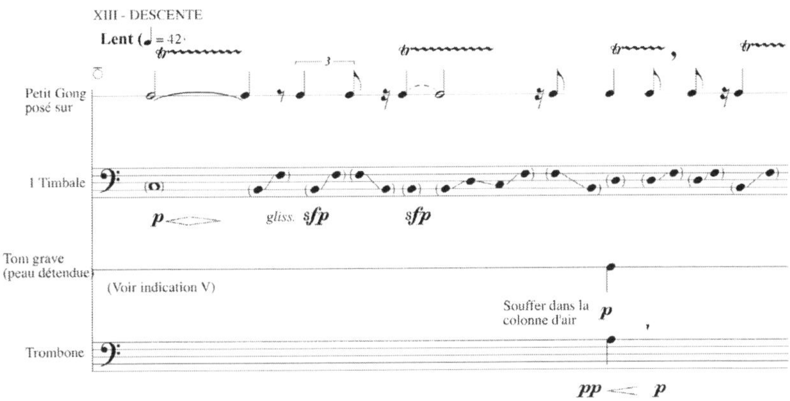

Fig. 4.6 Constant, *14 Stations* (Mvt. XIII, opening sounds)

Fig. 4.7 Ohana, *Études chorégraphiques* (Mvt. III, Chinese cymbals)

Chapter 5

SERIALISM

Permutating Indefinite-Pitched Instruments

World War II's devastation was most severe in Italy and Germany; less so in the other continental European countries. Yet, soon after the surrender of the Axis powers that ended World War II, musical activity of the avant-garde was again apparent. "Though the final months of the war had been catastrophic for Germany's cultural infrastructure, budding initiatives soon reestablished a lively new music community throughout the country."[1] In Germany, the Internationale Ferienkurse für Neue Musik (International Vacation Course for New Music) was held for the first time in the summer of 1946 "with the support of the city of Darmstadt (then 90 percent destroyed), the state government of Hessen, and the American military."[2] The Darmstadt courses, devoted to the performance and interpretation of new music, were held for two weeks each summer (now every other year). In 1950 the annual Donaueschingen Festival that had begun in 1921 was reactivated under the name Donaueschingen Festival of Contemporary Music. Traditionally a festival for the performance of chamber music, it had a prestigious history of important commissions and premieres. Both Donaueschingen and Darmstadt, with the help of German radio stations, reestablished interest in new European music after the war. Darmstadt, located just ten miles from the city of Frankfurt, became a meeting place for like-minded composers from Germany, Italy, and other European countries as well as the United States. In the 1950s and 1960s, many of those composers followed the lead of Schoenberg and Webern by embracing serial techniques.

Tonal music became atonal and composers, such as Pierre Boulez from France and the German composer Karlheinz Stockhausen, championed this new compositional approach. "Serialism is defined as the compositional procedure by which an order of succession is established for the values appropriate to one or more parameters (components) of the musical process; these orders of succession or permutations of them are then repeated throughout the composition."[3] The serial concept was first applied to pitch by Arnold Schoenberg, producing twelve-tone or dodecaphonic music. In the 1950s, serialization of other parameters (rhythm, dynamics, timbre) became common, and the term "serial music" was widened to include them.

One of the composers who adopted the serial compositional approach was Karlheinz Stockhausen. In the late 1950s, Stockhausen not only looked for ways to organize pitch, but also explored the possibility of organizing every parameter in a given work, thus, "the unification of all the properties of sound under a single principle of organization,"[4] or total serialization.

Born before the war in the town of Mödrath, Stockhausen began his musical training in nearby Cologne's Musikhochschule and, after the conflict ended, continued on at its university. Jazz piano became his favorite performance medium; he cites improvisation as being an important compositional impetus. Stockhausen became an important figure in the field of electroacoustic music and, with the musicologist Herbert Eimert (1897–1972), he directed the Studio for Electronic Music of the West German Radio (WDR). His work in electronics will be discussed in a later chapter. (See chapter 7 on electronic music.)

An early Stockhausen work for piano and two timpanists, *Schlagtrio*, was first performed in 1952. (A final revised version is dated 1972.) The title was chosen to indicate a chamber music work comparable to other chamber works. The six notes of the timpani, three drums per player, are tuned either a quarter-step above or quarter-step below the corresponding notes of the piano. Attack sounds and their resulting resonances prevail; soft drumrolls are used to enhance and extend these sounds. The notation is traditional. In this work, Stockhausen serializes not only pitches, but also dynamic levels and durations. By the end of the 1950s, he added three more significant percussion-involved works to the repertoire, expanded the concept of serialization, developed a new notation system for percussion, and incorporated "chance" procedures into his compositional structures.

In 1959, Stockhausen proposed that solo percussion be part of the Kranichstein Music Competition. *Zyklus* was written by the composer to serve as the competition's obligatory work. Dedicated to the director of the Darmstadt Vacation Course for New Music, Wolfgang Steinecke (1910–1961), it premiered on August 25, 1959, in Darmstadt with Christoph Caskel (b. 1932) as soloist. The composer provided a detailed analysis of *Zyklus* and suggestions on how to prepare the work for performance in a 180-page booklet included with the 1993 CD comprised of three works, *Zyklus, Refrain,* and *Kontakte.*[5]

Zyklus means "cycle" in English. The concept of a closed circle is at the core of the work's structure, including the positioning of the required percussion instruments. A marimba, vibraphone, four tom-toms, two African log drums, snare drum, high-hat, four pitched cowbells, button gong, tam-tam, suspended cymbals, triangle, guiro, and a string of Indian bells are arranged in a circle in whose center the player stands. During the course of the work, the percussionist completes a single oscillation turning either clockwise or counterclockwise. The score, written on sixteen spiral-bound pages, has seventeen periods of equal length, one to a page, except for the first page, identified as such by the composer analysis, that contains both period one and seventeen. (Fig. 5.1) There are thirty time units positioned across each period, the duration to be decided by the player (44 bpm is recommended by the composer).[6] A player may start at any point in the score and continue through the seventeen periods, ending with the first sound of the initial period. One can invert the score as well and play the work in reverse. Inspired by the schematic symbols used in electronic circuitry designs, Stockhausen created pictograms to easily identify each instrument regardless of how one positions the score. Other graphic indicators included are slanting up-and-down arrows identifying accelerandos and ritardandos and twelve sizes of notes indicating degrees of intensity. The score instructions describe nine structures, each offering the performer a degree of choice as to the selection of material for a given section, thus adding a degree of randomness to the work's form. In the clockwise version, the structures move from fixed material to increased randomness. Invert the score and the movement progresses toward greater fixity. Stockhausen had designed an earlier piano work, *Klavierstück XI,* in which melodic groups of various lengths were spread across the page of music. The pianist would, at a glance, or by the blink of an eye (Ger. *Augenblick*) select a group of notes to perform and, after doing so, move to the next group, ending the piece when the first group was repeated. In *Zyklus,* the visual "structures" offer the percussionist a similar degree of freedom in the selection of which material to play. In the triangle-shaped structures, the player determines the order of the notes contained therein. If there are several bracketed staves, only one is selected for a given performance. A series of rectangles contain groups of notes that offer even greater freedom of choice as to how and when they should be played. Due to the percussionist's need to choreograph his or her physical actions, how and when to change mallets and sticks and so on, the idea of *Augenblick* was not practical and Stockhausen came to realize that fact. He later recommended that the soloist predetermine the selection of material found within his system of structures and memorize that version for a given performance. *Zyklus* is a seminal work for solo percussion. It occupies an important place in percussion literature as well as in Stockhausen's development as a composer.

Stockhausen's *Refrain*, written for the Berliner Festwochen 1959, calls for three players: (1) piano and three pitched wood blocks, (2) celesta and three crotales, and (3) vibraphone and three pitched *almglocken* plus three glockenspiel bars. The sustained resonance of the keyboard instruments is at the core of the work's structure. Unique to the work is the use of alveolar tongue clicks used in some African and Australian languages and "called syllables" notated phonetically (such as [ta], [pa]). Both clicks and syllables are used to color the attacks of selected instrumental sounds and are notated in red in the score. Also unusual is a movable, transparent plastic strip fastened at the center of the score on which notes and figures are engraved: "The strip pivots like a compass needle over part of the score which is curved to accommodate it."[7] This plastic engraved strip, "the refrain," contains trills, tremolos, and bass piano notes. Positioned uniformly in each player's score, it interrupts the flow of the sustained sounds. "The refrain of the title is a notation of disturbances which discreetly ruffle the surface of the music at intervals."[8] The vibraphone is treated here as an equal to the other two keyboard instruments.

During the 1950s, Stockhausen was a dominant figure in Central Europe, acting as a source, transmitter, and codifier of new ideas. "His ideas about musical form, compositional process, musical notation, extension of musical resources, and classical electronic music studio techniques were often pioneering."[9] His electronic/percussion music, *Kontakte* and *Mikrophonie I*, from this same time period will be discussed in a later chapter. (See chapter 7 on electronic music.)

As part of the Axis coalition, Italy suffered greatly from the invasion of the Allied troops. Post–World War II saw the end of Mussolini's Fascist regime and the beginnings of a democratic society: "Italy became a democracy, however imperfect, and remained a democracy throughout the post-war decades."[10] In 1946, the famed conductor Arturo Toscanini (1867–1957) reopened the city of Milan's opera house, La Scala, with the sound of a solo snare drum (Rossini's overture to *La Gazza Ladra*), symbolizing Italy's cultural rebirth. Italy has a long tradition of lyric opera and Milan is its epicenter. It is also the home of the Milan Conservatory of Music where, in 1945, composer Luciano Berio (1925–2003) began his studies. In the summer of 1952, with the aid of a Koussevitzky Foundation scholarship, he traveled to the United States for a month to study serial composition with the Italian composer Luigi Dallapiccola (1904–1975).[11] Back in Milan, Berio found work as a composer at the Italian radio and television network, RAI, and became interested in electronic music, establishing in 1955, along with composer Bruno Maderna (1920–1973), Italy's first electronic music studio, Studio di Fonologia. Berio soon became part of the post-Webern group of young European composers. A Fromm Foundation commission produced one of his most successful chamber works, *Circles* (1960). Written for dramatic soprano, harp, and two percussionists, it was premiered by his wife, the American soprano Cathy Berberian (1925–1983), at the 1960 Berkshire Music Festival in Tanglewood, Massachusetts.

Circles is a setting of three poems, "Stinging," "Riverly Is a Flower," and "n(o)w," by the American poet E. E. Cummings (1894–1962). Written in five movements, *Circles* creates a palindromic arch form (12321) by repeating the first two poems in reverse order. The text of each poem is not fragmented, but rather set verbatim. An approximate tempo is given. The meter is free in the first three movements with the instrumentalists following and coordinating their parts with the vocal line. The soprano lengthens certain words, letters, and syllables, often using melisma to ornament them. She also employs *Sprechstimme*, a quasi-singing/speaking technique used in Schoenberg's *Pierrot lunaire* (1912). The work's structure reflects, at many levels, the idea of a circle, including the percussionists who are each surrounded by an array of more than fifteen different instruments. On stage, the two percussionists are centered with the harp between them. The soprano, first located at a music stand downstage, moves to a second location closer to the instrumentalists near the end of the middle movement. Playing finger cymbals while walking, she joins the players for the fifth and final movement. The theatrical setting adds to the dramatic nature of the music.

The two percussion arrays are very large, utilizing wood, metal, and skin sounds, pitched and unpitched, with the instruments positioned in a circle around the players. In addition to the standard percussion instruments, Berio scores for Mexican bean pods, four Chinese gongs, two congas, kick drum, wood and glass wind chimes, and a *lujon* (a "pitched American metallophone").[12] For each percussionist, the instruments producing resonant metal sounds are positioned closest to the harp with the wooden instruments at the far extremes of each setup. This arrangement of sounds is reflected in the score's notation where each instrument is notated on a single line. "*Circles* by Luciano Berio was one of the first pieces to employ an extensive array of instruments in a line-score system."[13] Berio utilizes a variety of notational devices throughout *Circles* including traditional and proportional notation, dotted vertical lines, and numerous caesurae to help coordinate the four parts. The setting of the lengthy middle poem, "n(o)w," uses "box notation" extensively, giving the two percussionists a greater amount of improvisational freedom. (Fig. 5.2) In each box, Berio indicates the instruments the player must use, pitch requirements (if any), dynamics, and the density of the sounds. No written explanation is given in the score as Berio assumed that the visual representation was adequate.

During the 1960s, Berio toured with his ensemble throughout Europe and the United States performing *Circles*, featuring his wife, Cathy Berberian, as soloist. With her definitive performances and the work's subsequent publication, *Circles* became one of the twentieth century's iconic works for percussion and voice written during the postwar period. "Berio's *Circles* was composed in the transitional years following World War II. It has the distinction of being one of the earliest and most successful uses of proportional notation, in the unprecedented orchestration and notation of the elaborate arrays of percussion, and . . . for the authority granted to text over the timbral, gestural, and structural organization of the piece."[14]

Berio did not fully embrace total serialism, but took from its discipline what he needed to create his own unique music, often lyrical and always interesting. An example of this would be his melodious work for two pianos and two keyboard percussion instruments, *Linea* (1973), written for the dance. In sections, players are allowed to improvise and reorder a given "row" of notes. Many of his later works were symphonic in nature.

The United States benefited from World War II in a number of ways. Due to the wartime mobilization of its industries, the U.S. economy grew strong, alleviating much of the prewar depression. The GI Bill helped raise the educational level of the general population. Finally, a great influx of war refugees, a sort of "intellectual migration," brought many musicians, among others, to its shores. Some, like Schoenberg and Stravinsky, became citizens, contributing greatly to the nation's musical arts.

Charles Wuorinen (1938–2020) is an American composer who created music utilizing and extending the twelve-tone system of Schoenberg and who patterned his early music after Stravinsky's. Born and educated in New York City, Wuorinen began composing at an early age. He was awarded the New York Philharmonic's Young Composers' award at age sixteen. After 1968, Wuorinen began using the twelve-tone system formulated by the American composer Milton Babbitt (1916–2011) that controls not only pitch, but also time structures. Babbitt's "time-point system is a structural design where there is a correlation between the distance between pitches (interval) and the distance between attack points in time."[15] Very prolific, with a body of over 260 works, Wuorinen has written extensively for percussion, as seen in most of his orchestral scores. His early percussion ensemble, *Prelude and Fugue for Four Percussion* (1955), is a modest work requiring five Chinese temple blocks, two suspended cymbals, a tam-tam, snare drum, and three timpani. The *Prelude* is in three sections marked by a change of tempo featuring interplay between temple blocks and timpani glissandos. The *Fugue*'s subject is a simple eight-bar phrase first stated by the snare drum. (Fig. 5.3) The subject is then played on a large, suspended cymbal that is hand-damped and played with a triangle beater. The syncopated counter-subject and rhythmic variations of both subjects adds interest to the movement. Wuorinen's 1962 work, *Invention for Percussion Quintet* (1962), is much more complex, featuring pitched percussion (xylophone, glockenspiel, vibraphone, chimes, and timpani) plus celesta and piano. It is brief (five minutes, forty-two seconds), with a tempo throughout of 60 beats to the quarter note. In the score, the composer positions each note visually with the aid of vertical lines (tactus symbols), giving some flexibility to the rigid meter.

In his 1966 work, *Janissary Music,* for solo percussion, Wuorinen presents the player with extraordinary technical and logistical problems. It is also an excellent example of the serialization of both pitched and relatively pitched percussion within a single work. The title is a historical nod to the importance of the Turkish janissary bands of the seventeenth and eighteenth centuries and their influence on Western European music. *Janissary Music* is scored for a four-octave marimba, three-octave vibraphone with variable speed motor, one kettledrum in F, twelve graduated membranophones (two bass drums, field drum, tenor drum, medium drum, snare drum without snares, five bongos), and twelve graduated metallophones (three tam-tams, three suspended cymbals, three cowbells, three triangles). In constructing a playable setup, the soloist must accommodate the marimba and vibraphone plus distribute the thirteen drums so they are within arm's reach. The tam-tams and triangles can be suspended vertically while the suspended cymbals are normally positioned horizontally. Unlike Stockhausen's *Zyklus,* in which the player turns slowly within a prescribed circle of a large percussion array, here, the player must position each of the instruments so as to be within reach of every single note or sound instantaneously. Compounding the logistical problem is the question of where to locate the single timpano. Used only twice as an ending note to each movement, the kettle must be located nearby. (Fig. 5.4) Mallet choices are left to the player's discretion, with the exception that the metal instruments are to be struck with a soft beater (for the tam-tams) or a hard beater, preferably metal. The rotation speed of the vibraphone baffles is indicated as slow, medium, and fast and pedal indications are given in the score. Wuorinen uses a standard five-line staff for notating both the keyboard instruments as well as the skin and metal ones. This approach works well for the pitched percussion, vibes, and marimba but seems inadequate for the others. Because of the technical and setup problems found in *Janissary Music,* the work requires dedication on behalf of the soloist. Memorization is a requirement. "At the time of this piece, he [Wuorinen] believed in writing parts of high complexity so that they had to be memorized, thus demanding adequate rehearsal time."[16]

Wuorinen continued to write for percussion employing serial techniques, including *Ringing Changes* (1969), a work for twelve players. Regarding *Ringing Changes,* Wuorinen comments: "What I wanted was to write a piece in which relative pitch played as much of a role as absolute pitch."[17] His forty-minute *Percussion Symphony* (1976) is in five movements requiring twenty-two players. The writing for the two outer movements is dense and contrapuntal combining both pitched and relatively pitched percussion. The duration of the slow, loud center movement is almost as long as movements one and five combined. In the other two movements, "Entr'acte I" and "Entr'acte II," Wuorinen reworks and orchestrates Petrarch's sonnet "Vergine bella," a musical setting from the early Renaissance written by the French composer Guillaume Dufay (ca. 1400–1474). According to Wuorinen, the two lightly scored "Entr'actes" serve as sonic relief from the surrounding powerful and dramatic movements.

In writing for percussion, Wuorinen uses conventional percussion instruments, many from the keyboard percussion family. Unlike the timbral explorations apparent in the percussion symphonies of Lou Harrison and Henry Brant, he rarely calls for any extended techniques or employs "found" instruments as sound sources. Wuorinen espouses the cause of twelve-tone music as the legitimate successor to the tonal system. His use of Babbitt's time-point system, which measures the distance from one attack sound to the next, enabled him to control both pitched and nonpitched sounds as well as rhythm and duration. He states: "It is my profound conviction that the twelve-tone system in all its ramifications is the legitimate successor to the tonal system."[18]

One of the twentieth century's largest percussion works was written by the Argentine composer Alberto Ginastera (1916–1983). *Cantata para América mágica* (1960) was written for dramatic soprano and fifty-three percussion instruments. Although best known for his early works, a number of ballets and operas based on Argentine folk music, Ginastera wrote *Cantata* in the style of Schoenberg and his followers. "His *Cantata para América Mágica* (1960) for soprano and 53 percussion instruments [13 players], reveals the influence of Webern."[19] The work was premiered on April 30, 1961, at the Second InterAmerican Festival in Washington, D.C., by the National Symphony Orchestra conducted by Howard

Mitchell with Raquel Adonaylo, soloist.[20] The text for the six-movement work, written by Mercedes de Toro (Ginastera's first wife), was inspired by fragments of pre-Columbian poetry. The first movement is an invocation to the sun god followed by a love song. Movement III, titled "Canto para le partida de los guerreros" ("Song for the Warriors' Departure"), is loud and fast (quarter note equals 160) with overlapping eighth and sixteenth notes played on the drums. An instrumental interlude follows, "Interludio fantástico," with dynamics of pianissimo to pianissimo. Here Ginastera employs the form of a palindrome, using "a symmetrical series reminiscent of Webern, with its second hexachord a transposed retrograde of the first."[21] The two halves of the movement are separated by a seven-second hold featuring all twelve notes of the scale. (Fig. 5.5) In the fifth movement, "Song of Agony and Desolation," explosions of instrumental sounds set off lengthy recitative passages. The finale is titled "Song of Prophecy." Together "the six movements of the work trace a narrative arc from invocation and romance to battle, defeat, and apocalyptic prophecy."[22]

Ginastera divides his instrumentation into three large groups. Timpani, drums (both membrane and wooden), and metallophones (cymbals and tam-tams) make up one group. This group is manipulated serially. "The series is used not only in the so-called pitched instruments such as the pianos, but there is also a relationship of six different pitches between the six kettle drums, six tambours, three cymbals, and three tam-tams."[23] A second large group of small instruments is divided among three players. The third group consists of xylophone, marimba, glockenspiel (three octave), celesta, and two pianos. Some of the indigenous instruments are described in the preface to the score with substitutes given, if necessary, including Indian drums, wood drums, *reco-reco* (scraper), claves, *chocalho* (metal shaker), maracas (played *sourdine*, or muffled), two fist-sized sea stones, and a sistrum. The last is a metal shaker still used in Ethiopian Orthodox Church services. The multitude of resources needed for Ginastera's *Cantata para América mágica*, the skills required of the players, the atonal soprano writing, and the need to balance these dynamic sonic forces made this work extremely challenging and unique in the percussion repertoire of its day.

The Greek composer, architect, and mathematician Iannis Xenakis (1922–2001) contributed a number of significant works to the percussion solo and ensemble literature of the twentieth century. Xenakis eschewed the serialism of Schoenberg and Babbitt. His compositional approach, with results as determinist as that of Wuorinen's, evolved from the mathematics of communication and the shapes and structures of architecture. "Xenakis became determined to 'formalize' the act of musical composition by focusing on the logical processes underlying the creative processes that could be expressed in the universal language of logic—mathematics."[24] Though interested in music from a young age, Xenakis officially pursued a career in engineering, graduating from Athens's Polytechnic Institute in 1946. Greece had hoped to be neutral during World War II, but was drawn into the conflict as a result of the Italian invasion of 1940. Xenakis, like many of his fellow students, joined one of the resistance groups and was seriously injured during the postwar struggle for the political control of his homeland. Fearing for his life, he fled to France. "Upon arriving in Paris, which became his permanent home, he landed a job as an engineer for Le Corbusier [pseud. of Charles-Édouard Jeanneret-Gris, 1887–1965]."[25] Xenakis's work with the famed architect brought him recognition as co-architect of the Philips Pavilion at the 1958 Brussels World Fair. The pavilion featured Edgard Varèse's *Poème électronique* (1956–1958) played through 425 loudspeakers. While working as an architect, Xenakis continued his interest in music, approaching it from a mathematical viewpoint. Using a stochastic process from probability theory, he was able to create a new music, one closely related to his work as an engineer. His music often considered not only the normal parameters—pitch, rhythm, timbre—but also location and direction. "Building on his experiences with the multispeaker sound projection for the Philips Pavilion, Xenakis had become increasingly interested in staging and spatialization."[26]

In 1969, he completed the sextet *Persephassa*, commissioned for the first Shiraz Festival held in Iran. Written for the French percussion ensemble Les Percussion de Strasbourg, *Persephassa* was first staged at the site of the ancient ruins of Persepolis in Greece. For *Persephassa*, each player's setup requires percussion instruments of skin, metal, wood, and stone, plus a mouth siren. The arrays are positioned some distance from one another in a hexagonal formation within which the audience sits. Some pitched instruments are needed (four timpani and seven pitched Thai gongs), but rhythm, not pitch, is the basis for the work's construction. The sonic range of *Persephassa* is considerable, from low, resonant drums and gongs to high, discrete wood and metal timbres. Some sound sources need to be constructed: *affolants* (sheets of thin metal, ca. twelve inches square), *simantra metalliques* (small resonant metal bars), and *simantra bois* (thin suspended wooden bars ca. two feet in length), one for each player. Each player's large array of instruments and the required distance between them is problematic. "With little direct regard for the difficulties . . . [Xenakis] created an extraordinarily virtuosic study of rhythm and tempo."[27] In performing *Persephassa* without a conductor, an electronic aid, such as a click-track, would be useful. Powerful drum sounds dominate the work, strongly pulsed or fragmented and nonmetrical.

Periods of silence and brief improvisatory sections ("stochastic clouds"),[28] utilizing mouth sirens and wood, metal, and stone timbres, interrupt the rhythmic flow and give relief from the drum timbre. At measure 91, the players begin a unison fortississimo quarter-note pulse at 40 bpm. (Fig. 5.6) Slowly, players begin to tear away from the pulse at prescribed tempi. (Here metronomes or electronic aids seem necessary to insure accuracy.) Earlier, beginning at bar 62, Xenakis creates a similar rhythmic effect using fragmented groups of five to interrupt the half-note pulse.

Throughout *Persephassa*, the listener is conscious of the movement of various timbres traveling clockwise and counterclockwise as they are passed from one player to the next. With similar timbres in each setup, Xenakis exploits these spatial phenomena. "Each percussionist having the same basic instruments provides the opportunity for rhythmic patterns, pulses, and gestures, identified by a particular timbre, to move around the listeners."[29] The concluding section features an extended accelerando with individual timbres whirling and spinning around the listener, creating a spectacular climax. In the decades following the premiere of *Persephassa*, Xenakis composed a number of other unique percussion works including ensembles, duets with other instruments, and two popular unaccompanied solos, *Psappha* (1975) and *Rebonds* (1989).

When first published, the solo *Psappha* presented players with considerable technical problems to solve and a new notation system to decipher. Xenakis often sketched his music on graph paper.[30] In *Psappha*, the score appears as a series of vertical and horizontal lines similar to graph paper with the vertical lines indicating the pulse. Note heads without stems are placed on the horizontal lines, either intersecting the vertical pulse line or halfway between. The opening pulse is indicated as 152 bpm. Other tempo changes in the work seem to demarcate formal sections. Attack sounds are most important, not their resonant decay. Their placement is based on a system Xenakis calls Sieve Theory, which he described in a 1976 interview: "They [attacks] are not derived from stochastics, but rather from the 'Sieve Theory' that I have developed. Time is considered as a continuous horizontal line on which you place dots that correspond to the attacks of percussion. On the relationships of the intervals of the dots is based the rhythmic organization."[31] Duration is measured from one note to the next: "duration functioning solely as measurement from one attack to the next."[32]

The instrumentation for *Psappha* calls for nine sound registers of skin and wood instruments, plus seven metallic. Xenakis lists a number of possible timbres from which the player constructs his or her own setup. In interviews, he suggests that the timbres be uncommon: "not tam-tams, but rough metal such as railway lines and pieces of iron or steel."[33] A bass drum with foot pedal solves one of the technical problems the work presents when an extra hand would be helpful. But, at bar 2023, Xenakis adds two slashes to each note-head with instructions that two or three strokes be used to play each note ("2 ou 3 coups par point"). This may be physically impossible and the player must be able to create the illusion of a continuous sound, a roll. A final climax is created by a loud bass drum ostinato (bass drum with foot pedal) plus the introduction of a new timbre (high metallic sounds). He uses a Fibonacci sequence to mark a series of accents leading to the work's conclusion. "The pattern of accents follows the series, expanding from a distance of two beats through to fifty-five (2–3–5–8–13–21–34–55), the final accent ending the piece."[34] In the last two decades of the twentieth century, *Psappha* became a popular recital work as young percussionists solved its physical challenges and coped successfully with its unusual notation.

Schoenberg's influence on composers of the postwar era was considerable. Some embraced his atonal, dodecaphonic approach, others applied its principles to musical parameters other than pitch. Still others found alternative ways to mathematically create the sound structures they needed. In fact, composers continued to create and explore various systems and mathematical schemes to define the structures of their individual works well into the next century.

Other works to consider: *Marginal Sounds* (1957) by Ernst Krenek (1900–1991); *Diacoustics* (1970) by Robert Kelly (1916–2007); *Fantasy-Variations* (1961) by Michael Colgrass; *Interactions for Vibraphone & Percussion* (1963) by John Bergamo (1940–2013); *Five Scenes from the Snow Country* (1978) by Hans Werner Henze (b. 1926); *Beaten Paths* (1988) by Milton Babbitt; *Rebonds* (1987–89) by Iannis Xenakis.

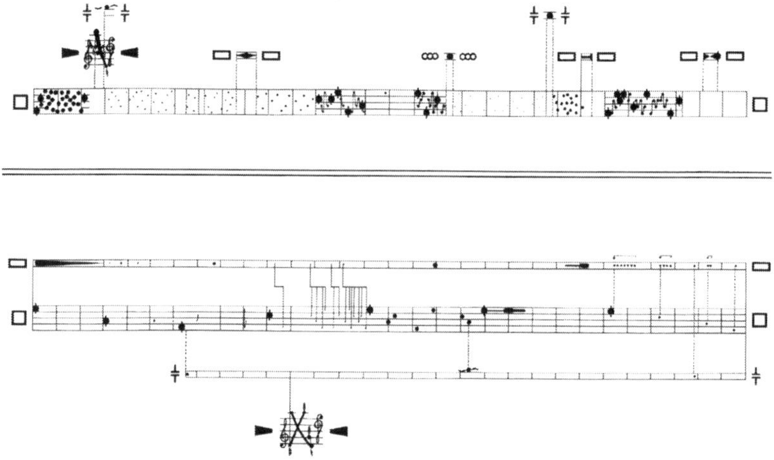

Fig. 5.1 Stockhausen, *Zyklus* (p. 1, periods 1 and 17). Copyright © 1960 by Universal Edition (London) Ltd., London/UE 13186.

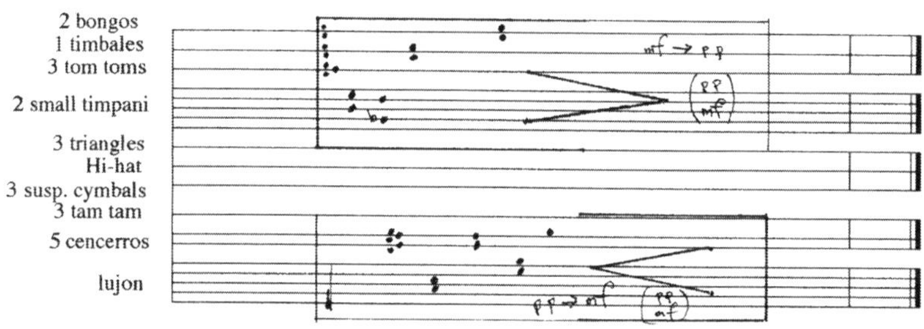

Fig. 5.2 Berio, *Circles* (box notation example)

Fig. 5.3 Wuorinen, *Prelude and Fugue for Four Percussionists* (fugue subject)

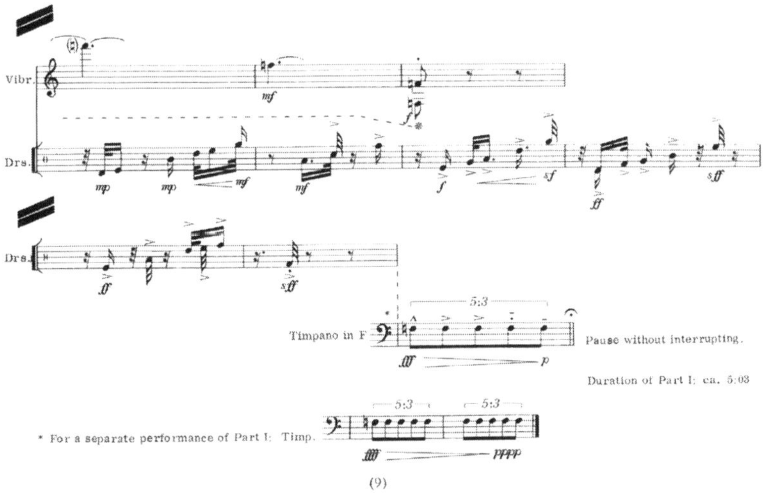

Fig. 5.4 Wuorinen, *Janissary Music* (p. 9, final two systems). Copyright © 1966 by C. F. Peters Corporation. Used by permission. All rights reserved.

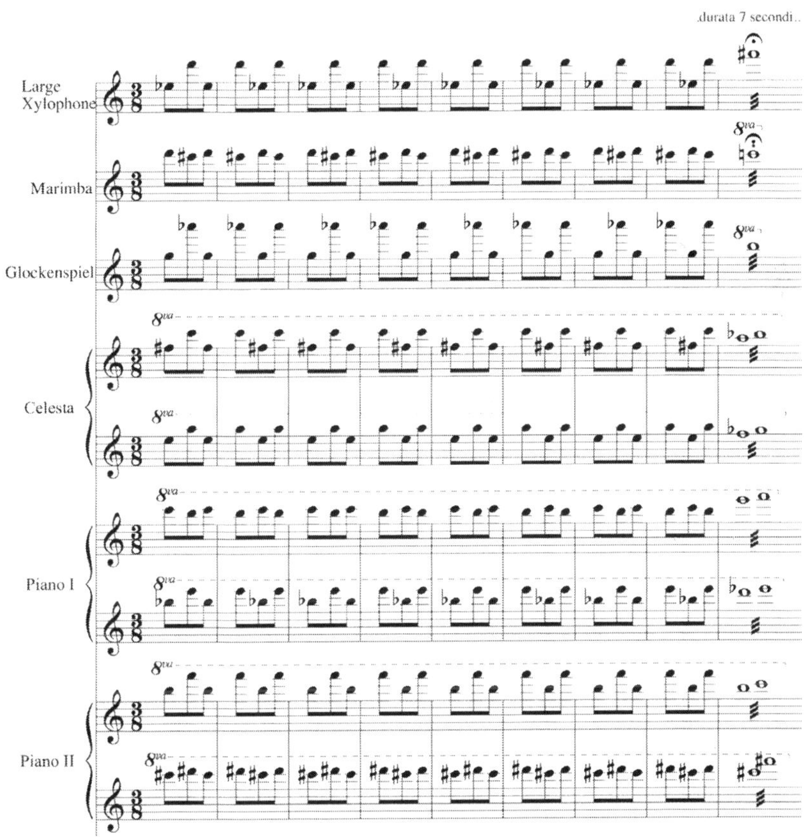

Fig. 5.5 Ginastera, *Cantata para América mágica* (Mvt. IV, "Interludio fantástico," meas. 123–134)

Fig. 5.6 Xenakis, *Persephassa* (meas. 191–205). Copyright © by Éditions Salabert, Paris, France. All rights reserved. International Copyright Secured. Reproduced by kind permission of Hal Leonard Europe S.r.l., Italy.

Chapter 6

CHANCE AND INDETERMINACY IN MUSIC

In serialism, the resulting music is fully determined by the parameter values each composer invents and utilizes. In the previous chapter, selected examples of music by Stockhausen, Berio, Wuorinen, and Xenakis demonstrated this compositional approach. Also, I noted that each composer was able to incorporate seemingly random notes and/or sections of improvisation within their compositional structures. In *Zyklus*, Stockhausen gave the performer numerous choices of material from within nine structures, each one of equal validity. "Between completely fixed and extremely polyvalent formation there are in *Zyklus* nine different degrees of polyvalence."[1] Berio's *Circles* afforded the percussion players opportunities for improvisation by indicating pitch, dynamics, timbre, and density, all notated graphically within boxes drawn across the time grid. Xenakis, in his ensemble work *Persephassa*, filled the score with stochastic clouds of dots for each performer to "realize" on selected groups of instruments. Each example elicited the aid of the performer to complete the composition. Composers relied on the players' understanding of the work's compositional style and their ability to respond to and interpret any unique or unusual notation.

The incorporation of degrees of chance in the creation and realization of music captured the imagination of composers in the late 1950s and early 1960s. This was partly in response to the seemingly dogmatic use of serialism in the works of many composers. It was also due, in part, to the influence of the American composer John Cage, the most prominent champion of chance and indeterminacy. "There is no question but that he was a welcome and liberating influence in a time dominated by Serialism and other forms of musical strait-jacketing."[2]

The year 1945 was one of many changes for Cage. Within three years after returning to New York City, Cage realized that his dream of establishing a center for experimental music was doubtful absent the hoped-for support of CBS. Also within this period, he divorced his wife, Xenia, and began a lifelong personal and professional relationship with the dancer Merce Cunningham. In this time of change and stress, Cage also began to question his approach to composition. "In 1946, Cage met an Indian musician Gita Sarabhai, who introduced him to Indian philosophy and music."[3] With the help of Sarabhai (1922–2011) and later, Dr. Daisetsu T. Suzuki (1870–1966), a leading advocate of Zen Buddhism, he found relief from his personal anxieties and a renewed interest in Eastern philosophy. A book by Ananda K. Coomaraswamy (1877–1947) led Cage to embrace the concept that "all art should imitate nature in her manner of operation."[4] He abandoned the idea that music was meant to communicate the emotions of its creator and began to look for ways to isolate compositional choices from his conscious and unconscious mind. Developing a process through which every parameter of music was decided in some random way, Cage started to write music that was based on chance operations. In 1951, composer Christian Wolff (b. 1934) gave Cage a copy of the ancient Chinese *Book of Changes*, the *I Ching*. This book consists of a set of hexagrams composed of six lines, broken or unbroken, that one can select by tossing coins. "To find, i.e., to 'cast a hexagram' one tosses three coins resulting in four possible outcomes: three heads, two heads [one tail], two tails [one head], and three tails."[5] One then follows a set of rules outlined by the *I Ching*. For years, Cage used this tedious process in his creation of new works—symphonic, chamber, electronic, solo—until the advent of the computer that could do that work for him at the push of a button.

In 1956, Cage completed a work for solo percussionist titled *27′ 10.554″*. It was part of a series of works (*Ten Thousand Things*) that Cage envisioned, but never completed, for solo instruments, each "with a title defining a precise duration."[6] For *27′ 10.554″*, Cage utilized chance operations to determine a number of musical components including the duration of both sounds and silence, the number of sounds within a given section or phrase, and the types of sounds, sustained, glissandi, and so on. It appears that he used the imperfections of the manuscript paper to determine where to place the notes, adding staff lines as needed. (Fig. 6.1) Players select the instrumentation from the following four categories: M = metal, W = wood, S = skin, and A = all others, with examples for the last given as electronic devices, mechanical arrangements, radio, whistles, and so on. The vertical position of notes above or below the staff line indicates volume, with the line representing a dynamic level of *mezzo forte*. Cage specifies, "A virtuoso performance will include a wide variety of instruments, beaters, sliding tones, and an exhaustive rather than conventional use of the instruments employed."[7] He goes on to describe various extended techniques that may be used to alter an instrument's timbre and calls for a variety of beaters and mallets. The score's twenty-eight pages, each sixty seconds in duration, are divided into twenty-eight subunits indicated by dotted lines. Each subunit stands alone and can be played individually or combined with other units for any given performance. The piece can also be "performed as a recording or with the aid of a recording."[8]

Cage's exploration of using chance means to compose continued to evolve after the 1950s. Abandoning all forms of traditional notation, his later works often contained only instructions on how to create a given performance. His solo work for organic percussion, *Child of Tree* (1975), offers four pages of written instructions describing how, and with what, a percussionist needs to realize the composition. To begin, the player identifies ten items capable of creating a sound made exclusively from plant material, for example, sticks, twigs, dry leaves, claves, *teponaztli*, and so on. Cage specifies the use of one or more dry pods from the Mexican poinciana tree identified as "pod rattles," which can be counted as one instrument of the ten required plus a cactus (or part of one) having spines that are amplified and plucked with a "needle or toothpick." "No conventionally pitched instruments are to be used and none made of animal or metal materials."[9]

The score itself is difficult to read and the directions are somewhat unclear. (Fig. 6.2) "That's partly because the score is a text meant to make it possible for performers to build their own performance score and Cage . . . wanted it to be a difficult task."[10] He specifies the work's duration to be eight minutes. This time frame is to be divided into parts "by means of the oracle of the I Ching."[11] The instruments are allocated in similar fashion. Once the player has created his or her own score, the directions are: "Using a stop watch, the soloist improvises clarifying the time structure by means of the instruments. This improvisation is the performance."[12] Cage followed *Child of Tree* with the solo percussion work *Branches* (1976) and a number of other similarly composed works.

John Cage was one of the most controversial, widely read, influential figures of twentieth-century art and music. Upon his death in 1992, the critic Allan Kozinn (b. 1954) wrote: "In the music world . . . Mr. Cage's influence was extremely far-reaching. He started a revolution by proposing that composers could jettison the musical language that had evolved over the last seven centuries, and in doing so he opened the door to Minimalism, performance art, and virtually every other branch of the musical avant-garde."[13]

Composer Morton Feldman (1926–1987) was a close friend of John Cage and a part of the so-called New York School. Though not formally a school,

Feldman and Cage, along with composers Christian Wolff and Earl Brown and pianist David Tudor, are often associated with a number of poets and visual artists loosely regarded as part of the group. Held in common was their desire to find new ways of making music, poetry, and art. Feldman was greatly influenced by the visual artists in the group and began notating sounds using graphic symbols. He embraced both indeterminacy and, like Cage, the concept that a single sound could stand alone. "He compared himself to Mondrian . . ., an artist who did not want to paint 'bouquets, but a single flower at a time.'"[14] In the summer of 1964, while on a Long Island beach, he composed a work for solo multiple percussion titled *The King of Denmark.* His approach to the work was radically different from that of Xenakis, Stockhausen, and others who exploited the attack sounds of percussion. In the *King,* Feldman requires the player to use fingers, hand, or arm to activate the instruments, mitigating any percussive attack. "What's interesting about *The King,*" Feldman said, "is that percussion was always used in the sense that what was exciting about percussion was a kind of fantastic availability of all these different kinds of attacks—and here, I take out the aspect of attack." He goes on: "I wrote the whole piece on the beach. And I can actually conjure up the memory of doing it—that kind of muffled sound of kids in the distance and transistor radios and drifts of conversation from other pockets of inhabitants on blankets, and I remember that it did come into the piece." The title, *The King of Denmark,* pays tribute to Christian X, the Danish monarch during World War II who, in an act of defiance to the occupying German forces, rode his horse unaccompanied through the streets of the capital. "The title came *after* the piece."[15]

A list of nine instructions help to interpret the score, which appears as a series of "time boxes"[16] graphed three-high, containing a variety of symbols, numbers, and grace notes. The tempo is slow to moderate indicated as a metronome marking of 66–92 per box. "With a total of 386 boxes, this piece could range from 4′ 12″ to 5′ 51″."[17] The score instructions prohibit the use of sticks or mallets. "The performer may use fingers, hand, or any part of his arm."[18] Feldman asks that the dynamics be soft and as equal as possible. A list of symbols gives the player an idea of the types of timbres that he envisioned: B = bell-like sounds, S = skin instruments, C = cymbal, G = gong, and so on. Approximate frequency range is indicated by a note's position on the graph, that is, top line for high sounds, bottom line for low. Numbers represent the amount of attacks within a time box, roman numerals simultaneous sounds. The score appears sparse at times, but there should be no real silence as the resonant sounds of the sustaining percussion create "wisps" of fading timbres. In the final moments of the piece (Fig. 6.3), a flurry of sounds, a vibraphone cluster, glockenspiel note, and antique cymbal are heard as a complex timbral wash that serves as a sense of closure.

The King of Denmark is the only solo percussion work that Feldman wrote. The piece has no apparent structure; the sounds exist for themselves. "In Feldman's [*King*] it is the isolated sounds themselves that are the essential experience, intentionally unrelated and disassociated from one another, thus creating a new time sense, previously unknown in Western music."[19]

The graphic percussion scores by the Austrian/Polish composer Roman Haubenstock-Ramati (1919–1994) provide the performer multiple opportunities for creative interpretation and are excellent examples of the genre. Born in Krakow, Poland, Haubenstock-Ramati immigrated to Israel in 1950, returning to Europe in 1957. A gifted artist and composer, he was appointed music editor for the Vienna-based publisher Universal Editions, which subsequently released a number of his works worldwide. In 1959, he organized the first exhibition of graphic music in Donaueschingen, Germany. "Haubenstock-Ramati was known as an innovator of musical notation from which he drew mobile forms."[20] Four of Haubenstock-Ramati's percussion works are part of a series he described as *Mobile*.[21] Included in the series are: (1) *Liaisons* (1958), a duet that can also be performed as a solo with prerecorded tape; (2) *Jeux 2*, a duet written in 1965; (3) *Jeux 4*, a quartet from 1966; and (4) *Jeux 6* (1960) written for the percussion sextet Percussions de Strasbourg.

In *Liaisons*, Haubenstock-Ramati combines both traditional, proportional notation and original graphic drawings. There is a minimum of dynamic markings present in the score as the performer relies on note size to convey intensity. The score appears as one large page divided into squares and rectangles (Fig. 6.4), some of which are empty, indicating silences of from three to five seconds in duration. Arrows drawn within the blank squares afford the player an opportunity to change direction as one journeys through the score. No tempo is indicated though figures written in traditional notation are beamed in such a manner as to suggest pace of movement. Played as a duet, one player requires a marimba and a vibraphone, the other a xylophone (or xylorimba). Two endings are offered; both respond to the sound of a tam-tam signaling the work's conclusion.

Realizing *Liaisons* or any of Haubenstock-Ramati's other works requires a careful reading of the performance directions and dedication to uncovering the composer's structural intentions. *Liaisons* has but one page of instructions; his duet, *Jeux 2*, has thirteen. *Jeux 2*'s performance chart includes thirteen graphically designed ellipses detailing the activation of the strings inside a piano that both players share. Similarly, various octagons regulate the actions for groups of tom-toms. Squares and triangles are embellished to control duration, dynamics, and rhythm. Added to the mix are electro-acoustic devices and letters and numbers to be spoken in one's native language. To properly perform *Jeux*

2, players must learn an entirely new notational system symptomatic of graphic scores from the second half of the century.

The composer Herbert Brün (1918–2000) was born in Berlin. He immigrated to Palestine in 1936 and, in 1962, made his way to the United States where he became a member of the music faculty at the University of Illinois. While in Palestine, Brün studied composition with Stefan Wolpe (1902–1972) and "worked as a jazz pianist."[22] He returned to Germany in 1955 where he found employment as a composer, writing music for a theater in Munich. A concert of new music at Munich's Herkules Saal greatly impressed Brün, as the program "contained the first harvest of the electronic music studio in Köln [Cologne], pieces by Stockhausen, [Gottfried] Koenig, [Henri] Pousseur, and others."[23] From 1955 to 1961, Brün explored the possibility of composing electro-acoustic music. He continued his research at the University of Illinois, composing a number of works utilizing electronic means. In 1967, Brün created, with the aid of a computer, three solo percussion works titled: *Plot for Percussion, Touch and Go*, and *Stalks and Trees and Drops and Clouds*. "For each of the three pieces, a FORTRAN program was written by the composer and run on the IBM 7094. The output tape contained instructions for the CALCOMP PLOTTER to draw the score of symbols to be interpreted by the performer."[24]

For *Stalks and Trees and Drops and Clouds* there are thirteen different instrument symbols—seven symbols for *Stalks and Trees* and six for *Drops and Clouds*. The symbols for *Stalks and Trees* indicate nonreverberating sounds and sprout up on stems like flowers from the bottom timeline. Those for *Drops and Clouds* are reverberating, ringing sounds and hang like fruit from the top. (Fig. 6.5) The distance of the symbol from its timeline indicates the degree of intensity. The score indicates that the farther away, "the greater the applied force of attack."[25] The symbols, all of which are part of the plotter's library, also vary in size: as they get larger a "more voluminous timbre should be achieved."[26] The timbral subtleties and control of each instrument's duration suggested by Brün are aided by the use of a great variety of mallets and beaters. The position of each symbol in relation to the timeline designates the ictus of each sound. The score contains thirty-one pages, each eighteen seconds in duration, grouped into eighteen sections. Some of the pages are to be played *attacca;* others have notated silences of up to twelve seconds that must be observed. The timeline is printed across the top and bottom of each page. Estimated duration of the work is seven minutes, thirty seconds.

Brün worked closely on the three solos with three dedicatees: Michal Ranta (b. 1942), G. Allan O'Connor (1942–2019), and William Youhass (b. 1943). He wrote a general preface explaining a practical approach to preparing the work for performance. Three periods are suggested. The first requires the player to get acquainted with the details of the score, select the instruments, look for or invent phrases and so on, and preserve a strict adherence to the timeline. As the score indicates, a period of inaction follows: "For a week or so, do not look at the piece, don't touch it."[27] In the final period, the player hones the phrases, somewhat ignoring the timeline in making the piece his or her own.

The three solos necessitate the closest of cooperation between composer and performer. The phrase "making the piece their own" elicits the question: Who is the composer? Brün felt that composer and performer should become "co-conspirators" in an effort to fulfill his compositional concept and to realize the very best performance.[28] Brün wrote a number of other works featuring percussion including the 1977 trio, *More Dust with Percussion*, requiring four-channel or two-channel tape, plus solos for snare drum, marimba, and timpani.

The works described in this chapter approach both the idea of compositional indeterminacy and performance indeterminacy in different ways as both composer and performer participate in the creation of these works. Relinquishing control of many aspects of their compositional process, a number of composers in the 1960s and 1970s relied on the performer's instrumental expertise, musical acumen, and ability to decipher the composer's intent when realizing their works. Part of the performer's task was to conceptualize and create a unique event from the options presented by the composer. In many of these compositions players had numerous options that they could exercise—a choice of ranges, timbres, dynamics, duration, sequence of events, and so on. This was especially true of composers whose works were largely pictorial or graphic. Unlike Cage's approach with *Child of Tree*, once a graphic score is printed, it presents the performer with a fait accompli. Each work brought new challenges to the percussionist. There were no standards for graphic notation, though many used the left-to-right axis for the sequence of events, up and down for pitch range, and large or small notes to represent dynamics. By century's end, a set of pictograms designating the various percussion instruments became available for those composers employing commercial computer music notation programs. With the exception of a few symbols, such as the one for triangle, no international standard has been established.

Other works to consider: *Interiors* (1964) by Robert Moran (b. 1937); *Calder Piece* (1964) by Earle Brown (1926–2002); *Obelisk* (1970) by David Cope (b. 1941); *Arrangements for Percussion Player(s)* by Toshi Ichiyanagi (b. 1933); *Time Fields* (1969) by William Duckworth (1943–2012); *Sonora* (1968) by León Schidlowsky (b. 1931); *Polymer* (1980) by Satoshi Ohmae (b. 1943).

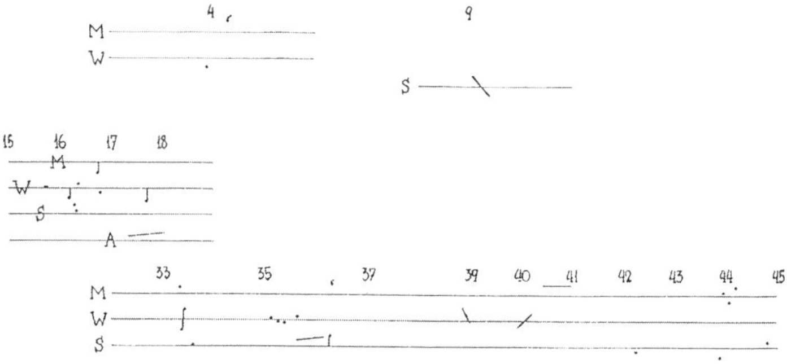

Fig. 6.1 Cage, *27′ 10.554″*, (p. 1). Copyright © 1960 by Henmar Press, Inc. Used by permission of C. F. Peters Corporation. All rights reserved.

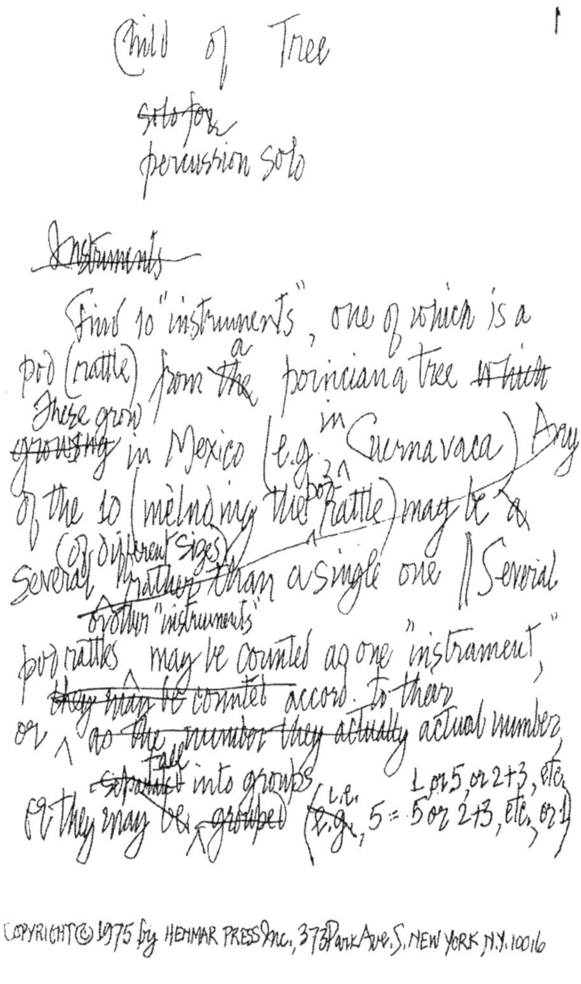

Fig. 6.2 Cage, *Child of Tree* (p. 1). Copyright © 1975 by Henmar Press, Inc. Used by permission of C. F. Peters Corporation. All rights reserved.

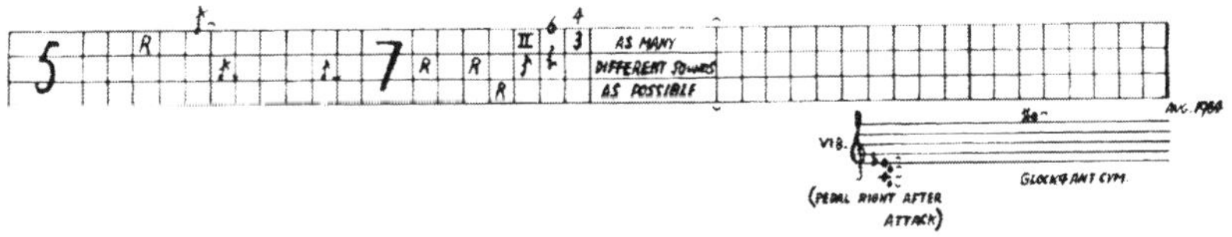

Fig. 6.3 Feldman, *The King of Denmark* (final system).

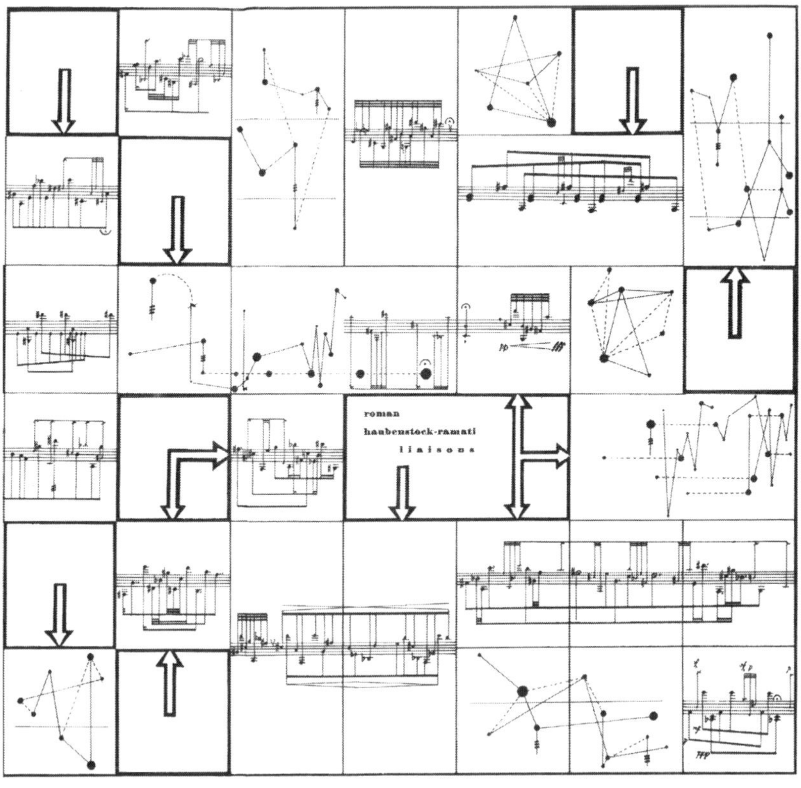

Fig. 6.4 Haubenstock-Ramati, *Liaisons* (partial score page).

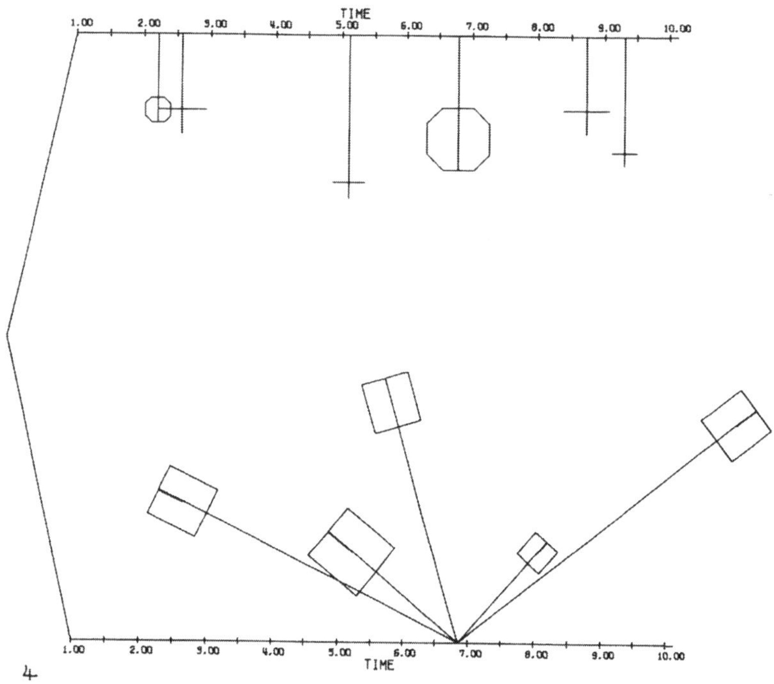

Fig. 6.5 Brün, *Stalks and Trees and Drops and Clouds* (p. 4). Copyright © Sonic Art Editions, c/o Smith Publications, 54 Lent Rd., Sharon, VT 05065. Used by permission.

Chapter 7

ELECTRONIC MUSIC

The term electronic music, later designated as electro-acoustic music, includes several categories by which the music is produced: *musique concrète,* classical electronic music, tape music, synthesized music, and computer music. Regardless of the label, its evolution in the twentieth century was dramatic. For the purpose of this chapter, the term electronic music will be used as described by one of the pioneer composers of the genre, Otto Luening (1900–1996): "Electronic music is a generic term describing music that uses electronically generated sound or sound modified by electronic means, which may or may not be accompanied by live voices or musical instruments, and which may be delivered live or through speakers."[1] With the end of World War II came the rebirth of European radio. Stations in France and Germany were at first supported by the occupying Allied forces and later by the newly formed governments of each country. In 1948, in Paris, France, the radio station Office de Radiodiffusion Télevision Française (ORTF) established a studio dedicated to research in electronic music. It was built and directed by the engineer/composer Pierre Schaeffer. Schaeffer and his colleague Pierre Henry (1927–2017) created numerous musical works by manipulating prerecorded sounds using the studio's disk recorders, and later, tape machines. One of Schaeffer's early compositions was *Etude aux chemins de fer* (1948) created from railroad sounds. Music written by these two composers is categorized as *musique concrète,* or "real music," a type of music made from sounds that exist acoustically in the world that are recorded and then altered. The idea was not new. Prior to the establishment of a dedicated electronic music studio, the Egyptian American composer Halim El-Dabh (1921–2017) wrote a work in 1944 using a wire recorder. "Experiments with discs had been conducted before the war, notably (and independently) by Milhaud, Hindemith, and Varèse, but it remained for Schaeffer to discover and to utilize the basic techniques of electronic transformation: reversing a sound by playing its recording backwards, altering it in pitch, rhythm, and timbre by changing the speed of playback, isolating elements from it, and superimposing one sound on another."[2]

In 1951, a West German radio station, Westdeutscher Rundfunk (WDR), located in the city of Cologne, established a studio as well. It too was dedicated to research in electronic music, though its approach was, at first, different than that of Schaeffer's Paris studio. It began to explore making music via electronic means. Using sine wave, pulse, and white-noise generators, the WDR studio produced electronic music through the process of synthesis, either additive (superimposing sine waves), or subtractive (filtering the signal output of white-noise). "The German studio initially leaned toward the use of tone-generating devices and filters, reflecting the German interest in working directly with the physics of musical tone production."[3] Magnetic-tape machines, two- and four-track, were used to store the signals. Composers working in the studio developed pieces in a manner similar to that of film editors working in motion pictures by editing and splicing the magnetic tape, a more easily manipulated medium than the recording disks used by Schaeffer. Other equipment used to produce, manipulate, and edit sounds was added to the Cologne studio's capabilities over the next fifty years. The studio closed in the year 2000.

Many works for tape alone were created during the second half of the twentieth century resulting in a large and diverse repertoire. For many listeners, attending an early electronic music concert was a challenge. No matter how unusual and ear-catching the music, the experience was often less than rewarding. In a conversation with the author Thom Holmes, John Cage remarked: "I was at a concert of electronic music in Cologne and I noticed that, even though it was the most recent electronic music, the audience was all falling asleep. No matter how interesting the music was, the audience couldn't stay awake. That was because the music was coming out of loudspeakers."[4] Concert audiences have deep-seated traditional expectations. "Audiences expect to see as well as hear a performance, and loudspeakers aren't much to look at."[5]

Typically, the stage setting for an early electronic music concert would be bare except for two loudspeakers. Entering the auditorium, one noticed a slight hum emanating from the speakers. As the house lights dimmed, a click was heard followed by a noticeable hissing sound announcing that the work had begun. For recorded sounds to have a "presence," considerable volume was required. The high decibel level often drove audience members to the exits. With another click, the hiss disappeared, the work was over, and the remaining audience, conditioned to respond to a performance with applause, had to react to a new, somewhat alien experience. It wasn't until the digital age, with its more sophisticated electronics, that most of these mechanical problems were solved.

At the time, one way to help engage the listening audience was to mix live and electronic elements, or, like Varèse, juxtapose the two. Early on, composers of electronic music began adding live musicians to their electronic creations. The audience response was positive. Soon, solo and ensemble works with tape were added to the literature, including some that featured percussion.

As noted earlier, Cage, working in the recording studio at the Cornish School, experimented with recordings of electronic sounds. In 1939, he created his *Imaginary Landscape No. 1*, using the studio's resources—a variable-speed turntable and frequency recordings. In 1942, he composed *Imaginary Landscape No. 3* for electronics and percussion. Some of the sound material came from prerecorded 78 rpm records or discs. Many radio stations across the country owned sets of recordings useful for generating various types of signals such as a sine wave. The station engineers used these signals to test their equipment. Cage found a more creative use for them.

Cage's *Imaginary Landscape No. 3* calls for two arrays of empty tin cans (five in each set), an electric buzzer (commonly used during the period for home doorbells), two button gongs (or two large temple blocks), a marimbula (amplified by contact microphone), and an amplified coil (a length of coiled copper aerial wire inserted into a phonograph cartridge). The coil hangs freely and is slightly unwound so as to vibrate when gently activated, producing a low reverberant sound. *Imaginary Landscape No. 3* also requires an audio frequency oscillator and a continuously variable frequency record. This work is a little over three minutes in duration.

As in the *First Construction (in Metal)* described earlier, Cage uses his "square-root" formula for *Imaginary Landscape No. 3*. The rhythmic structure is listed in the score as: 12 x 12 (3, 2, 4, 3). One hundred and forty-three measures are divided into groupings of three, two, four, and three measures. The final group starting at rehearsal letter K appears to be reversed, to wit, three, four, two, and three measures. (Fig. 7.1) Cage may have done this to help provide a satisfactory conclusion, a noted difficulty when using the square-root procedure. To mark each section of the work's structure, Cage employs a variety of devices such as adding a new instrument, changing a dynamic mark, or introducing a new rhythmic pattern. His rhythmic cells include groups of eighth notes and sixteenth notes often beamed over the bar lines. Also, uneven groups of three-, five-, and seven-note figures are used throughout. Cage notes that the pitch of the graduated tin can sets will be altered through usage. This is either a cautionary note or evidence that the work is primarily concerned with rhythm, rather than with relative pitch. The active rhythmic sections are dominated by the percussion instruments in stark contrast to the two sections beginning at rehearsal letter C, where the electronic sounds stand alone. Despite the absence of rhythmic material that would create forward motion, Cage notates both a ritardando and an accelerando, illuminating the structural points at entrances with dynamic changes.

Cage's contribution to electronic music was considerable. "Cage's *Cartridge Music* (1960), the first substantial work to use live electronic techniques, uses contact microphones and record-player cartridges to amplify 'small,' otherwise inaudible sounds."[6] His inventive use of electronics to produce and enhance percussive sounds continued throughout his career.

During and after World War II, Edgard Varèse wrote very little, though his earlier pieces began to be played more often. "Varèse's music experienced a renaissance during the 1950s. The percussion piece *Ionisation* (1931) especially was widely seen as a bold anticipation of the sound world of electronic music."[7] For years, Varèse pursued his dream of having a place where he could scientifically investigate the very nature of sound. In a lecture given at the University of California in 1939, he spoke of the need for a machine that would allow him to realize his music electronically. "Personally, for my conceptions, I need an entirely new medium of expression: a sound-producing machine (not a sound-reproducing one)."[8] In 1949, he began composing *Déserts,* a work for wind and percussion ensemble that included interpolations for electronic tape. A nascent electronic music scene had emerged after World War II as composers began experimenting with the use of phonograph recording equipment and early models of tape decks. "In the United States composers began work with tape and tape recorders in about 1950."[9] In 1953, Varèse received an Ampex tape recorder as a present and began work the following year on the tape interpolations for *Déserts* with the French pioneer of *musique concrète,* Pierre Schaeffer. The work requires fourteen wind and brass players plus five percussionists, each with an array of instruments. New to Varèse's percussion palette is the addition of three dragon heads (temple blocks) and a vibraphone. The percussion sounds play a crucial role throughout the work, including the material that comprises the tape interpolations. The writing is vintage Varèse, demonstrating his use of fragmented groups of three and five notes within a single pulse. (Fig. 7.2) The premiere of *Déserts* was given by Hermann Scherchen and the Orchestre National, Paris, December 2, 1954, and was broadcast live on radio. Prior to the event, the announcer read an analytical text prepared by the composer/conductor Pierre Boulez (1925–2016). Boulez described the interpolations (interventions) as follows:

> The first intervention consists of sound recorded during research on factory noises, sounds produced by friction, percussion, etc. . . . Varèse is not in search of the picturesque, but rather seeks to produce sonic material that relates to the orchestra material. In the second intervention Varèse recorded an ensemble of five musicians playing various percussion instruments in the usual manner, without any sonic manipulations. The purpose of this intervention is to give a stereophonic dimension to a normal recording. The third intervention is a mixture of both procedures in which real sounds (a telephone ringing, among others) and instrumental sounds are brought together with a view to creating a double structure, highlighting the sonic possibilities in all of the forms these might take in the course of the work.[10]

As with earlier large-scale Varèse works, the percussion plays a separate and crucial role, serving here to transition from live sounds to electronic ones. In 1961, the tape parts were revised with the help of the composer Bülent Arel (1919–1990).[11] Though the method of composing for tape at the time was primitive compared to the technology at the end of the century, *Déserts* stands as an important step in validating music made by electronic means. Varèse's contribution to the genre, along with his exploration of music written for instruments of percussion, will always be part of his legacy.

In Germany, the WDR Cologne studio attracted a number of internationally prominent young composers who produced innovative, groundbreaking, electronic works including Herbert Brün, Mauricio Kagel, Luciano Berio, and others. Most prominent was the composer and one of the studio's directors, Karlheinz Stockhausen. His transformative 1959–60 composition for tape, piano, and percussion, *Kontakte*, was the source material for his solo work, *Zyklus*, discussed earlier. "*Kontakte* is often ranked as the most significant electronic composition ever produced in a tape studio."[12] Listed in Universal's catalogue as *Nr. 12 Kontakte*, for electronic sounds, piano, and percussion, the work has two versions: one for electronic sounds alone, intended for broadcast or as a recording; the other for four-track tape, piano, and percussion to be performed "live" with tape. The tape part is played through multiple loudspeakers with at least two of them placed behind the audience. The score used by the instrumentalists is drawn schematically and great attention is given to the timeline given in minutes, seconds, and tenths of seconds. Dotted and straight lines aid the players' efforts to coordinate their notated sounds with the tape. The score also includes photos of the instruments required and a picture of the performance setup. For the percussion needs, Stockhausen uses many of the same instruments employed in *Zyklus*, plus a set of bamboo wind chimes, crotales, and an inverted bongo with a few beans inside that roll around activating the drum's membrane (like a rattle). The pianist has a few percussion instruments to play and shares, with the percussionist, a station with a large tam-tam and a button gong located midway between the two players, adding an element of theater to the work.

Not all early electronic music used wire, disk, or tape recorders. Some works created with equipment normally used to amplify the sound of an instrument (or voice) were performed live without employing any type of recording device, disk, or tape. *Mikrophonie I* written by Stockhausen in 1964 is a good example. "The title *Mikrophonie* also points to the fact that vibrations that are normally inaudible (in this case those of a tam-tam) can be made audible by means of an active process of auscultation with microphones (in much the same way as a doctor uses a stethoscope)."[13]

For this work, six players are divided into two groups of three using two microphones, a band-pass filter, two potentiometers (for volume control), an array of loudspeakers, and a giant tam-tam. One player from each group activates the tam-tam utilizing a variety of implements. "The implements can be chosen from any material and in any form (household implements), and the manner in which they are used (knocked, hit, scratched, rubbed, wiped, scraped, and so on) is to be derived both from the words and from the graphic signs (for rhythm, dynamics, pitch range)."[14] (Fig. 7.3) An extensive list of over ninety descriptors, words such as groaning, creaking, baying, barking, are listed in the score. These directions are to be used creatively by the players as they excite the tam-tam eliciting the suggested sound. (The descriptors are reminiscent of those used by the Futurist Russolo.) Two activators, with their array of mallets and other implements, are complemented by two assistants who control the hand-held microphones used to pick up the tam-tam sounds. "As in the works of Cage, the amplification of the tam-tam reveals normally inaudible upper partials, significant in this instance because of the inherently complex inharmonic spectrum of that instrument."[15] Two other players are placed in the center of the performance space, each using a band-pass filter and potentiometer to control the sound emanating from various loudspeakers. Though some improvisatory passages are possible, the entire work is carefully calculated. Not only are the sounds of the tam-tam specified, but also the filtering of the sound and its dynamic level. To perform *Mikrophonie I* the players must create a plan for each performance using the score's list of materials and the directions for controlling the resulting audio. Stockhausen composed the work at his home, erecting the tam-tam in his back yard and experimenting with ways to exploit its sound capabilities. "Some years previously I had bought myself a large tamtam for my composition MOMENTE, and set it up in my garden."[16] The instrument, a 155-centimeter Paiste tam-tam, is pictured in the score. *Mikrophonie I* was premiered on December 9, 1964, in Brussels, Belgium, and is dedicated to Alexander Schlee, the director of Universal Publications in Vienna.

One of the composers whose reputation was enhanced by works combining electronic and live music was Mario Davidovsky (1934–2019), an American composer of Argentine birth.[17] In 1958, he met composer Milton Babbitt who "encouraged him to move to New York to work at the Columbia-Princeton Electronic Music Center."[18] There he produced a series of works entitled *Synchronisms*, combining live instruments and voice with electronics. *Synchronism No. 5* (1969) was written for a percussion quintet with tape. *Synchronism No. 6* for piano and electronic sounds won the 1971 Pulitzer Prize in music.

Synchronism No. 5 was commissioned by the Thorne Music Fund and is approximately nine minutes in duration. Its instrumentation is extensive including seven kettledrums, glockenspiel, vibraphone, marimba, and a number of drums, gongs, cymbals, and miscellaneous percussion. In the work, Davidovsky calls for a number of extended techniques including bowed tam-tam and bowed triangle. He also carefully specifies mallet and stick choices. At measure 50, he indicates that cowbells are to be played with "tight brush" that is, a jazz brush, not fully extended, so as to aid with rhythmic articulation. Later, at measure 56, the triangle is to be played arco using a violin bow. (Fig. 7.4) *Synchronism No. 5* begins slowly and softly with percussion alone; the sounds of pitched percussion, timpani, marimba, and vibraphone are dominant. A melodic line is evident here accompanied by both consonant and dissonant intervals. The score instructs the timpani rolls to be even, "close to a sound continuum." The quality should be songlike; Davidovsky asks that the "timpani sing like a melodic instrument," marking each timpano entrance cantabile. Following the opening, a six-measure section, marked pianississimo, features three keyboard percussion instruments, glockenspiel, vibraphone, and marimba. All twelve chromatic notes are presented in sequence by the glockenspiel, eleven by the vibraphone (the C sharp is missing), while the marimba sustains a cluster of four notes (including the C sharp). A transition section follows at a new tempo, 120 bpm to the eighth note, announcing the tape entrance at measure 65. A steady eighth-note pulse continues to the work's final measure with a number of holds along the way ensuring the coordination of the tape and the instrumentalists. The piece climaxes at measure 175. A short, coda-like section follows and the tape closes the work with a descending electronic figure. *Synchronism No. 5* was one of the most successful early works integrating live percussion sounds and tape. "This is chiefly because the sounds of percussion instruments . . . more closely resemble the basic electronic timbres favored by Davidovsky."[19]

The availability of tape recorders in Europe and the United States was paramount to the rapid increase in electronic music in the decades that followed World War II and the number of studios dedicated to the research and composition of electronic music grew at an exponential rate. "The earliest sound experiments of Cage, Pierre Schaeffer, and Pierre Henri were with disc recordings; however, it was the invention and availability of magnetic tape that made the electronic music movement a reality."[20] Even so, by the end of the 1980s, the computer had come of age and soon digital devices for creating, reproducing, and playing music heralded the demise of the tape machine. "The medium of magnetic tape recording remained the most viable and affordable audio recording and editing medium for 40 years until the availability of affordable digital audio technologies in the 1990s."[21] Composers embraced the new digital technology. It reduced both the size and cost of equipment needed to produce electronic music. It was no longer necessary to rely on institutional studios. With a modest investment in equipment, composers could work at home.

The American composer Steven Everett (b. 1953) has written a number of works that explore the use of computers in "real time." His percussion work, *Quiet Silence*, was composed in 1999 for a five-octave marimba and interactive electronics. Everett, who currently serves as executive vice president and provost at Adelphi University in New York, studied composition with the composer Salvatore Martirano (1927–1995), who "became widely known as the inventor of the SalMar Construction, a one-of-a-kind analog synthesizer designed for real-time performance composition."[22] The inspiration for Everett's marimba work came from "walking the narrow Roman paths" above the Italian Riviera coastline. "I was struck by an awareness of extremely slow pulses of time and light and sound, each exerting pressure on the other."[23] Slowly shifting cyclical patterns (similar to those found in gamelan music) using numerical relationships from an infinite series, "and spectral transformations and spatial movements generated in real-time," comprise the work.[24]

Quiet Silence requires a marimba with the range of five octaves (fairly common by the 1990s), plus a four-channel sound system and four microphones with short stands allowing them to be placed under the marimba: "The idea was that each of the four mics placed under different registers of the marimba would be used to quasi-isolate the instrument into four sound sources which could then be treated with different audio effects and moved separately to the four speakers placed in each corner of the room."[25] Using a computer and commercially available software of the time (Kyma or Max/MSP) allowed the audience to hear different melodies emerging from each speaker location. To perform Everett's *Quiet Silence,* the marimbist needs great physical dexterity: the entire five-octave range is in continual use throughout the work. (Fig. 7.5) As percussionists became more proficient on keyboard percussion instruments, composers began to write more difficult and challenging parts. Not only two-mallet, but also four- and five-mallet passages became part of the marimbist's repertoire.

Electronics had a significant impact on composers and performers throughout the twentieth century. Early on, a few composers envisioned a time when they could bypass the performer and bring their creations directly to the music audience through electronic means. Cage, Chavez, Varèse, and others predicted a future in which composers would create music through electronic means, thereby contacting the listening public directly much as a painter or sculptor does visually. From the early experiments of Russolo and his *intonarumori,* to the late 1990s, where digital audio workstations use algorithms to create sounds never previously heard, composers have pursued this dream. "An international survey published in 1974 estimated that more than 2,000 composers, working in some 500 electronic music studios, had by then produced more than 10,000 electronic compositions, not to mention their wide use in popular genres."[26] By century's end, the use of electronics to create, enhance, listen to, or perform music was global. Drum machines, electronic keyboard percussion with pads, and percussion synthesizers all became part of the percussionist's "bag" in addition to the many Western and non-Western acoustic instruments already included in their wheelhouse. Percussionists needed to acquire new skills in response to this ever-changing world of electronics.

Other works to consider: *Transposition/Improvisation* (1962) by Klaus Hashagen (1924–1998); *Machine Music (1964)* by Lejaren Hiller (1924–1994); *Structure* (1965) by Roger Hannay (1930–2006); *Cry of This Earth* (1977) by Konrad Boehmer (1941–2014); *Time Mark* (1987) by Scott Wyatt (b. 1951); *North Star Boogaloo* (1996) by George Lewis (b. 1952); *. . . from behind the unreasoning mask* (1975) by Roger Reynolds (b. 1934).

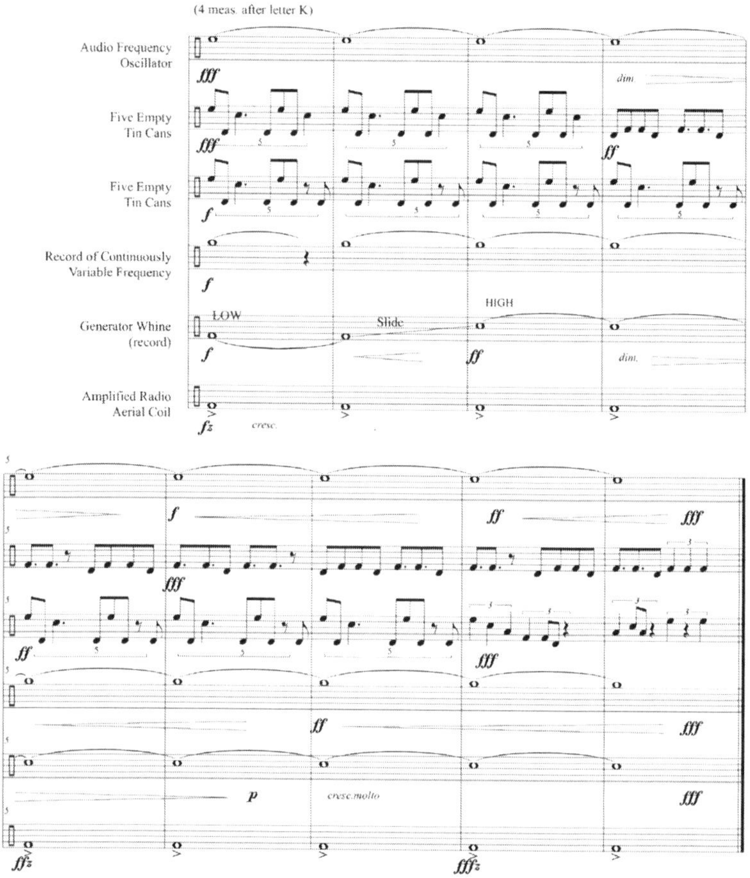

Fig..7.1 Cage, *Imaginary Landscape No. 3* (final nine measures)

Fig. 7.2 Varèse, *Déserts* (meas. 150)

Fig. 7.3 Stockhausen, *Mikrophonie* (photo of activators). Copyright © Klaus Barisch, photographer. Used by permission.

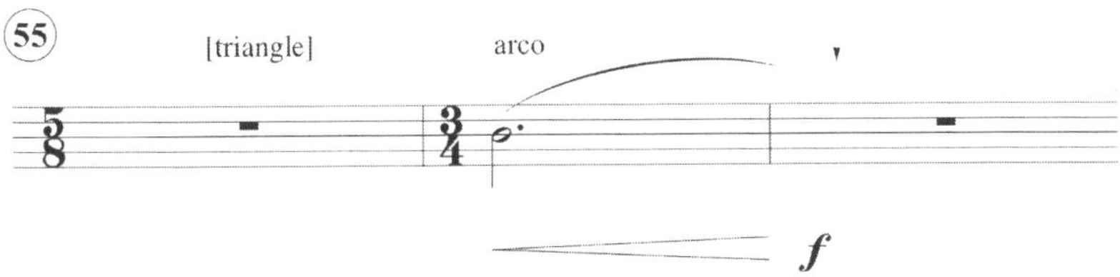

Fig. 7.4 Davidovsky, *Synchronism No. 5* (bar no. 54)

Fig. 7.5 Everett, *Quiet Silence* (meas. 244–246). Reprint courtesy of Steve Everett.

Chapter 8

MUSIC-THEATER

In the late 1960s, a renewed focus on the theatrical aspects of musical performance merged with political and social concerns to create a new genre. The times were, as noted by the songwriter Bob Dylan, "a-changin'." With an unpopular war in Asia, the civil rights movement in the United States, and student riots in France, young people across the globe challenged the authority of their governments. It was a time of societal unrest. The names given to this emerging music genre were many as were the various aspects of theater that composers appropriated. "Theater-music," "music-theater," "mixed- or multimedia" and "intermedia" are just some of the names found in the literature describing individual or groups of works that combined music with various theatrical components. These components could include elements such as lighting, theatrical gestures, stage action, social commentary, improvisation, electronics, staging, film, set design, and others, elements that involved more than just the aural aspects of music. To best illustrate this style of new music, this chapter will use the term "music-theater." "The inclusive meaning of the term can encompass the entire universe of performance in which music and theater play complementary and potentially equal roles."[1]

Music-theater of the 1960s is not opera. Rather, it identified with the works of post–World War II composers who began to exploit the drama and theatricality inherent in live music presentations. Its roots are found in the scandalous multimedia concerts staged by the Italian Futurists, the coupling of new music and modern dance in the first half of the century, and the theatrical side effects intrinsic to live music presentations. Within this new music-theater, instrumentalists may be asked to speak, sing, chant, dance, gesture, or move about the stage or performance venue. These works are designated music-theater, their actions dictated (or suggested) by the composer.

For the percussionist, theatricality is inherent in the action he or she uses to produce a given sound, an action that may be physically performed in a variety of ways, but with similar results. Different schools promote various ways of striking the timpani or snare drum, crashing the cymbals or playing the marimba. For the percussionist, the resultant sound is of the utmost importance no matter what approach one takes, but in music-theater the action is part of the composer's concept, one demanding the attention of the performer and the listening audience.

Theater as ritual has been part of the history of ancient cultures throughout the world. One of the composers who looked to ancient rituals for inspiration was the American iconoclast Harry Partch (1901–1974). Partch's musical and aesthetic influences included Congo rituals, Chinese theater, American jazz, Hebrew chants, Javanese gamelan, and ancient Greek philosophy. In his book *Genesis of a Music* (published in 1949), Partch recounted the life experiences that brought him to reject the "tempered scale" and many of Western music's traditions. By designing a scale comprised of forty-three tones to the octave, Partch embraced "just intonation." This decision would lead him to become not only a composer, but also an instrument designer, builder, and tuner because there were no standard instruments that could readily perform music written using "just intonation." One could add to Partch's list of skills conductor, librettist, publisher, record producer, teacher, and percussionist since he found that to succeed as a composer, he had to do everything himself. The path he chose was a difficult one. In the 1930s and 1940s, a worldwide economic depression would find Partch working at any odd job just to stay alive—picking fruit as a migrant worker, proofreading for a New Orleans newspaper, washing dishes, and others. For a short period of time, he "rode the rails" as a hobo while continuing to write music and chronicle his adventures, an experience that would later serve as source material for his *Americana* compositions. A series of small grants, including a Guggenheim, helped him publish *Genesis of a Music,* his justification for rejecting equal temperament.

As a young boy living in southern Arizona, Partch heard the music of the Yaqui Indians who lived near his home. He also remembers hearing Christian hymns and Chinese lullabies sung by his mother who, along with Partch's father, served as a missionary in China at the turn of the century. By age fourteen his family had moved to Albuquerque where Partch began writing music and playing piano and organ for silent movies. After moving to Los Angeles, and following the unexpected death of both of his parents, he briefly enrolled in the School of Music at the University of Southern California. Partch found schooling not to his liking and would instead explore the free libraries of whatever city he found himself in as he traveled across the country. "Having given up on both private music teachers and music schools, Partch began to read about music in public libraries and to compose music free of academic restrictions."[2] Partch writes that a book he found in the Sacramento public library, *On the Sensations of Tone*, by the German physicist Hermann von Helmholtz (1821–1894), "was the key for which I had been searching."[3] He says that by 1923 he had abandoned the traditional, accepted way of composing and began searching for new scales, forms, and, eventually, instruments to support a style of vocalization unique to his music.[4]

The scale Partch arrived at is predicated on a tuning system called "just intonation." It is a system of tuning based on the vibrational ratios between two given pitches. In ancient Greece, the philosopher/mathematician Pythagoras of Samos discovered this vibrational relationship by dividing a monochord into two equal parts, producing an octave, expressed as the ratio 2:1. Dividing the half into three parts produces a 3/2 ratio, or a perfect fifth. Continuing with this process, one can eventually construct the entire chromatic scale. This process does not produce today's "equal temperament" scale, the scale used for tuning the piano and our keyboard percussion instruments. That takes a mathematical compromise that Partch was not willing to make.

Partch not only rejected equal temperament, but also most of the aesthetic principles of Western music. His oeuvre contains little music that is purely instrumental, a type of music he defined as "abstract." Partch felt that music began with the spoken word, "one voice," devoid of the "specialized idiosyncrasy known as 'serious' singing."[5] He denounced the Italian bel canto style of singing and the abstraction of vocal counterpoint. His lyrics were meant to be heard and to be understood. They were spoken or "intoned" with or without the support of his unique instrumentarium. Partch called this music "corporeal," which he defined as the opposite of "abstract." His research led him to create a unique body of work. "Having settled on a justly tuned scale of forty-three tones and a Monophonic and Corporeal vision of music's possibilities, Harry Partch never looked back."[6]

In 1928, Partch began his long apprenticeship as an instrument builder. He first adapted a viola by adding a longer neck into which he inserted brads as a tactile aid for locating pitches. Using the viola, and later a reworked guitar,

Partch began performing his own music created from disparate literary sources such as the poetry of Li Po (701–762), Shakespeare, and the Bible. He also found inspiration during his travels. Partch notes: "I wrote music exploiting the speech of itinerants (*Bitter Music*), hitchhiker inscriptions copied from a highway railing (*Barstow*), a cross-country trip (*U.S. Highball*), and newspaper boy cries (*San Francisco*), generally using an ensemble of my own instruments."[7] This ensemble included a small reed organ he called Chromelodeon, reconstructed by Partch in 1945. Partch used the Chromelodeon, which had a range of five octaves, to tune all his other instruments. He also built a series of plectra instruments inspired by Greek models including three kitharas (a type of lyre) and three harmonic canons, modeled after the ancient Greek monochords with moveable bridges to accommodate the modality needed for a specific work.

As his musical vision and repertoire expanded, Partch added percussion instruments to provide additional tonal range and rhythmic clarity for his orchestrations. " I realized a most urgent need—percussion built for this system of music, for these theories."[8]

The instruments Partch constructed were built for specific compositional needs as he began to compose large-scale dramatic works. "Not a ratio of vibrational lengths has been put on paper nor one piece of wood glued to another which did not have as its ultimate objective the creation of music."[9]

Over a number of years, Partch hand-built an entire keyboard percussion family: a thirty-six-bar instrument called the Diamond Marimba (1946), a bass marimba (1949–50), and his colossal Marimba Eroica (1951), comprised of a series of four sub-bass notes. The Diamond Marimba was constructed with bars made from Brazilian rosewood and Pernambuco wood. It is a practical realization of the theoretical tonality diamond. The thirty-six bars are arranged in the form of a tiered rhombus; strokes from top to bottom on the right side are otonalities (major), while those on the left are utonalities (minor). Twenty years later (1965), Partch built his Quadrangularis Reversum, a mirror image of the Diamond Marimba. Between the two came the bass marimba with bars made from Sitka spruce coupled with redwood resonators. Its lowest bar is fifty-two inches in length sounding a cello C. Partch eschewed the practice of turning up the lower resonator ends à la commercial bass marimbas. "Sound never liked corners."[10] As a result, the bars stood five feet from the floor and the player needed a bench in order to reach them. Partch used a standard five-line staff to notate the bass marimba's pitches. (Fig. 8.1) Notes that fall on lines are indicated on the instrument with red circles. Even lower in pitch than the bass marimba was Partch's mammoth Marimba Eroica, also made from Sitka spruce. The longest bar was tuned to twenty-two cycles, approximately F below the lowest piano note. Struck with large, fluffy mallets, the sound is more felt than heard. In 1972, for the production of his film *The Dreamer That Remains,* Partch built the Mbira Bass Dyad, two wooden blocks made from Osage orange wood and, like the Eroica, having their own resonators.

To his family of marimbas, Partch added a number of other tuned percussion: the Boo, or Bamboo Marimba, custom-made from sixty-four sections of Philippine bamboo; Cloud Chamber Bowls, crafted from the tops and bottoms of twelve-gallon carboys; the Eucal Blossom, made from thirty-three tuned tubes of bamboo mounted on a stand with its own music rack; the Gourd Tree and Cone Gongs, comprised of twelve bowl gongs with gourd resonators attached to a eucalyptus bough, "to give the impression of ripe fruit growing at various angles on stems, somewhat like a papaya tree,"[11] and a number of instruments inspired by or adapted from University of Illinois industrial design students. These included the Zymo-Xyl, a collection of marimba bars, inverted wine bottles, and three metal auto hubcaps; the Mazda Marimba, named after the Persian god of light, composed of three rows of various-sized, suspended light bulbs; and the Crychord, a single string whose tension is controlled by a lever and struck with a length of covered dowel rod. On a hand-made stand, Partch mounted a single marimba bar and suspended a number of other percussion sounds including pedal-operated flexatones, which he called "Whang Guns," a guiro, a wood block, two Cloud Chamber bowls, and seven brass artillery casings. He titled this grouping "The Spoils of War."

Partch's interest in ancient Greek drama led him to create works inspired by Greek myths: *Oedipus* (1951), *Castor and Pollux* (1952), and *Ulysses at the Edge* (1955). His large music dramas include *Revelation in the Courthouse Park—After "The Bacchae" of Euripides* (1961) and *Delusion of the Fury—a Ritual of Dream and Delusion* (1966) in two acts. "Act I, based upon a Japanese story dating from the eleventh century . . . is intensely serious. Act II, based upon an African tale . . . is highly farcical."[12] His final composition was for the sound track of a film, *The Dreamer That Remains* (1972), in which Partch talks about his life's journey while demonstrating many of the instruments mentioned above.

One of Partch's most original works, *U.S. Highball,* is a 1943 musical account of a transcontinental journey, hitching freights and thumbing rides, from San Francisco to Chicago. The word *highball* in the title refers to a signaling device used on U.S. railroads during the time of steam locomotives to alert train engineers and control traffic. A "low ball" was a signal "to stop or slow down, to beware."[13] A "highball" meant the track ahead was clear. "In time, the latter term became a verb, and any hobo knows that 'Let 'er highball, engineer!' means 'Let's get going.'"[14] In 1955, Partch revised and reorchestrated *U.S. Highball* utilizing a number of percussion instruments including the sound effect of a train whistle constructed from a set of bellows, an old 1912 auto exhaust horn, and three organ pipes. Partch called the resulting "contraption" a Bloboy. Played with a "smear" (a short glissando) on the Chromelodeon, it realistically sounds like the whistle of an old freight train in the distance.

U.S. Highball is composed in three large parts, fast-slow-fast (what Partch calls "a hobo allegro form"),[15] with a text consisting of the names of towns and states through which the train passes, plus interjections from hobo conversations, boxcar graffiti, and hitchhikers' inscriptions. There is no storyline. It begins with the words "leaving San Francisco" intoned by the protagonist, Slim (changed to Mack at a later date). The instruments, especially the bass marimba, provide forward motion with steady quarter, eighth, and sixteenth notes. The main text is vocalized by a tenor with the instrumentalists occasionally adding comments and interjections. The work ends with the word "Chicago" softly whispered as Partch's journey ends. As with all of Partch's work, *U.S. Highball* provides the listener with both a theatrical and a musical experience. The instrumentalists, dressed in black, provide action as they play, speak, and chant. The instruments themselves, lit with colored stage lighting, appear as sculptural objects. The gestalt is theatrical and the experience corporeal.

Partch's influence was limited during his lifetime, in part by the lack of consistent support and a home base from which to work. During his most productive years he found it necessary to move his studio from place to place across the face of America. Despite invitations from enthusiastic supporters at various universities, including those in Wisconsin and Illinois in the 1960s, his stays were usually limited to one or two years as permanent positions were denied.[16] "Music departments generally remained hostile and unsupportive."[17] Also, the necessity of having his works performed exclusively on his handcrafted collection of specially tuned instruments created production problems and limited mobility. Yet, his work was performed, became known, and was influential. The idea of ritualized music-theater as conceived by Harry Partch continues to resonate today.

One of the composers who worked with Harry Partch for a period of time and embraced just intonation as a compositional starting point was Benjamin Johnston (1926–2019). Johnston's career included thirty-five years of teaching composition and music for dance at the University of Illinois, ending with his retirement in 1986. With the exception of a few works, Johnston avoided the necessity of creating his own set of just-tuned instruments. "I knew there was no sense in my trying to build instruments; I just don't have any of the right talents."[18] He wrote a few wind pieces and then settled on writing for the instrumental family that, with minor adjustments, is able to perform music using just intonation, namely the strings, especially string quartets. His works for percussion include a concerto written for the dance, a snare drum solo, and two versions of a work he titled *Knocking Piece.*

Knocking Piece was first conceived as part of incidental music for a play titled *In 3 Zones* by Wilford Leach (1929–1988). Johnston's music was to be provided by an onstage chamber orchestra with two percussionists and included a part for just-tuned piano. Unfortunately, due to lack of financial support the play was never produced. Its first act was based on the same story used by Stravinsky in *Histoire du soldat,* a retelling of the Faust tale described in an earlier chapter. In Leach's version, the soldier falls asleep, dreaming that, upon returning home, his entire village has been destroyed with the exception of one house, which miraculously is his home. He finds the house locked and climbs all over it to get in. To mimic this action, Johnston proposed that the two percussionists cross the stage to the piano and begin exploring the sound possibilities of its interior with sticks and mallets; their theatrical actions were to be seen as an attack on one of music's most revered instruments, a grand piano. The music written for the percussionists was eventually published as a duet entitled *Knocking Piece* (1962). Its rhythmic scheme was taken from an earlier Johnston work, *A Sea Dirge,* from Shakespeare's *The Tempest.*[19]

In *Knocking Piece,* Johnston uses the time-shifting process known as "metrical modulation," made popular by the American composer Elliott Carter (1908–2012). He extracted the pitch ratios found in *A Sea Dirge* and used them as the basis for one of the most rhythmically challenging percussion duets written up to that time. "I was interested . . . in exploring a transfer of ratios of the pitches in a just-tuned composition to ratios of superimposed metrical patterns in a percussion piece."[20] In converting the pitches to rhythms, Johnston interpreted unisons as 1:1, octaves as 2:1, perfect fifths as 3:2, minor sixths as 8:5, and so on. The sequence of intervals found in *A Sea Dirge* became the polyrhythms of *Knocking Piece.* Appearing as two surgeons about to operate, one percussionist is positioned at the keyboard so that he or she is able to reach inside the piano as well as control the sustain pedal. The other player stands in the well of the piano. Both players require a number of different mallets used to strike and hammer the piano's body, metal harp, soundboard, and occasionally, for color, the strings, taking care not to damage the instrument. The tempo is set as player one plays two eighth notes in the first bar. (Fig. 8.2) Equal signs across the second and third bars signify that the player is to keep the eighth-note pulse steady. In bar 2, the second player plays three eighth-notes against the first player's two notes and in the third bar, five eighth-notes against the four notes of player one. At this point, the equal signs are given to the second player who keeps the speed of his five eighth-notes steady into the next bar as player one plays three notes against his four. The result is a slight increase in tempo in the fourth bar. This back-and-forth interplay of polyrhythms (or cross rhythms) causing accelerandos and ritardandos continues throughout the piece, with each player in turn assuming control of the basic pulse. Players must rely on each other rather than compete, as the challenges found in *Knocking Piece* are considerable. "The players must be friends; in quick alternation each must support the other."[21] Audience reactions to early performances of *Knocking Piece* were mostly hostile. Johnston wrote: "It was easy, in the late 1960s, to make a startling impact on an audience with a cleverly-made theatrical piece."[22]

The composer Mauricio Kagel (1931–2008) was born in Buenos Aires, Argentina, on Christmas Eve, 1931. His musical training was traditional with the exception of composition. As a young man "he took theory, singing, conducting, piano, cello and organ lessons . . . but was self-taught as a composer."[23] He met Pierre Boulez on a visit to Argentina and was able to show the famed French composer some of his early works. Boulez encouraged Kagel to pursue his studies in Europe. "Apparently impressed, Boulez made clear to Kagel that in order to pursue a career as a composer he would have to leave Argentina."[24] Kagel applied for and was able to procure a scholarship for study at WDR's electronic music studio in Cologne. This was fortunate for Kagel since the studio was one of the leading centers for experimental music at that time: "Cologne in the late 1950s was arguably the capital of new music with the electronic studio of the WDR at its centre."[25] Kagel became a German citizen, active as a composer and teacher, and in 1974 was appointed professor of new music-theater at the Cologne Musikhochschule.[26]

An early work of Kagel's, *Transición II* (1958–59) for piano, percussion, and tape, included many new, at that time, notational ideas, such as graphics, proportional notation, and so on and detailed directions on how to prepare the piano. The score has sixteen pages of instructions. In *Transición II*, the percussionist modifies the piano strings as directed and plays inside the piano providing, through his or her actions, both sounds and theater.

A later and more theatrical work, *Match* (1964), places the percussionist center stage. Written for two cellists and a solo percussionist, the work explores a detailed list of extended performance techniques. Kagel collected string playing techniques, coupling them into 112 combinations, and distributing them over the cello parts according to a randomized number series.[27] The two string players, dressed in formal concert attire, are positioned on podiums at stage left and right. The percussion setup includes a marimba, bass drum, snare drum, suspended cymbal, sizzle cymbal, and cymbals à 2, plus a number of sound effects: dinner bell, *sistrum*, castanets, dog bark, police whistles, and a wind-up bell like an old-time alarm clock. The percussionist is positioned center stage between the dueling cellists and acts as a referee in an imagined athletic event, keeping the players in line, cueing entrances, and sometimes interrupting them. At one point, a cellist appearing to be asleep is awakened by the percussionist's alarm clock effect. At another time, the percussion soloist interrupts the action with a police (or referee) whistle. The percussion part is a tour de force. The physical actions created by the performer's normal movement are part of the theatrics as well as those caused by the virtuosic, sometimes impossible, demands that Kagel notates. He labels this type of work "instrumental theatre." It is meant to carry meaning, both musically and sociologically. "On the whole, his work (contrary to Cage's), is deeply committed to exploring the capacity of art for communication and expression (if in mediated fashion), which entails referencing existing musics or wider cultural, social, or historical contexts."[28]

Kagel's percussion trio *Dressur* (1976–77) is dedicated to "Cercle de Percussion à Paris" (Les Trio Cercle). The instrumentation is extensive for this approximately twenty-five-minute theatrical work written for three players, much of which needs to be memorized. All instruments used in *Dressur* are made of wood, including many ethnic instruments. Some are normally found in the percussionist's trap case: claves, wood blocks, castanets, maracas, guiros, temple blocks, ratchets, and whip. Others are more unusual: Asian angklungs, wooden elephant bell, African coconut rattle, *wasamba* rattle or *sennpo* (sistrum from the Ivory Coast), and a stamping tube. Also needed are the following wooden items: a whistle, wind chimes, nutcracker (and three nuts), a mortar, and two pairs of clogs. There are a few items that need to be handcrafted such as a nut rattle, a bouncing ball box, and others. Props including a table, a chair, and lengths of wood and carpeting help set the stage and provide varying sounding surfaces for the stamping tube and wooden shoes.

A circus tune played on the marimba opens *Dressur*. The melody references a *galop*, *Souvenir de Cirque Renz* (Fig. 8.3), by the nineteenth-century composer Gustav Peter (ca. 1833–1919). Staging is vital to a successful performance of *Dressur* as are the choreographed actions of the three players. Kagel's *Dressur* stands as one of the most elaborate music-theater works in percussion ensemble literature. As in Partch's compositions, the sounds, the instruments, and the movements of the players are vital parts of the work's gestalt. "In many ways, then, Kagel's instrumental theatre strives to rediscover what has been lost in Western classical music: the visual and kinetic nature of performance, the physicality of music-making, the bodily presence of the performers, the three-dimensional space of the stage, the spectacle of stage events."[29]

In 1981–82, Kagel composed *Rrrrrrr . . .*, a set of forty-one pieces (the titles all begin with the letter R) that included the following six percussion duets. *Railroad Drama* (a railway accident) opens with one player imitating the sound of a steam locomotive. Holding a paper perpendicularly to his mouth, the player turns his or her head back and forth while blowing briefly each time the mouth passes the paper, increasing the tempo as the engine "picks up steam." This figure is repeated later using two birch switches with exaggerated arm movements à la a rudimental open-to-closed roll. Various whistles, a lion's roar, and friction drum add accompanying sounds. *Ranz des vaches* (a Swiss cowherd's song) requires a prerecorded tape of sounds one might hear on a dairy farm. Along with the tape, sets of almglocken are played by funneling sand over their surfaces or by using vibe mallets. *Rigaudon* (an early French folk dance) calls for reco-reco, wood blocks, tenor drum, tambourine, *tumbas,* and a pedal bass drum. Repetitive sixteenth- and eighth-note figures overlap and move at a rapid tempo marked vivace. The movement starts and ends pianissimo forming a dynamic arch. *Rim Shots & Co.* is written for two snare drums placed on stage at a distance from one another. Here, Kagel explores the technique of finger rolls followed by rim-shots and accents played in bursts of sound. In *Ruf,* for tubular chimes, inverted snare drum, bass drum, maracas, ratchet, and sleigh bells, Kagel's performance notes ask that the chime notes marked tenuto be struck with a dead-stroke while the pedal is damped, a seemingly contradictory action resulting in an unusual sound. The inverted snare drum is played with fingers, as is a slack-headed bass drum. The drums play ruffs of various lengths at a very soft dynamic level while the chimes perform a dirgelike melody. *Rutsher,* the final movement in this pastiche, is marked *galop.* A tuneful xylophone solo, accompanied by snare drum, high-hat, and wood block, acts as a rousing finale.

Kagel wrote music for orchestra, chamber music, voices, radio plays, and film. Many of these works include percussion; most explore the theatricality inherent in musical performance. His theater works from the 1960s and 1970s helped define this unique genre. "It is in the domain of music theatre that Kagel left his mark most unmistakably and that his influence is felt most clearly."[30]

In the 1970s, Stockhausen "began a series of instrumental works that use lighting, costumes, mime, and other aspects of ritual."[31] The electronic music wizard had, from the beginning of his compositional career, a sense of theater apparent in early works like *Zyklus* and *Mikrophonie.* It resonated fully in his final creation, *Licht,* a cycle of seven operas to be performed inside and outside of the normal performance space requiring multiple orchestras, soloists (including percussion), choruses, mimes, dancers, actors, electronics, and four helicopters. His 1975 theater work, *Music im Bauch,* was somewhat less ambitious. Inspired by his daughter Julike, who reportedly was amused by the sounds of her father's stomach rumblings, *Music im Bauch* (Music in the Belly) is an ideal example of the music-theater genre from the time period. For this work, Stockhausen wrote twelve melodies, one for each sign of the zodiac. These melodies were converted into custom music boxes made available by a Swiss company. Three chromatic octaves of crotales, orchestra bells, a set of pitched bell plates (*Klangplatten*), and a low f-sharp marimba complete the instrumentation. Staging and lighting are crucial to the piece and Stockhausen's score provides detailed directions. A larger-than-life birdman figure, clothed in shirt and slacks, is suspended center stage. The marimba is positioned stage left, the Klangplatten stage right. Behind the birdman figure are the crotale sets and downstage a set of orchestra bells is positioned, as well as three small tables on which the music boxes will eventually be placed. The work requires six percussionists. Three of the players act out an elaborate ritual, moving about the birdman figure, whipping it rhythmically with switches, performing an "ecstatic dance with wild leaps"[32] until one of the players cuts open the birdman's belly and removes one of three music boxes hidden inside. It is placed on a downstage table, its lid opened, and, with amplification, it begins to be heard. Two other players follow suit keeping the music boxes active until all three are sounding.

For a given performance, three of Stockhausen's original zodiac melodies are selected, one melody for each music box. (Fig. 8.4) One of the selected melodies is played on the marimba; all three chosen are played by the Klangplatten. The marimba players' normal movements are stylized and mechanical in appearance. As in a trance, they play their selection once through over the duration of the piece (ca. thirty-five minutes). The Klangplatten player plays all three melodies in a specified sequence and controls the overall action, signaling the other ensemble members by activating a musical spinning top or by striking the tubular chimes. "*Musik im Bauch* unfolds simultaneously on different time-scales. The marimba, with two performers acting in concert like automatons, plays a stretched version of one of the chosen melodies which lasts the entire length of the performance; on the opposite side of the stage, the bell-plate player performs stretched versions of all three chosen melodies in sequence, each in turn determining the duration of one scene."[33] *Music im Bauch* incorporates music, lighting, staging, choreography, and electronics. It is without narrative, as are many examples of this genre, but the combination of set design, lighting, action (in this case ritualistic), and sound makes for a satisfying aesthetic experience.

One of the founding members of the French percussion group Les Trio Cercle, composer Jean-Pierre Drouet (b. 1935), has championed contemporary music since 1959, at which time he began a close association with the composer Luciano Berio. His early career as a pianist was short lived due to an accident. In response to this tragedy, Drouet turned to the trumpet and drums, studying at the conservatories of Bordeaux (where he was born) and in Paris where he joined the composition class of André Hodeir (1921–2011). Drouet's published works include a number of technical studies for percussion as well as solo and ensemble works. His trio *Combien de cercles superposés* (1974) reflects his early interest in music-theater as does his work from 1991, *Variations sur un texte de Victor Hugo*.

A twenty-five-minute tour de force for percussion quartet, Drouet's *Variations* requires skills not usually demanded of the contemporary percussionist. Written for the French percussion group Quatuor Hêlios, it combines acting, singing, and dancing as well as musical expertise of the highest order. The text includes quotes from Hugo's classic novel, *Les Misérables*, calling for vocal sounds that range from dulcet to guttural. Drouet invokes irony as the work reflects upon the optimism of Hugo's protagonist, Jean Valjean, who in 1832 joins a group of protesting French students manning the barricades in Paris as they fight for freedom and democracy. Valjean encourages them with words of hope spoken in unison by the ensemble as the musicians softly tremolo on tuned almglocken: "Men will no longer have to fear, as they do now, a conquest, an invasion, a usurpation, a rivalry of nations." Hugo writes: "Citizens, the nineteenth century is great, but the twentieth century will be happy."[34] Given the great wars of the twentieth century, Hugo's hopeful vision did not come to pass. In his *Variations*, Drouet reminds us of the follies of humankind and its continuing hope for a peaceful future.

Variations sur un texte de Victor Hugo is composed of three parts. It opens with a section featuring four floor tom-toms played with hands, fingers, and mallets. Each player sits on a swivel stool with a tray stand behind, accommodating almglocken, shakers, rattles, sound effects, castanets, and tambourines. The players swivel back and forth from tom-toms to tray stands at intervals indicated graphically in the score. Facing forward, the players perform in a normal manner. When they swivel to the rear, their actions and words become erratic: "Drouet articulates the dichotomy between the façade that we live in and the reality that we deny."[35] The extended techniques that Drouet calls for include changing the pitches of the tom-tom by applying pressure to the drum's head with elbows, hands, and almglocken. The notation in the middle part is unique, consisting of stick figures coupled with notated rhythms. (Fig. 8.5) The players slowly transition to part two of the *Variations* featuring rhythmic dancing, including flamenco and tap dance. One of the players breaks away from the dance and moves behind the tray stands and begins playing a loud four-mallet ostinato figure on a marimba. The other three players join in sequence and a complex sixteen-mallet section ensues. This dissolves into an extended section with the four players using rosined bass violin bows to activate the marimba bars. Voices and marimbas end the work playing a mournful chorale against sparse metallic taped sounds. *Variations sur un texte de Victor Hugo* is an ambitious work, as was Hugo's novel, *Les Misérables*, each bearing a universal message.

The Vietnam War, the plight of Native Americans, slavery, Japanese Noh drama, modern dance, and North Indian rhythms are a few of the touchstones that influenced the creative works of American composer Michael Udow (b. 1949). A successful percussionist and teacher, Udow displayed his compositional talents early in his career, writing his first works by age fifteen. While a high school student at Michigan's Interlochen Arts Academy, he attended composition classes with Warren Benson (1924–2005) and continued his studies at the University of Illinois with a number of composition faculty members including Herbert Brün, Thomas Frederickson (1928–2017), and Edwin London (1929–2013). In 2011, Udow retired after a thirty-year tenure as the director of percussion studies at the University of Michigan. His mature compositional work includes percussion ensembles, solo pieces, works for orchestra and wind ensemble as well as chamber music for mixed instrumentation. For many of his pieces he designed and constructed new instruments, created new notation systems, and invented rhythmic structures based on polyrhythmic strata. In 1987, Udow composed his first large-scale work for voice and percussion, *The Shattered Mirror*. An opera in two acts with a duration of just under two hours, it has all of the genre's trappings: dramatic singing (including soloists and chorus), dance, and instrumental accompaniment (primarily percussion with piano and synthesizer) in a grand theatrical presentation. The cast of characters includes the Sun, the Moon, the Wind, and Four Grandfathers, each representing one of the cardinal directions, East, North, West, and South. Eight percussionists, piano, and synthesizer comprise the orchestra. The orchestration relies heavily on pitched percussion, marimbas, vibraphone, MalletKAT, glockenspiel, chimes, tuned gongs, and almglocken, plus two water gongs, bass drum, a set of Indonesian angklung, strike rods, and two sets of specially tuned crotales pitched at 440 and 447 cycles per second. Percussion permeates the stage area as well. Each chorus member carries two sets of microtonal wind chimes, a rainstick, and wind tubes. The Four Grandfathers are equipped with an array of tuned metallic bells, crotales, and cymbals, plus Japanese *odaikos* and African *djembes*. Many of the instruments used in *The Shattered Mirror* were created specifically for the work.

The Shattered Mirror tells no story in the traditional sense, but rather evokes the emotion and sentiment of the poems Udow chose to use in place of a traditional libretto. Program notes to the premiere state: "The corpus of this poetic libretto was written by John Gracen Brown and reassembled in a narrative style by the composer." Other poems by various authors were used as well. The work is a multicultural mix. The Four Grandfathers evoke the spiritual traditions of Native Americans from the Great Lakes region in Canada and the United States, the stages of life, and the need for balance in the world. Together, the Sun, the Moon, and the Wind narrate the birth of dawn and the coming of darkness as they comment allegorically on the meaning of life and the passage of time. The score is constructed in part on a North Indian *kaida*. (Fig. 8.6) The sixteen-beat pattern, played by the Four Grandfathers, opens Act One. Udow uses the kaida later in the movement in canon and in Act Two as well. Like Harry Partch, Udow's *The Shattered Mirror* presents the listener with a total theatrical package.

Udow's antiwar work, *Understanding* (1969), requires a traditional stage with lighting, costumes, electronics, props (starter pistol, basketballs, and a rifle), and a stage pit that can be lowered during the performance. It begins with a two-minute excerpt from any popular antiwar song followed by the dramatic entrance of a line of black-hooded and -robed drummers, each carrying a field drum covered in black crepe, playing a simple dirgelike cadence. Six soloists and the conductor emerge from the line and position themselves on stage behind an array of equipment. Each soloist's instruments are nonspecific, chosen within certain limitations, namely loudness, duration, and avoidance of pitched sounds. There is no score to *Understanding*. Each player has six pages covered with fairly dense graphics similar to that of the 1960s action painter Franz Kline (1910–1962), each page representing one minute of music. Lines, dots, and smears of black ink represent sound, with the rhythms, dynamics, and timbres interpreted by each player according to the composer's directions. The conductor serves as a timekeeper, giving cues as needed. As the work moves toward its conclusion, the six soloists mount a mock attack on the conductor who, in turn, shoots each one. He then points the rifle at the audience, speaks the word "everyman," fires, and falls to the floor as the stage lift retreats as if a coffin is being lowered into a grave. At this point in the action, strobe and stage lights begin to flash. The players, who have now discarded their robes, climb out of the pit with basketballs and dribble off stage to the sounds of the march *American Patrol* by the composer Morton Gould (1913–1996). Udow remarks in the score: "This theater piece is dramatic with forces of demented hatred, and death, and then a turn-around ending. The acting must be convincing."[36] In a 1985 interview, the composer commented: "*Understanding* was written in 1968 when people were very conscious about what was happening in Viet Nam . . . it was theater music."[37] Other twentieth-century music-theater works by Udow include *As the Wind Colors* (1980) for gong players and four canoes, an outdoor work that references Native Americans. In the same decade, he created two paired works for claves and a conductor, *Reality I* and *Illusion I*, which combined theater music and minimalism, the latter a topic for chapter 10.

Other works to consider: *Paradigm* (1968) by Lukas Foss (1922–2009); *Three Rituals for 2 Percussion and Lights* (1969) by Lejaren Hiller (1924–1994); *Targets* (1970) by Paul Steg (1919–1995); *Poebells* (1972) by Edwin London (1929–2013); *War Games* (1976) by Walter Mays (b. 1942); *14 Stations* (1969) by Marius Constant; *Les corps à corps* (1978) by George Aperghis (b. 1945); *Sources III* (1967) by David Burge (1930–2013).

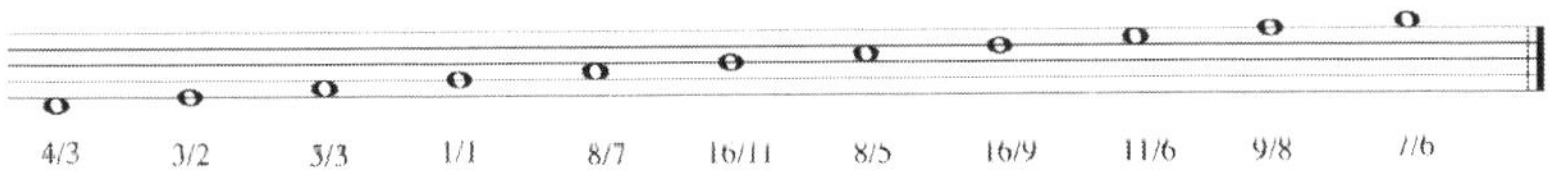

Fig. 8.1 Partch, *U.S. Highball* (bass marimba pitches)

Fig. 8.2 Johnston, *Knocking Piece* (title page). Copyright © Smith Publications, 54 Lent Rd., Sharon, VT 05065. Used by permission.

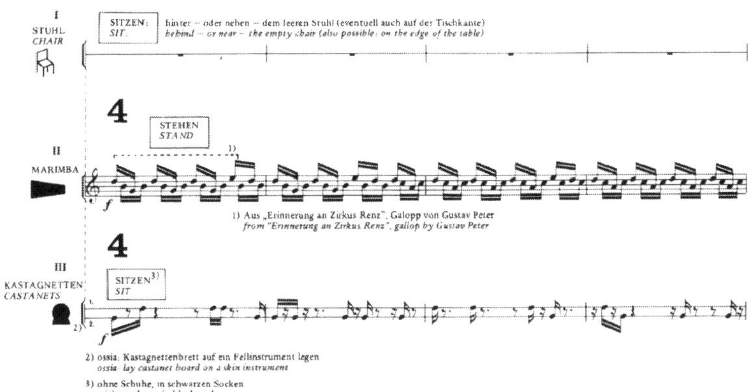

Fig. 8.3 Kagel, *Dressur* (p. 1, system one). Copyright © 1977 by Henri Litolff's Verlag. Used by permission of C. F. Peters Corporation. All rights reserved.

Fig. 8.4 Stockhausen, *Musik Im Bauch* (3 melodies). Copyright © Stockhausen Foundation for Music, 51515 Kürten, Germany. www.karlheinzstockhausen-stiftung.de.

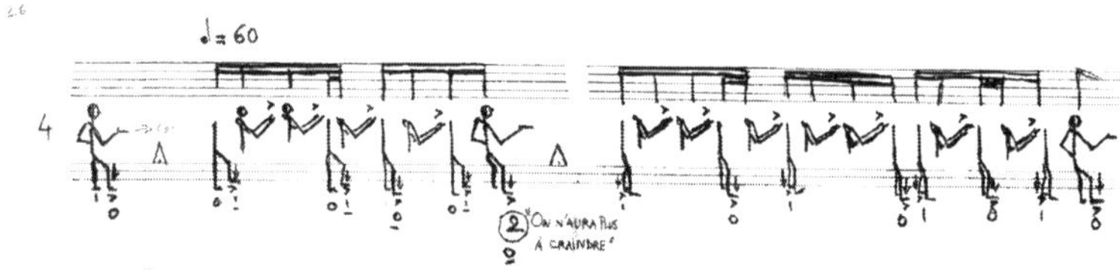

Fig. 8.5 Drouet, *Variations sur un texte de Victor Hugo* (stick figure notation example). Reprint courtesy of Jean-Pierre Drouet.

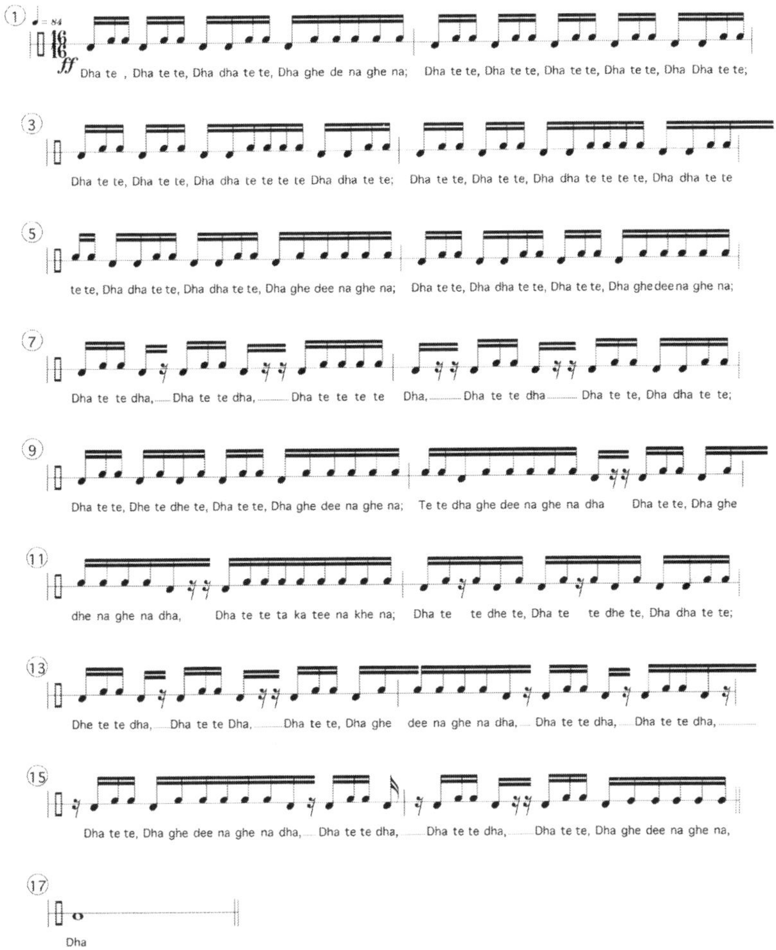

Fig. 8.6 Udow, *The Shattered Mirror* (kaida excerpt). Reprint courtesy of Michael W. Udow.

Chapter 9

SONORISM

The Color of Music

Timbre, that is, tone color (*Klangfarbe* in German), is the characteristic of sound that helps us discern the difference between an auto horn and a xylophone. Acoustically it is the arrangement of overtones that, with the help of a transient "attack sound," makes it possible to differentiate between even closely related instruments (for example, between a cymbal and a tam-tam). For a number of twentieth-century composers, timbre became a key element in their work, both structurally and conceptually. For Anton Webern, it meant assigning notes of a musical line to different instruments, adding color (timbre) and texture to a melody that he could serialize. Others treated this important musical element intuitively, or, much as we do in spoken language, emotionally, coloring both melodic and rhythmic lines. In his article "No Ear for Music: Timbre in the Early Percussion Music of John Cage," author/composer Christopher Shultis writes of Cage's careful attention to timbre. He decries those who fill their instrumental shopping cart without care for the quality of sound: "Unfortunately, when performers interpret Cage's early music, in particular his percussion pieces, their method of sound source selection is often highly uncritical, choosing whatever instruments happen to be at hand without giving consideration to their sonic properties in relation to their historical past. In my opinion, this approach is painfully flawed."[1]

In Poland in the 1960s, a school of composition labeled "sonorism" arose that focused on the timbral and textural characteristics of sound. The school's radical approach to composition was made possible by an easing of aesthetic restrictions forced on artists by the Soviet communist regime of the postwar era. Following the war, Poland and six other countries had come under the political domination of the USSR. Their respective governments were controlled from Moscow and were subjected to the whims of the dictator Josef Stalin (1878–1953), who insisted on compliance with Communist Party ideologies. In the arts, this meant acceptance of socialist realism whereby composers, writers, and other artists were to create works solely for the masses. "Cultural officials encouraged composers to direct their creative production towards the 'working masses' through the composition of mass songs and other accessible works."[2] Beginning in 1956, a series of protests by Polish workers demanding higher wages and better working conditions, coupled with the recent death of Stalin, led to a relaxation of centralized artistic control, though Poland's economic miseries continued until the dissolution of the USSR at the end of the 1980s. Taking advantage of this thaw in governmental relations with the communist hierarchy, Polish musicians instituted an annual fall festival during which more adventurous music began to be heard.

Beginning in 1956, the Warsaw Autumn (as the festival became known) programmed works by Western composers, such as Stravinsky and Schoenberg, that would not have been allowed earlier, as well as new, more radical works by Polish composers. The 1961 festival saw the premiere of *Threnody to the Victims of Hiroshima* (1961) written by the Polish composer Krzystof Penderecki (b. 1933). Written for string orchestra, Penderecki's work is an excellent example of sonorism. Its use of extended techniques included slapping the body of string instruments and bowing behind the bridge and on the instrument's tailpiece to create subtle (and not so subtle) changes in timbre. Orchestrated into thick clusters of notes, the resultant sound became almost electronic in nature. Penderecki's work influenced a number of other Polish composers, including Henryk Górecki (1933–2010) and Kazimierz Serocki.

The Polish composer Kazimierz Serocki (1922–1981) was born in Toruń on the banks of the Vistula in north-central Poland. He studied music at the Łódź Academy of Fine Arts and in Paris with Nadia Boulanger. His early works followed the aesthetic dictates of socialist realism. In 1956, he cofounded the Warsaw Autumn festival with his compatriot Tadeusz Baird (1928–1981). From that point on, his compositional output became more experimental, influenced by the international styles of the time. His percussion sextet, *Continuum*, written for the Strasbourg Percussion Group, "anticipates Xenakis' *Persephassa* in its placing of six percussionists around the perimeter of the hall."[3] The setups for each of the six players require keyboard percussion instruments, membranophones, and metallophones selected from the standard orchestral arsenal, with the addition of nine tuned Thai gongs and three suspended glass bottles. Seventeen sound activators are indicated graphically from triangle beaters, to bell mallets, to fingernails. Cluster bars made from both wood and metal are needed for the keyboard percussion instruments.

Each player performs from the score. The score's layout is an excellent example of clarity in that it enables each percussionist to easily coordinate entrances. Durations are given in seconds for each of thirty-six sections in which the sounds are notated proportionally. Serocki used a variety of notations, from traditional to avant-garde. He built extended sections of complex textures by additive means. At rehearsal number 32, each player enters in sequence playing irregular repetitive rhythmic figures notated within a box. Unique are the empty note heads for the keyboard percussion instruments that indicate playing not on the keyboard, but on the metal resonators—single notes as well as glissandi. (Fig. 9.1) Though timpani, chimes, and other pitched instruments are used in *Continuum,* their importance is minimal, mostly applied to register change. The score instructions give alternate layouts for positioning the six players; however, the one in which the audience is placed in the middle is central to the composer's creative vision. Single sounds and gestures pass over and around the listener to great aural effect. Unlike Xenakis's *Persephassa,* Serocki's work eschews the constant rhythmic pulse. Instead the composer uses a kaleidoscope of timbres, changes of textures, and a wide range of dynamics to move the work forward. *Continuum,* with its wide palette of colors combined with varying textures and extreme dynamic contrasts, creates a dramatic, satisfying sonic experience.

The American composer George Crumb (b. 1929) definitely had an ear for timbre coupled with a love of percussion. The majority of his compositions utilized percussion instruments, as well as other instruments used in a percussive manner. His music has been described as atmospheric, vividly expressive, and ritualistic—expressions that are normally descriptive of the graphic arts or theater. He explored the sonic possibilities of instruments of the percussion family with fervor, creating new, extended techniques and unique combinations of sounds. Trained academically (degrees from Mason College and the Universities of Illinois and Michigan), Crumb's music often quotes from past masters such as Bach, Debussy, and Mahler, and is influenced by literary imagery, especially the poetry of the Spaniard Federico Garcia Lorca (1898–1936). "Eleven of Crumb's compositions have connections with Lorca."[4] Beginning in 1965, Crumb wrote a series of chamber works for voice titled *Madrigals I, II, III.* This series was successfully premiered by the American mezzo-soprano

Jan DeGaetani (1933–1989), whose artistry greatly impressed Crumb. A larger work, *Ancient Voices of Children* (1970), was written expressly for her. In these works, Crumb integrates percussion into the fabric of the piece in true chamber music style. In the first madrigal, written for soprano, vibraphone, and bass, the vibraphone is struck both with mallets and fingernails. Occasionally, using a hard and soft mallet, a vibraphone pitch is "bent down" by pressing the hard mallet on the node and sliding it across the bar while striking it with the soft mallet. In his madrigals and other works, Crumb continued his exploration of the sonic possibilities of percussion instruments, consistently looking for ways to elicit new and unusual timbres from them.

In 1974, Crumb completed *Music for a Summer Evening (Makrokosmos III)*. The first two works in the series, *Makrokosmos I and II*, were for piano alone. Like Bartok's 1937 *Sonata* discussed earlier, *Makrokosmos III, Music for a Summer Evening* is scored for two pianos and two percussion. (The title, *Makrokosmos*, is also a nod to Bartok's piano series, *Mikrokosmos*.) *Music for a Summer Evening* calls for a large battery of percussion instruments including some that are unusual: Tibetan prayer stones, thundersheet, Japanese temple bells, sistrum, bell tree, glass wind-chimes, quijada, slide whistle, alto-recorder, African log drum, and a jug that the percussionist blows so as to create a moaning sound. The two pianists become percussion players in the fourth movement playing guiro and mbira (African thumb piano).

Crumb describes the overall structure of *Music for a Summer Evening* as a "large expressive curve over its approximately 40-minute duration."[5] Of the five movements, one, three, and five are the most elaborate with the other two movements being "dream-like pieces functioning as intermezzos."[6] Movement I, titled "Nocturnal Sounds (The Awakening)," quotes the Italian poet Salvatore Quasimodo (1901–1968)—"I hear ephemeral echoes, oblivion of full night in the starred water." In this movement, Japanese temple bells, glass and bamboo wind-chimes, vibraphone glissandi, and other percussive sounds are interjected between piano riffs. At the *a tempo*, a vibraphone tremolo and sleigh bells create support for an extended crescendo. The movement ends with crotales placed on a timpano head. As they are struck, the timpani pedal is moved back and forth creating harmonic glissandi. Movement II, "Wanderer-Fantasy," opens and ends with a plaintive call played on slide whistles. The percussionists play the whistles into the piano while the pedals are depressed, adding resonance and activating sympathetic vibrations. "Two slide whistles are played directly over the piano strings . . . producing distant, plaintive congeries of tones and overtones."[7] The whistles' notated intervals and range make the part extremely challenging. The middle movement, "The Advent," has a quote from the *Pensées* (Thoughts) of the French genius Blaise Pascal (1623–1662)—"The eternal silence of infinite space terrifies me." In Movement III, sustained metallic sounds—vibes, glock, chimes, and thundersheet—dominate the percussion writing. A cymbal is placed bell-down on a timpano and struck while the pedal is moved back-and forth, creating glissing harmonics. In the second section, "Hymn for the Nativity of the Star Child," the percussionists sing, harmonizing two short phrases. Movement IV, "Myth," is a percussion quartet. The tempo marking, "adagio *isorhythmico*: lonely, bleak," gives notice that Crumb utilized isorhythmic structural control "which consists of simultaneously performed taleas of 13, 7, and 11 bars."[8] In this movement, the two pianists join the percussionists with Piano I striking the metal crossbeams of the piano, striking the bass strings with crotales, scraping the guiro while holding it against a crossbeam, and voicing percussive rhythms. Piano II plays the mbira, holding it firmly against one of the piano crossbeams, which helps amplify its sound. Both pianos are electronically amplified. The two percussionists play a variety of instruments. Percussion I plays five sixteenth-notes over a dotted whole note by placing a clave on the head of the bass drum and striking it with the other clave. (Fig. 9.2) Percussion II provides moaning sounds and bends the pitch of a jug while blowing across its mouth. All the players vocalize, sometimes shouting to color the attack tones of the percussion instruments. Bowed tam-tams and jug glissandi are two of the many extended performance techniques Crumb uses to educe just the timbral effect he desires. The final movement, "Music of the Starry Night," quotes the poet Rainer Maria Rilke (1875–1926): "And in the nights the heavy earth is falling from all the stars down into loneliness. We are all falling. And yet there is One who holds this falling endlessly gently in His hands." The three quotations given in *Music for a Summer Evening* exemplify Crumb's emotional thoughts as he composed the work, as does the J. S. Bach excerpt quoted from the *Well-Tempered Clavier Book II* (Fugue No. VIII). In the fifth movement, the fugue subject is passed from pianos to vibraphone until two loud chords, "The Fivefold Galactic Bells," interrupt and the final "Song of Reconciliation" begins. It is marked "Joyous ecstatic, with a sense of cosmic time," completing the work's emotional journey. A bowed harmonic from a small tam-tam blends with the timbre of three Japanese temple bells and the sound of open fifths, played by the pianos, fade out, bringing *Music for a Summer Evening* to its conclusion.

Crumb mined masterworks from music history and the literary canon to inspire and construct his many creations. Ignoring counterpoint and other traditional compositional processes, he suspended time so that ear-catching timbres dissolved and mutated. For many, his pieces were both sonically attractive and emotionally understandable. Richard Taruskin, in his book *Music in the Late Twentieth Century,* comments:

> Crumb was one of the first composers (in the 1980s their number would multiply) to make timbre his primary creative preoccupation, varying and nuancing it with great subtlety and resourcefulness while reducing the music's formal structure to simple repetitive or strophic designs and stripping its sound surface down to bare nomadic or heterophonic textures. Critics marveled at the way in which timbre, often thought a decorative "nonessential," could successfully replace the more "substantial" elements of music—the elements out of which most of the standard techniques in the modernist arsenal were assembled.[9]

The young Polish American composer Marta Ptaszynska (b. 1943) created a number of works for both solo and ensemble percussion in the latter half of the century. Born in Warsaw, Ptaszynska completed her theory and composition degrees at the Warsaw Academy of Music and went on to continue her studies with Nadia Boulanger in Paris and later at the Cleveland Institute of Music in the United States. Trained as a percussionist, her writing is both idiomatic to percussion instruments as well as uniquely original. Speaking about her own music, she states that she is "fascinated by the logic of the digital universe, by the elegance of mathematical progressions, and, above all, by the beauty of geometric symmetries."[10] She found inspiration in the paintings of Wassily Kandinsky (1866–1944) and the surrealists Max Ernst (1891–1976) and Yves Tanguy (1900–1955). "Some sounds and harmonic structures seem to convey to my mind some characteristic colors . . . I am able to hear music which I feel already exists in a painting."[11]

Space Model (1971) is an early solo percussion work by Ptaszynska that utilizes tape as an accompaniment to the live performance. Three multiple-percussion setups are arranged so as to encircle the audience. The first movement requires nine different percussion timbres ranging from tom-toms to maracas. Written mostly in traditional notation, using time signatures and bar lines, it is performed without accompaniment. As the movement concludes, the soloist moves to the second setup while playing maracas. A prerecorded version of the first movement is then used to accompany the second movement, which calls for marimba, vibraphone, timpani, and a sizzle cymbal. The two movements interlock to create a duet—live and tape. Playing a cymbal (in hand), the player moves to the third setup, which contains both pitched and unpitched percussion. A tape recording of the duet version is coordinated with this third and final movement, creating a trio played by one performer. The work, though not difficult to perform, sounds complex as each sound layer is added. Ptaszynska used this concept again in a much larger and more elaborate 1974 work for percussion ensemble titled *Siderals.*

Written for the University of Illinois percussion ensemble, *Siderals* is scored for ten players divided into two quintets, 117 different percussion instruments, magnetic tape playback, and lighting. It was conceived as an audio-visual, or mixed-media work, though it can be performed as a concert piece without the light show. Ptaszynska obviously took her musical inspiration from astronomy as the title refers to space, the stars, and the galaxies. The large number of percussion instruments helped her create a multiplicity of sound constellations that differ from one another by texture, color, complexity, and motion.

Performance preparation includes arranging the unpitched percussion families in order from high to low; thus the tom-toms, wood drums, and tam-tams need to be scalar within each of the quintets. The third movement should be rehearsed first and, when performance level is reached, a tape recording needs to be made of the initial portion of the movement. The two quintets are to be positioned on stage right and left, though antiphonal procedures do not dominate the work.

The first movement is written in variation form, A, B, A1, B1, A2, B2 and so on. Twelve sections, marked with rehearsal letters A to L, alternate between contrasting segments. The segments are both controlled (bar lines and tempo markings) and free (additive textures, created ad libitum, with durations given in seconds). If the lighting display is used, each section would be assigned contrasting color values: A sections—warm hues (red, orange, yellow); B sections—cool colors (green, blue, violet). The display of light is to be "twinkling points of various colors."[12] Ptaszynska's references for the lighting are the paintings of the English Impressionist Alfred Sisley (1839–1899).

Movement II is dreamlike in nature with long, sustained sounds created by glass, metal, shell, and wood wind chimes, marimba, and glass bowl. Glissandi are written for flexatone, pipe rack, lion's roar, guiro, RotoToms, vibraphone, saw, and bowl gong. The bowl gong is placed on a timpano and struck while moving the pedal. (Fig. 9.3) In this movement, the color projection is to be passive: black shadows and white shapes "moving slowly, and fusing with one another, resembling the picture of cosmic nebulae."[13]

The final movement has seven sections. The first five are characterized by a monolithic sound structure constantly growing, which corresponds to a crescendo form. Conversely, the last two sections are in the form of a diminuendo. The full force of Ptaszynska's instrumentarium is utilized with the drums, both skin and steel, predominating. The prerecorded tape enters ten seconds after the start of the movement and continues in canon through most of it. Near the end, a bolero-like rhythm begins and both live performance and tape coordinate creating a palpable sound mass. A final explosion of sound and color, marked "Prestissimo—Improvisation ad libitum," in which all 117 instruments are utilized, precedes a short coda that ends the work.

The three composers highlighted in this chapter approach the use of timbre in differing ways. Their compositional styles vary dramatically from one another, yet they have one thing in common, that is, their reliance on the timbre of each notated sound as integral to the work's structure, not just as aural decoration.

Other works to consider: *Patterns and Processes* (1971) by James Fulkerson (b. 1945).

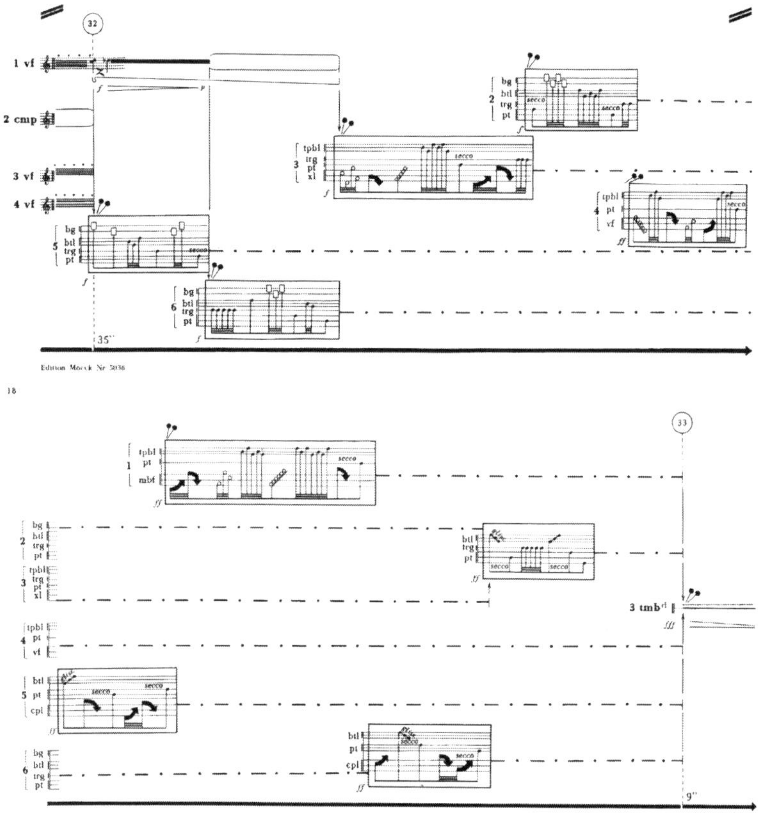

Fig. 9.1 Serocki, *Continuum* (reh. no. 32).

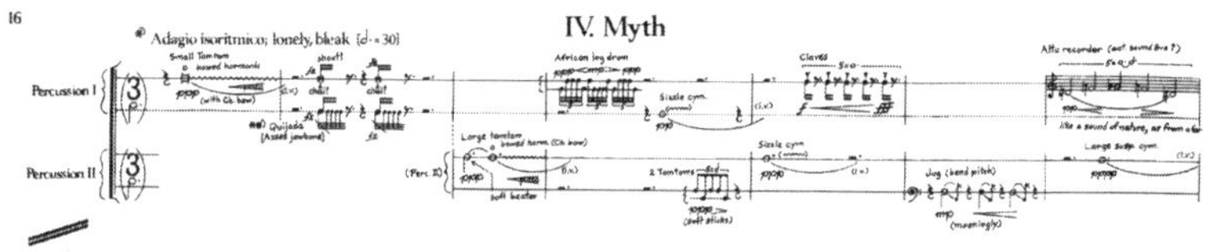

Fig. 9.2 Crumb, *Music for a Summer Evening* (Mvt. IV, "Myth," p. 16, first system).

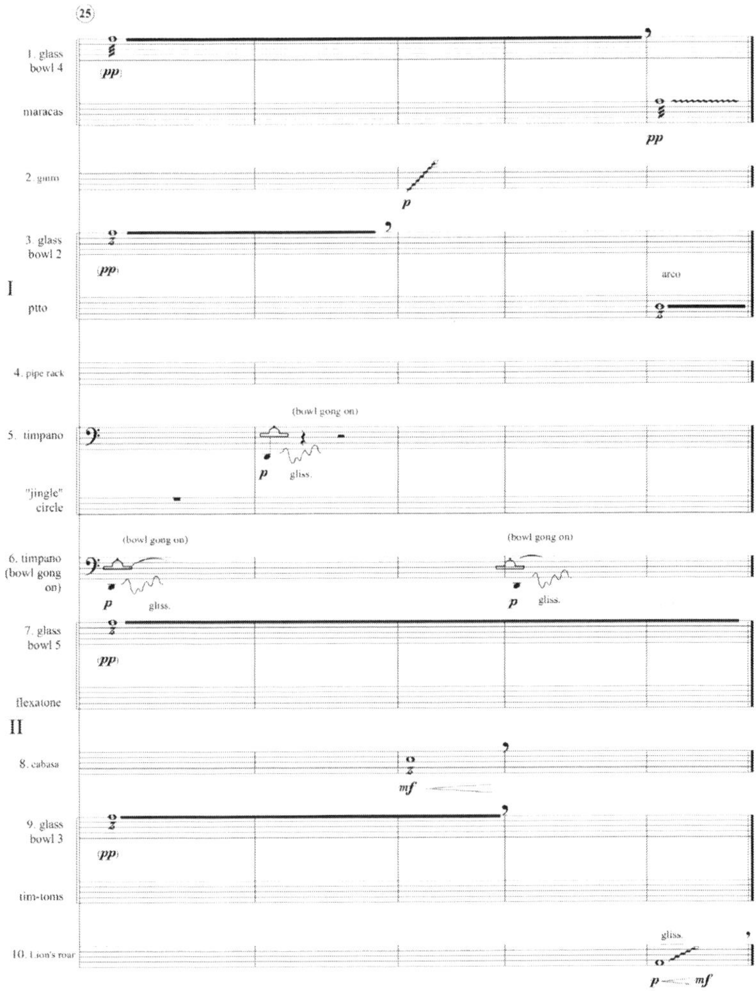

Fig. 9.3 Ptaszynska, *Siderals* (Mvt. II, first 5 bars)

Chapter 10

MINIMALISM

In the 1960s, the American composer La Monte Young (b. 1935) founded a music collective, the Theatre of Eternal Music, as a showcase for his drone-based music, which uses a minimum of musical resources, producing sounds and textures that change at an extremely slow pace. "Minimalism proper begins with La Monte Young, the master of the drone."[1] The label "minimalism" was used by critics to describe Young's music as well as an art movement from the same time period. His music was restricted to occasional performances by Young himself (he improvised on a soprano saxophone over the drones) and was normally devoid of percussive sounds. There is one recording available in which Young and his wife, the artist Marian Zazeela (b. 1940), played a tam-tam (or gong) using bass bows for over twenty minutes in duration. The restricted sound source and the emphasis on the minute variations in overtones that slowly appear and constantly change helped to label the work as "minimal."

A notable member of Young's performance collective was the composer Terry Riley (b. 1935), whose iconic work, *In C*, came to personify the minimalist genre. "More than any other single piece, *In C*, written in San Francisco in 1964, gave voice to the minimalist movement in America."[2] Written for any number of players, *In C* consists of fifty-three small melodic cells and phrases repeated at will. The piece ends when all the players reach the final sound module; in practice, it can last from a half-hour to an hour and a half or longer. An eighth-note pulse played on a piano (high octave C) holds the ensemble together and was crucial to the work's success. The first performance of *In C* was held on November 4, 1964, at the San Francisco Tape Music Center and included the composer Steve Reich (b. 1936), who helped Riley prepare the work and suggested the use of the repeated high C. In an interview, Reich, who later became one of the leading minimalist composers, commented: "I certainly learned a tremendous amount from putting the piece together, and I think it had a strong influence on me."[3] The success of Riley's *In C* premiere brought fame to the composer, who apparently could not handle it. "I responded by dropping out and going to Mexico for three months," he recounted.[4] For the rest of the century, Riley's compositional focus was varied: string, saxophone, and choral works plus improvisatory music that included elements of popular music, which he mostly performed himself using multitrack recordings.

Steve Reich was born in New York City and his musical training began at an early age with piano lessons. Upon hearing jazz music for the first time, he decided to pursue drum lessons with the goal of starting a band. His tertiary schooling included Cornell University, the Juilliard School of Music, and Mills College, studying composition with William Bergsma (1921–1994), Vincent Persichetti (1915–1987), Luciano Berio, and Darius Milhaud. While at Mills, Reich discovered a book by A. M. Jones, *Studies in African Music,* that was "quite a revelation for me in terms of seeing a brand new musical technique laid out on paper."[5] During Reich's stay at Mills he also investigated the possibilities of electronic music. He constructed tape works using the spoken voice, which he edited into short phrases. Making tape loops of the material, Reich accidently discovered a process he labeled "phase shifting," an interesting aural phenomenon that results when two tapes, played simultaneously on two tape recorders, slowly get out of synchronization. Reich used this technique to create two of his early works, *It's Gonna Rain* (1965), spliced out of a recording of a gospel sermon delivered by Brother Walter, a San Francisco street preacher; and *Come Out* (1966), made from the recorded voice of a Harlem teenager who, while being beaten by New York City police, opened a wound on his leg so as to bleed, giving him a trip to the hospital and out of police custody. Reich's work with these early tape pieces provided him with insight as to how to apply these techniques and how to use them to create live music. *Piano Phase* (1967), for two pianos, was an early result. (Note: The work can be, and often is, played on two marimbas.) *Piano Phase* is in three parts, the first of which consists of twelve sixteenth-notes divided into two groups of six. One player begins by playing the opening bar ostinato figure, and the other joins in unison, fading in gradually. While one holds the tempo steady, the other player slowly moves his or her tempo forward incrementally, creating at first an echo-like resonance.

Eventually, player two arrives at the midpoint, forming a composite rhythm of thirty-second notes, and then continues on until he or she is one sixteenth-note ahead (namely reaching the second note of the original twelve), creating a canon as the two players are once again in phase. Reich explains, "My music is canonic: 'phase' is merely a word for a new canonic procedure."[6] This process continues until the players return to the initial combined figure. One player then fades out and the other player deletes two notes from each group of six, ending with an eight-note phrase. The tacit player then joins back in and the process of moving out of phase begins again. A final section is reduced to just four notes. For the next few years, Reich continued to explore the possibilities of this compositional technique including *Four Log Drums* (1969), a work that uses a phase-shifting pulse gate. In 1971, he completed *Drumming*, a percussion ensemble scored for eight tuned bongos, three marimbas, three glockenspiels, plus female voices and piccolo. To ensure that *Drumming* and his other early works were performed accurately, Reich formed his own ensemble and began to tour. Surprisingly for a percussion chamber work, *Drumming* soon became part of the mainstream repertoire of contemporary music and over the next three decades was performed in both classical and popular venues throughout the world. Accolades followed. "*Drumming* [is] perhaps minimalism's first masterpiece."[7]

Part one of *Drumming* begins with a single forte bongo stroke repeated three to six times. A second drummer joins in unison and together they slowly add notes until an eight-note rhythmic pattern is established, one that is basic to the entire work. (Fig. 10.1) "This pattern undergoes changes of pitch, phase position, and timbre, but all the performers play this pattern, or some part of it, throughout the entire piece."[8] The other two drummers enter adding notes until a steady stream of eighth notes is heard. Reich uses the phase technique described earlier, notated here by measures of dotted lines. Audible rhythmic and melodic patterns emerge from the interplay of pitches and are highlighted by individual players fading in and out. The movement closes as bongos fade away and three marimbas fade in, imitating the drum rhythms and pitches. During the second movement, Reich uses the same phasing technique, but this time the resulting patterns are accentuated by the soprano and alto singers vocalizing nonsense syllables. "By exactly imitating the sound of the instruments, and by gradually fading the patterns in and out, the singers cause them to slowly rise to the surface of the music and then to fade back into it, allowing the listener to hear these patterns, along with many others, actually sounding in the instruments."[9] Eventually all nine percussionists are playing on three marimbas creating a rich, sonic texture. Part three features the glockenspiels with the piccolo replacing the singers. Along with whistling (performed by either a singer or one of the percussionists), a piccolo accentuates the patterns, now too high a tessitura for the vocalists. Part four combines the forces, both instruments and vocalists, ending with a written crescendo to fortissimo.

The compositional process represented by *Piano Phase* and *Drumming* is best described by the composer who, in 1968, wrote what could be described as a manifesto outlining his personal approach to minimalism and music composition. Titled "Music as a Gradual Process," it first appeared in an exhibition catalog for a 1969 show at the Whitney Museum of American Art in New York City.[10] By process, Reich means the music itself. "What I'm interested in is a compositional process and a sounding music that are one and the same thing."[11] For Reich, the compositional process (can we call it "structure"?) is heard as the music unfolds. To be able to perceive this, the sounds need to change at a slow rate; thus repetitiveness is essential to the process. To hear the changing structure in a minimalist work, the material used needs to be memorable and concise. "In its most extreme form, the use of repetition in pattern-pulse works has represented a basic simplicity to musical syntax and rhetoric.[12]

The pulse, used by Reich and others during this time period, was incessant, reminding many listeners of the music of India, Indonesia, Africa, and 1960s rock. Combined with a steady dynamic level (often loud) and the lack of climax, it made the music hypnotic for some and boring for others. To add interest to his work, Reich exploited what he calls "mysteries," the psychoacoustic phenomena caused by the interaction of rhythmic and tonal patterns. "These mysteries are the impersonal, unintended, psycho-acoustic by-products of the intended process. These might include sub-melodies heard within repeated melodic patterns, stereophonic effects due to listener location, slight irregularities in performance, harmonics, difference tones, etc."[13] In his manifesto, "Music as a Gradual Process," Reich compared his compositional approach to chance music and serialism:

> John Cage has used processes and has certainly accepted their results, but the processes he used were compositional ones that could not be heard when the piece was performed. The process of using the I Ching or imperfections in a sheet of paper to determine musical parameters can't be heard when listening to music composed that way. The compositional processes and the sounding music have no audible connection. Similarly, in serial music, the series is seldom audible.[14]

Reaching the audience and having them enter his compositional world was important to Reich and he created a process that made it possible. "While performing and listening to gradual musical processes one can participate in a particular liberating and impersonal kind of ritual. Focusing in on the music process makes possible that shift of attention away from *he* and *she* and *you* and *me* outwards towards *it*."[15] By the mid-1970s, Reich could no longer call his work minimalistic. The forces needed to perform his new compositions grew, becoming more complex and making it more difficult for listeners to audibly follow their structures. "*Drumming* was the last of the phase pieces and the end of that way of thinking."[16]

American composer Philip Glass (b. 1937) was born and raised in Baltimore, Maryland. "Along with Reich, Riley, and Young, he was a principal figure in the establishment of minimalism in the 1960s."[17] As a boy, Glass studied violin and flute and tried his hand at composition. He entered the University of Chicago program for gifted students at the age of fifteen. His schooling continued at New York's Juilliard School of Music (MA in composition, 1961); at Colorado's Aspen Music Festival, where he worked with Milhaud; and eventually, in France with Nadia Boulanger. "He spent two years in France, and this is where he had his musical epiphany."[18] While in Paris, he was hired to transcribe the music of sitarist Ravi Shankar (1920–2012) for a film by Conrad Rooks (1934–2011). The experience made Glass realize that music could be structured in a different way: "The thing I learned from Ravi is that the rhythmic structure could become an overall music structure."[19] Back in New York, Glass began studies with Alla Rakha Qureshi (1919–2000), a tabla virtuoso and Shankar's accompanist. From this experience came Glass's first work for percussion, *1+1*, a 1968 work for amplified table-top. Glass's other percussion piece that belongs in the minimalist camp was extracted from incidental music he wrote for the play *End Game*, by Samuel Beckett (1906–1989). The *Prelude to End Game* exemplifies "minimalism" with its reduced forces of just two players (timpani and double bass), its simple, repetitive rhythmic modules (alternating between 2/4 and 6/8 throughout the entire work), its static tempo (quarter note equals 144 bpm), and constant dynamic (none indicated in the score). (Fig. 10.2) The music is appropriate to the construct of the play. *End Game* requires only four characters who speak mainly one word at a time, and move with repetitive, ritualized actions on a spartan, gray-lit stage (an empty room with two small windows). The play, along with Beckett's *Waiting for Godot*, is part of the post–World War II Theater of the Absurd movement. Glass would not produce another percussion work until his 1999 *Timpani Concerto*, followed by the 2000 *Concerto Fantasy* for two timpanists and orchestra.

Composer and theorist Per Nørgård was born on the 13th of July 1932 in Gentofte, Denmark. Following his studies at the Danish Academy of Music in

Copenhagen, he traveled to Paris in January of 1956 to study with Nadia Boulanger and to experience the city's avant-garde scene. "But it was an alien world. Listening to the pianist David Tudor knocking on the underside of the grand piano didn't provoke much more than a shrug of the shoulders from me. It was a style I couldn't relate to at all,"[20] he recalled. Nørgård's compositional output throughout the century concentrated on large orchestral works initially written in a traditional style. Eventually, he began to explore various twentieth-century stylistic trends, including serialism and minimalism. In 1969, he created *Waves* for a percussion soloist. The work was dedicated to and premiered by one of Denmark's leading percussionists of the time, Bent Lylloff (1930–2001). The instrumentation for *Waves* calls for four conga drums, large tam-tam, a chromatic set of tuned gongs, marimba, suspended cymbal, tom-tom, and a pair of kettledrums. The score includes three pages of preliminary exercises designed by Lylloff to aid the soloist in understanding and executing the work's notation.

Waves opens with a forte stroke on the tam-tam. As the sound fades, a four-note figure played over four congas gradually emerges. Starting inaudibly, each individual drum makes a crescendo and diminuendo, overlapping, then finally uniting and accelerating to a two-note figure. "In *Waves*, Nørgård immerses the listener (and the musician) in a meditation on the floating, weightless shifts that happen when the stresses in a four-beat pattern are slowly and gradually displaced from one beat to another."[21] Eventually the inner two drums fade away and the outer drums slowly fall out of phase as indicated graphically in the score, similar to the notation used by Xenakis in his *Persephassa*. A dotted-eighth sixteenth-note figure begins with the sixteenth note being played but not heard, à la "ghost" strokes in jazz drumming. "This notation indicates that before any sound is heard the note in question should only be realized in movement, thus letting the rhythm be preceded by a visual rhythm."[22] The other two drums slowly fill in the missing sixteenths and Nørgård takes us through another version of the opening ostinato. A tam-tam strike serves as a transition into the next section. As the tam-tam note fades, the player touches it carefully with a triangle beater to produce a "sizzle" effect. (Fig. 10.3) Three sections follow: tuned gongs, drum and cymbal, and marimba, as Nørgård notates permutations of his initial concept for each. A final theatrical section features rubber (or golf) balls to be bounced on the timpani creating overlapping reverberations—"a correspondingly organic wave pattern arising from the material itself.[23] The work can last up to a half-hour. Nørgård's use of the phase process, limited resources, and long, repetitive sections places this work in the minimalist camp. He contributed more than a dozen works to the percussion literature canon, both solo and ensemble, during the latter part of the century.

Works written in a multiplicity of styles by the American composer James Tenney (1934–2006) reflect the composer's broad aesthetic interests and his training. Born in Silver City, New Mexico, Tenney attended Bennington College (BA) and the University of Illinois (MA). He lists numerous composition teachers including Varèse, Cage, Partch, Chou Wen-chung, and others. Following his tenure at Illinois and his studies there with Lejaren Hiller Jr. (1924–1994), Tenney moved to New York, finding work exploring digital synthesis at Bell Telephone's pioneering research laboratory.[24]

In 1971, Tenney wrote a defining minimalist work entitled *Having Never Written a Note for Percussion.* On a postcard, he notated a single whole-note with a tremolo indication and the words "very long" written above to be played beginning *pppp*, slowly intensifying to *ffff* and back to *pppp.* Written for the percussionist/composer John Bergamo (1940–2013), it inevitably was performed on a large tam-tam, though the published score indicates "for any percussion instrument(s)."[25]

A more ambitious work, *Three Pieces for Drum Quartet,* honors three historic American composers, Charles Ives, Henry Cowell, and Edgard Varèse. The first piece, "Wake for Charles Ives," is scored for four identical tenor drums. The opening two-bar motif, sounding like a funeral dirge, is composed of just six notes. (Fig. 10.4) It mimics the rhythm Ives used in his setting of a poem by Vachel Lindsay (1879–1931) titled "General William Booth Enters into Heaven" (1914). As the music unfolds, Tenney incrementally adds thirty-second notes before each beat, slowly increasing the texture over sixteen bars, at which point the second canonic voice enters. By the time all four drummers have entered, the texture is dense and the dynamic level has risen. A final crescendo ends the movement. The second work, "Hocket for Henry Cowell," positions four identical bass drums in the corners of the performance area, surrounding the audience. It opens with the four voices entering every two bars. Soft tremolos with crescendos and diminuendos create waves of sound of varying intensity that pass from player to player creating a continuous rumbling texture. Tenney slowly adds single strokes to this mix leading to a hocket section where the notes are rapidly passed from drum to drum. (Fig. 10.5) The term "hocket" refers to a stylistic device from the thirteenth and fourteenth centuries, also used in some African music.[26] Tenney returns to bass drumrolls, ending the movement as it began. In the third piece, titled "Crystal Canon for Edgard Varèse," the voices enter three beats apart. Tenney quotes the very recognizable *tambour militaire* excerpt from *Ionisation.* Fragmented at first, the piece slowly adds notes until the famous passage is quoted in its entirety beginning with the pickups to measure 14. (Fig. 10.6) The other three voices follow until near the end where a stretto-like section brings them into unison for a powerful, final statement.

The percussion music examined in this chapter exhibits many of the traits that define the genre minimalism. The constant, repetitive pulse (both written and tactile), reduced forces (sometimes to an extreme as in Tenney's *Having Never Written a Note for Percussion*), slowly changing rhythmic modules (as in Glass's incidental music for *End Game*), and canonic constructs are evident in much of the music labeled "minimalist." La Monte Young has stayed true to the definition, while Riley, Reich, and Glass have moved on, but they are still identified with the genre they helped to create. Minimalist composers are few, as are minimalist painters, but many others have borrowed their concepts to create new and interesting works. "Minimalism has unquestionably been the most influential, worldwide, of any musical movement born since the Second World War."[27]

Other works to consider: *Les moutons de Panurge* (1969) and *To the Earth* (1985) by Frederick Rzewski (b. 1938); *Nine Bells* (1973) by Tom Johnson (b. 1939).

Fig. 10.1 Reich, *Drumming* (basic rhythmic pattern)

Fig. 10.2 Glass, *Prelude to End Game* (pattern example)

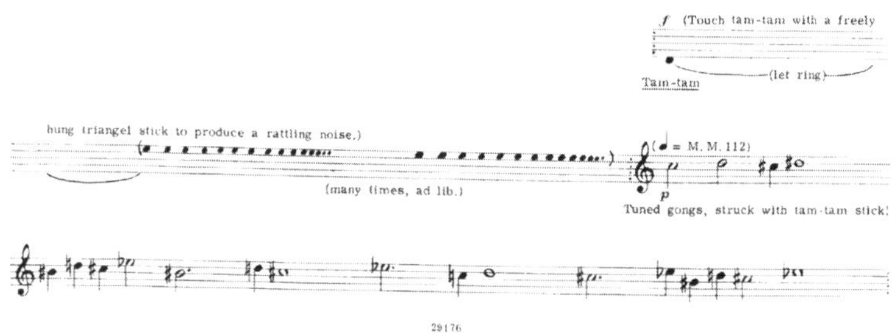

Fig. 10.3 Nørgård, *Waves* (p. 3, tam-tam and gongs). Copyright © 1972 by Edition Wilhelm Hansen AS, Copenhagen. This arrangement Copyright © 2019 by Edition Wilhelm Hansen AS, Copenhagen. International Copyright Secured. All rights reserved. Reprinted by permission of Hal Leonard LLC.

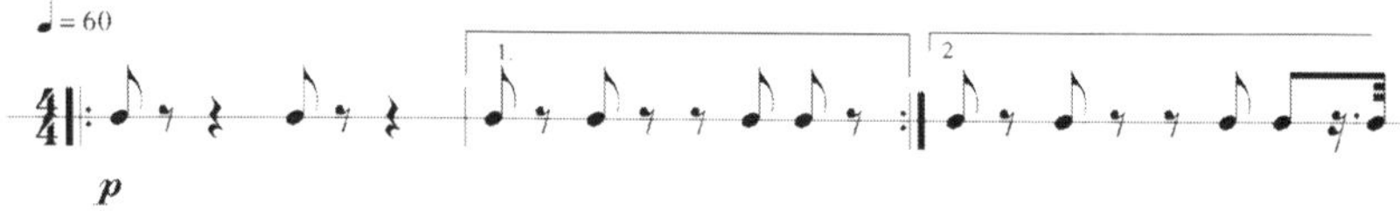

Fig. 10.4 Tenney, *Three Pieces for Drum Quartet* (Mvt. 1, meas. 1–3)

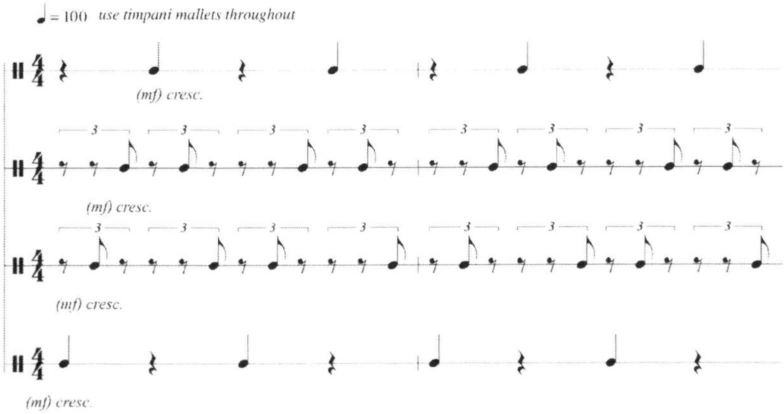

Fig. 10.5 Tenney, *Three Pieces for Drum Quartet* (Mvt. II, meas. 63–64)

Fig. 10.6 Tenney, *Three Pieces for Drum Quartet* (Mvt. III, meas. 10–11)

Chapter 11

THE SOLO PERCUSSIONIST—CENTER STAGE

After World War II, solo works for timpani, keyboard percussion instruments (especially marimba), and groupings labeled "multiple percussion" began to appear on recitals, both professional and student. "Not long ago the very notion of a percussion soloist would have seemed ludicrous."[1] Eventually, symphony orchestras in Europe, Asia, and the Americas began programming concerti featuring solo percussionists. Beginning in 1950 and continuing into the latter decades of the century, the increase was dramatic. In the past, composers, with few exceptions, had avoided the problems that nonpitched instruments presented as a vehicle for a solo work. In the twentieth century, many found ways to exploit the rich sonic treasure trove of instruments that we call percussion and began expanding the repertoire for the virtuoso percussionist.

Historical records demonstrate that the notion of the percussion soloist is not unique to the late twentieth century. Solo works for timpani, written and improvised, were heard in Europe during the 1700s and, for centuries, keyboard percussion music was part of various cultures throughout the world. The sound of the solo snare drum, commanding the great armies of both East and West, was the workhorse of the military signal corps from ancient times. However, the idea of combining many dissimilar percussion instruments into a unified array, thereby creating a complex solo force labeled "multiple percussion," was novel to the twentieth century.

TIMPANI

A strong case can be made that the sight of four or more giant copper kettles, coupled with the balletic movements of a skilled timpanist placed center stage, is as impressive as a black grand piano with a Liszt-like figure seated to one side. The history of the kettledrums, their importance to the armies of antiquity, their mechanical development, and their eventual preeminence in the Western orchestra's percussion section is well documented. As a solo instrument, timpani, with a literature and a listening audience, may not be as well chronicled or as well known but it appears that as far back as the eighteenth century, solo kettledrums attracted both composers and listeners. "As the pomp and spectacle of timpani performance grew in popularity among England's theater-going public, its performers achieved great, albeit brief, notoriety. Solo timpani recitals were not unknown in England during the first half of the eighteenth century. A particularly interesting consequence of this notoriety was the creation of showcase pieces, described as concerti, for multiple timpani soloist."[2]

This activity seemed to go out of vogue in the 1800s, though early timpani concertos, written by composers from the eighteenth and nineteenth centuries, continue to be performed and recorded today. With the growing popularity of the "early music" movement during the twentieth century, it was natural that contemporary timpanists would resurrect the few available works from earlier times, such as *Partita in C Major for Six Timpani* by Georg Druschetzky (1745–1819) and Johann Carl Christian Fischer's (ca. 1733–1800) *Symphonie with 8 Obbligato Pauken*. It is interesting to note that both Druschetzky and Fischer were timpanists as well as conductors and composers.

William Kraft[3] was one of the twentieth century's most eminent composers. Following the tradition of composer/conductor/timpanist, Kraft added a number of solo works for timpani to the repertoire. His 1983 *Concerto for Timpani and Orchestra* was commissioned by Indiana Percussion Projects led by Thomas Akins, principal timpanist with the Indianapolis Symphony, to whom the composition is dedicated. Written for five drums, the work begins quietly with the timpanist first striking the drums with just the index finger covered with soft felt (cotton), then with the middle finger covered with a harder material (leather), and finally progressing to various types of timpani mallets (staccato, ultra-staccato, wood). It is evident that Kraft is concerned not only with dynamic control (soft to loud), but with subtle changes in timbre as well: "Starting with felt-covered fingers, the timpanist moves to leather, then to the whole gloved hand, and then to sticks of increasingly hard coverings, until we have reached uncovered wood. Likewise, the musical material grows."[4] Movement II, subtitled "Poem for Timpani, Two String Orchestras, Celeste, and Percussion," is a lament dedicated to the composer's mother who died during its conception. Here Kraft effectively explores the distinct sound of the timpani glissando. The drums' continuous tremolos and pitch changes create a sound and textural mix that combines with string choirs to great effect. The third movement, in rondo form, begins with a four-note motive that the orchestra takes up and, along with the timpani and percussion, develops into a virtuosic display of skill for all. The movement includes some improvisation and a brief contrasting section that requires four-mallet technique. (Fig. 11.1) A short cadenza near the end completes the solo.

Earlier in the century, another timpanist, composer, and sometime conductor, Werner Thärichen (1921–2008), composed *Konzert für Pauken und Orchester* in 1954 for his son, Nicolai. The elder Thärichen studied music at the Berlin Hochschule für Musik, specializing in composition and conducting. In 1948, he became a member of the prestigious Berlin Philharmonic where he established himself as one of the world's leading timpanists. His *Konzert für Pauken und Orchester* consists of three movements marked allegro assai, lento, and allegro moderato. In the concerto's first movement, the timpanist presents rapid, syncopated motives, which the orchestra answers, especially the muted brass and winds. Also, high strings and timpani interact with a rapid flurry of notes that challenge both parties. Throughout the movement, the soloist uses a variety of timpani mallets, sometimes four at once, and snare drum sticks. (Fig. 11.2) A quieter second movement is dominated by tremolos using soft mallets. Here the soloist makes a number of pitch changes to both the inside pair and outer drums. Movement III effectively displays the dexterity of the soloist with passages of cross-sticking and rapid movement between drums. There is a short cadenza near its close. Thärichen's tonal language is somewhat dissonant, yet within the traditions of the late Romantic period. The form is the classic concerto, three movements, fast-slow-fast, with movements II and III played attacca.

Not all the solo timpani pieces written in the twentieth century were composed by professional timpanists, nor were they all concerti with orchestra accompaniment. Some were designed to be played with brass, wind, piano, or electronic accompaniment. Many more were written for timpani alone. The surge of new works for solo timpani was, in part, a result of the conservatory and college training programs that blossomed after World War II. In such schools, students pursuing degrees whose instrumental emphasis was percussion, were required to demonstrate their performance skills. Students in the

1950s and 1960s, searching the extant solo timpani literature for unaccompanied works, found few options. A few students, like Michael Colgrass, were talented enough to create their own. Others solicited works from faculty members of their school's composition department or searched the reviews of new works published in professional journals of music societies such as the National Association of College Wind and Percussion Instructors (NACWPI) and the Percussive Arts Society (PAS).[5]

In the 1950s, an ideal set of recital works for timpani was written by the iconic American composer Elliott Carter. His classic set of *Eight Pieces* methodically explored the timbral and technical possibilities of the kettledrums while challenging the player with their rhythmic complexities. Carter composed six pieces for timpani in 1949–50, revising them in 1966, at which time he added two more solos. Of the original six pieces, the two titled *Recitative* and *Improvisation* were published first and became readily available. Each having a performance time of just over three minutes, the two solos perfectly fit the test criteria for a student's graduate recital. The other four remained in manuscript form with limited distribution until 1966.

A protégé of the composer Charles Ives, Carter pursued his musical studies at the Horace Mann School and Harvard University, with composition lessons from Walter Piston (1894–1976), Gustav Holst (1874–1934), and Nadia Boulanger. Carter's early works were written in a neo-Classical and neo-Romantic style. It wasn't until the 1950s, when he began using a process called "metric modulation" while composing his *First String Quartet,* that his style became original. By chance, the timpani pieces were written as a result of sketches Carter made in preparation for creating his quartet. In an interview, Carter stated: "The *Eight Pieces* . . . were written to develop notions of metric modulation as a sort of experiment. Because I then wrote my big First Quartet which uses all the little metric modulations that you find here in the *Eight Pieces* on a simplified basis. So, this was kind of sketch for a string quartet—if you can believe it!"[6]

In 1965, noted percussionist Jan Williams performed Carter's timpani works at New York City's Carnegie Recital Hall with the composer in attendance. Impressed with Williams's performance, Carter suggested that they collaborate on a revision of the six solos. The eventual result of this collaboration was the publication of the original six works titled: *Saeta, Perpetual Motion, Recitative, Improvisation, Canaries,* and *March,* plus two new titles, *Adagio* and *Canto.*

The *Adagio* is one of the collection's more challenging solos and reflects Williams's knowledge and skill as a timpanist. Written senza misura, it is the only solo in the collection without a time signature. The tempo is slow and the music is to be played "very freely." The pitch changes over the four drums are accurately notated; some are discretely covered by the resonance of loud drum strokes. Producing timpani harmonics is one of the more difficult performance techniques and it is called for throughout the movement, sometimes just a single note, but often a rapid series of harmonics. (Fig. 11.3) Williams experimented with various ways to create the harmonics and recommended the following: "1. Straddle the center (node) of the drum head, with the thumb and middle finger of either hand held about 4 to 6 inches apart, lightly touching the head. 2. Strike the drum at the very edge, but not directly on the rim of the bowl. 3. A split second after striking the drum, quickly lift the fingers from the head. The harmonic will sound one octave higher than the pitch to which the drum is tuned."[7]

The final solo in the collection, *March*, is one of the most popular. The four drums are tuned to two sets of perfect fourths, G/C and B/E, intervals found in many symphonic works. "The Classical and Romantic Eras in Western music are filled with examples of timpani parts that employ the pitch interval of a perfect fourth—an interval that reinforces a tonic-dominant relationship."[8] *March* begins in duple time (quarter note equals 105 bpm) with a quarter-note pulse played by the G/C drums setting the initial marching tempo. Against this pulse, the other perfect fourth, B/E, performs figures comprised of dotted eighths creating a ternary pulse. To help keep these two lines audibly separate, Carter designates the butt end of the sticks for the G/C (left hand) and the head of the stick for the B/E (right hand). Slowly, the ternary figures begin to dominate the pulse and at measure 14 their pulse becomes the new tempo, increasing it from the initial 105 bpm to 140 bpm. This manner of altering the tempo is the essence of Carter's metric modulation. It does not refer simply to changing the meter but functions as a means to alter the tempo. "Tempo modulation, often called 'metrical modulation' . . ., is Carter's trademark innovation."[9] Each of Carter's *Eight Pieces* present unique challenges for the timpanist, both technically and musically. "Elliott Carter offered a profusion of creative ideas in the *Eight Pieces* and they continue to be a major influence in the modern canon of timpani literature."[10]

Carter wasn't the only twentieth-century composer to probe the musical possibilities of the kettledrums. A number of other composers produced solo timpani works that fall into the classifications discussed in this book, including electro-acoustic music. The Czech composer Jan Hanuš (1915–2004), who is known for his symphonic and opera works, composed an early work for solo timpanist, assistant, and tape. The work, *Concertino for Timpani and Tape, Opus 69*, was composed in 1970 and combines both live and recorded timpani sounds, the latter manipulated à la *musique concrète*. Four movements, "Energico," "Con Fantasia," "Scherzando," and "Drammatico," present the timpanist with technical challenges previously unseen in the literature. The composer suggests that two players may be employed "according to their own abilities and the instruments (timpani) they have at their disposal."[11] Producing extensive and rapid pitch changes over four or five drums, while coordinating with the taped accompaniment, requires great skill. (As an aid, a pulse of 60 bpm is used throughout.) Hanuš varies the drum timbres by using a variety of mallets (soft, hard, wood, rubber, snare) and beating spots (normal, center, and edge), and by covering the kettledrum heads with a cloth to both dampen and alter the drum's timbre. In the first movement, "Energico," a twelve-tone quasi-melody is played using one mallet accompanied by a steady ostinato rhythm with the other mallet, a favorite device used by composers when writing a solo timpani work. (Fig. 11.4) Later, this passage is inverted. In the second movement, four mallets are used to play arpeggiated chords. In both gestural and rhythmic passages, Hanuš's *Concertino* is well constructed and unified as the timbre of the tape source (though electronically manipulated) is similar to the kettledrum's timbre. The *Concertino* is an early and excellent example of music for tape and timpani.

Other works to consider: *Concerto for Five Kettledrums and Orchestra* (1955) by Robert Parris (1924–1999); *Concerto for Timpani and Brass* (1957) by Peter Tanner (b. 1936); *Variations for Solo Kettledrums* (1964) by Jan Williams (b. 1939); *Xoe* (1971) by Paul Zonn (1938–2000); *A Feast of Thunder* (1981) by Sherwood Shaffer (b. 1934); *Dunbar's Delight* (1985) by Robert Erickson (1917–1997); *Dinosaur Dance* (1991) by Michael Udow.

KEYBOARD PERCUSSION INSTRUMENTS

Xylophone

The origin of the xylophone is disputed as being either Asian or African. Found on both continents, as well as in Central and South America (where it most likely arrived with the slave trade), its native versions took many forms. In Europe, an early xylophone version was simply resonant bars of wood laid over a bed of straw, the "*holz und stroh*" version. "The xylophone, which had been known in Europe since the Middle Ages, was by the 19th Century associated largely with the folk music of eastern Europe, notably Poland and eastern Germany."[12] A Russian Jew, Michael-Josef Gusikov (1806–1837), was a xylophone soloist, and, for a brief time, captured the attention of Europe's musical elite, including Mendelssohn and Liszt, with his virtuosic ability. Part of a klezmer group, he performed concerts of popular and classical music on an instrument made of resonant wooden bars (*holz*) positioned over ropes made from straw (*stroh*). The xylophone entered the orchestra percussion section as early as the 1700s and gained acceptance in the classical orchestral repertoire by the late 1800s. As a solo instrument, it became popular throughout the Western world, in part due to the development of music recording devices.[13] Its unique acoustic signature was ideal for the rudimentary recording equipment of the time: "The xylophone had somewhat of an advantage in that it tended to record very well."[14] The repertoire of early xylophone recordings and the solos performed live, often on the vaudeville circuit, were mostly arrangements of classical selections, ragtime tunes, and popular songs. There were many outstanding xylophone soloists at the turn of the century whose artistry was recorded, Charles Daab, George Hamilton Green (1893–1970), and William Dorn (1891–1971) to name a few.

Before World War II, the Japanese xylophone soloist Yoichi Hiraoka (1907–1981) was employed by NBC Radio in New York City to play a fifteen-minute program of classical music every morning, six days a week: "He would have a regular show every morning except Sunday beginning March 15, 1931."[15] When the war broke out, Hiraoka and his family (and other Japanese nationals) were deported to Japan where he continued to perform, returning to the United States in 1962 to resume his career. On his return, Hiraoka commissioned a few extended works for xylophone and orchestra including the popular *Fantasy on Japanese Woodprints, Op. 211*, by Alan Hovhaness. This work references scales and compositional devices, such as *portamento* or sliding tones, found in Japanese classical music. The opening pentatonic scale used is the Japanese *In* scale, but, according to program notes included with the score, "No folk, no traditional melodies are used."[16] (Fig. 11.5) Hovhaness's inspiration was a set of "woodblock prints of old Japan."[17] For the most part, the work is strictly notated with few exceptions. There are senza misura sections to be improvised, including an extended one leading to the final allegro section that, with the help of the percussion section, drives the work to an exciting climax. As the century progressed, few serious xylophone commissions occurred as mallet soloists abandoned the xylophone in favor of its close cousin the marimba.

Other works to consider: *Concertino for Xylophone* (1965) by Toshiro Mayuzumi (1929–1997); *Sonata* (1965) by Thomas Pitfield (1903–1999).

Marimba

The evolution of the marimba seems to have had a different trajectory than that of the xylophone. The marimbas that arrived in the Americas resembled those of Africa with rows of wooden bars assembled into scales suspended on simple wooden frames with gourd (or wood) resonators. Each resonator included a mirliton device (a thin membrane covering a small hole in the resonator) causing the note to "buzz" when struck. Eventually, the bars were arranged to form a chromatic scale, enabling Western music to be played. The marimba became very popular in southern Mexico and the Central American countries, particularly Guatemala: "It is a commonly recognized fact that the marimba is an essential element of the musical life of Guatemala and has been since the mid-nineteenth century."[18] In 1908, a Guatemalan marimba band known as the Hurtado Brothers toured North America. Their concerts and later recordings on the Victor label helped to popularize the marimba in the United States. As with the xylophone, the marimba players first adapted literature from the classics and the popular music of the day.

Led by the artist and teacher Clair Omar Musser (1901–1998), an orchestra of 100 marimbas performed a concert on the Midway of Chicago's 1933 "Century of Progress" World's Fair. Musser's contribution to the popularity of the instrument was significant: "Musser has been the dominant figure in marimba development in the United States during this [twentieth] century, distinguishing himself not only as an innovator, designer, and manufacturer of the instrument, but also as a conductor, composer, arranger, educator, and marimba virtuoso."[19] Many of Musser's students became marimba teachers and performers including Ruth Stuber Jeanne (1910–2004), who premiered one of the first extended works written for a solo marimbist. In March of 1940, at New York's Carnegie Hall, Jeanne performed the fifteen-minute *Concertino for Marimba* by Paul Creston (1906–1985) accompanied by Frédérique Petrides (1903–1983) and her all-female Orchestrette Classique. The three movements are marked "Vigorous," "Calm," and "Lively." Two-mallet technique is needed for the outer movements; the middle one requires the use of four mallets. In this movement, Creston notates a lyrical melody supported by closely positioned chords. (Fig. 11.6) "The harmonic vocabulary consists of major and minor seventh chords in a closed position."[20] The *Concertino* circulated in manuscript form for many years before being typeset. Its number of performances with orchestra was modest, though a version with piano reduction was widely distributed and became a familiar recital work for college music students. The four-mallet middle movement, "Calm," was often played alone.

Another landmark composition for marimba was written in 1947 by the French composer Darius Milhaud. *Concerto for Marimba and Vibraphone* was commissioned by keyboard percussion artist John "Jack" Connor (1913–2001). Milhaud's *Concerto* introduced the vibraphone to the "legitimate" music world. Conner had participated in Musser's International Marimba Symphony

Orchestra of 1935 and, by the mid-1940s, was an accomplished keyboard percussion player. To convince a reluctant Milhaud to write the concerto, Connor traveled to Milhaud's California home and performed a number of classical transcriptions and some jazz on both marimba and vibraphone. Milhaud accepted the commission and finished the concerto quickly. Marveled Connor, "It took him two weeks to write it!"[21] Despite the rapid production, Milhaud was careful to consider the change in timbres produced by using various mallets. Precise mallet indications, including hard and soft rubber, linen thread and yarn, a section to be played with the butt end of the sticks, and five measures using only the hands (*avec les mains, sans baguettes*) evinced his concern. (Fig. 11.7) "The precision of Milhaud's indications demonstrated his willingness to explore new sounds."[22] Marked "Lent," the middle movement features the vibraphone. Here, a number of passages require rapid movement between both keyboard instruments, which is quite challenging as it is necessary to use the vibraphone's sustaining pedal. Milhaud's *Concerto* was not performed as often as Creston's *Concertino*: "Neither educators nor performers have provided Milhaud's opus with the exposure and popularity achieved by other marimba compositions."[23]

Marimbist Vida Chenoweth (1929–2018) has written, "Transcriptions, as a total repertoire, are in my opinion, a disservice to the instrument's musicalness."[24] As with the timpani soloist, marimbists in mid-century where anxious to find new concert literature to both showcase their talent and legitimize the solo capacity of their instrument. Oklahoma-born Vida Chenoweth, another Musser student, dedicated herself to promoting the marimba as a solo instrument. Her brief career had a significant impact on many aspects regarding the construction and utilization of the instrument. "She pioneered compositional, performance, and interpretive techniques commonly used on the instrument today, among these the performance of polyphonic music via independent mallets."[25] In 1956, Chenoweth commissioned a concerto from the American composer Robert Kurka (1921–1957), thus adding a major work to the nascent repertoire for solo marimba and orchestra. To familiarize himself with the instrument's capabilities, Kurka (who was to die of leukemia before the work's Carnegie Hall premiere) watched Chenoweth practice and was fascinated by the performer's physical movement. "After she finished, his primary comment was that he didn't realize the marimba was such a visual instrument."[26] Kurka's *Concerto for Marimba and Orchestra,* Op. 34, has three movements marked "allegro molto," "adagio espressivo," and "allegro con spirito." It is "mostly diatonic, filled with smart and leaping tunes, and it exploits the agility of its soloist to the utmost."[27] The outer movements challenge the performer with fast tempos and wide multiple octave leaps. (Fig. 11.8) The middle movement is chorale-like, normally played with four graded mallets so as to "speak" in the extreme ranges of the instrument. With spreads of over an octave in each hand, the use of extended shafts is recommended. Of the three major early works presented here, the Kurka may have had the most significant impact on the future of marimba concerti and on the career of Chenoweth. "The performance that catapulted Chenoweth to the forefront as an artist of stature, and also resulted in the critical acceptance of the instrument, was her performance of the Kurka *Concerto for Marimba* with the Orchestra of America in Carnegie Hall."[28]

The 1960s bore witness to a dramatic increase in solo works written for the marimba, many of them by young Japanese composers who responded to Western influences brought to their island nation following World War II.

> With the country's sense of urgency to rebuild after the devastation of the war, with the end of the American occupation in 1952 and strong conservative figures in music no longer in control, with determination prevailing to reconnect internationally but on an individual's own terms, the creative interest of individual [Japanese] composers went in multiple directions—from engagement with traditional music to experimentation with international modernist and avant-garde styles.[29]

Postwar Japanese composers absorbed the latest contemporary compositional trends and began writing music that reflected American and European influences, yet was uniquely Japanese: "Practically all Western movements have been quickly transmitted and have counterparts in Japan."[30]

The Japanese marimbist Keiko Abe (b. 1937), who began her musical career playing the xylophone, first heard the sound of the marimba played by a group of American missionaries. Captivated by the instrument's rich, sonorous sound, she eventually switched to the marimba and began a long and successful career as a solo artist. In the 1960s alone, Abe premiered eighteen new marimba works including two concertos. By the end of the 1990s, the number was over fifty. Abe revolutionized the use of four mallets while fostering a whole new repertoire through her own writing, recordings, commissions, and concerts that featured contemporary twentieth-century music.

A colleague of Keiko Abe and director of the Toho Gakuen music school in Tokyo was the composer Akira Miyoshi (1933–2013), who in 1968, at the request of Abe, composed the marimba solo *Torse III*. This unaccompanied solo can be viewed as a model for many that followed. Each of its four movements, "Thèse," "Chant," "Commentaire," and "Synthèse," are brief, two minutes or less in duration. The movement "Thèse" opens with a fortissimo gesture that begins the first of two four-bar phrases. Six more bars complete the movement. Miyoshi's writing includes sudden and dramatic dynamic changes that range from fortissimo to pianississimo. As in the Kurka composition, the player's lateral body movements over the course of the work require dexterity; Miyoshi utilizes the entire range of a four-octave marimba. The opening movement alone presents new marimba techniques (one-handed rolls—in octaves as well as on a single note), a new tonal language ("post tonal but not serial"),[31] and establishes a new idiomatic approach to writing for the marimba. Ignoring classical tonal harmony, the second movement, "Chant," opens with four-mallet chords playing tremolos moving in parallel motion. Movement III, "Commentaire," is toccata-like with rapid forward motion provided by moving eighth notes, strong accents, and a wide-ranging tessitura. The final movement, "Synthèse," lives up to its title as it combines compositional ideas from the previous three movements. As a nod to Kurka, Miyoshi essentially creates a bow on the work's last chord (Fig 11.9) as the player must bend over the marimba to reach the extreme ends of the instrument. Miyoshi contributed a number of other marimba pieces to the canon: an earlier five-movement suite titled *Conversation* (1962), a *Concerto for Marimba and Strings* (1969), and *Rin Sai* (1987), a work for solo marimba with percussion sextet.

From the 1960s forward, the volume of new works for solo unaccompanied marimba multiplied rapidly. Composed in a wide range of styles by amateur as well as professional composers, solo marimba works found a market with beginning players as well as with a growing cadre of marimba specialists who formed consortia as an aid to funding and commissioning new solos. Relatively few of these new solos were written to be played with orchestra or wind ensembles. Most were written for unaccompanied marimba, while others were written to be performed by smaller, mixed chamber groups.

Many accompaniments for marimba solos made use of other percussion instruments, as fellow percussionists were more open to performing this new music. The Japanese composer Maki Ishii's (1936–2003) *Marimbastück mit zwie Schlagzeugern* (1969) combined percussion instruments from both East and West. In this work, premiered by Keiko Abe, the marimba holds center stage flanked on both sides by percussionists with an array of instruments. Suspended cymbals, cowbells, and claves are joined with *yotsudake* (bamboo plates), *mokusho* (wood block), a range of Japanese *taikos* (drums), and other instruments from both sides of the Pacific in what was, at the time, a unique chamber setting. Ishii followed his *Marimbastück* with over thirty new works for both solo and ensemble percussion. His generation included fellow composers Minoru Miki (1930–2011) and Toru Takemitsu (1930–1996), who together added another nineteen percussion works within the twentieth century. Minoru Miki's *Marimba Spiritual* (1984) has become one of the most performed percussion chamber quartets featuring the marimba. The soloist is accompanied by a trio of percussionists playing wood, metal, and skin instruments. Though Miki suggests using Japanese instruments, Western substitutes are allowed. This work is also dedicated to Keiko Abe.

Toru Takemitsu's music stands apart from that of his Japanese colleagues. Self-taught in composition, his early pieces explored Western genres featuring improvisation and graphic notation. In 1976, he composed a concerto for marimba and orchestra, *Gitimalya,* and in 1981, the keyboard percussion trio *Rain Tree.* The latter work is one of Takemitsu's finest and was inspired by a novel written by Nobel Prize–winning author Kenzaburo Oe (b. 1935). In Oe's work, *Atama no ii, Ame no Ki,* the tree serves as a metaphor, gathering the night's rain and releasing it drop by drop throughout the next day: "The significance of 'the tree', . . . is a profound symbol of regeneration and spiritual renewal."[32] *Rain Tree* requires two marimbas placed on either side of a vibraphone, plus sixteen crotales (two of which need to be custom-made as they go below the standard two octave sets). Additionally, the composition requires lighting in the form of three spotlights that, ideally, are controlled by an offstage technician. The piece is atmospheric, descriptive, and episodic. Its tonal language is impressionistic with the vibraphone and crotales creating ringing resonances and the marimbas imitating discrete sounds of falling raindrops. Precise lighting cues are given in the score. *Rain Tree* begins in darkness; the crotales sound "very soft" single notes eventually growing in density until the vibraphone entrance (bar 30), at which time Takemitsu asks the two crotale players to improvise: "improvise with crotales softly and irregularly like a rain droplet from the leaves."[33] Throughout the piece the vibraphone plays a soloistic role as it builds complex chords with the use of its sustaining pedal. (Fig. 11.10) Most of the composition is metrically free. Takemitsu uses time signatures to coordinate specific sections, however, the composition's forward motion often stops as he creates beautiful, sonic clouds of metallic timbres. Throughout *Rain Tree,* the composed drops of rain are obvious and, as such, the addition of the blinking lights to simulate raindrops is unnecessary to fully enjoy the work.

Other works to consider: *Suite for Marimba* (1950) by Alfred Fissinger (1925–1999); *Toccata for Marimba* (1955) by Emma Lou Diemer (b. 1927); *Two Movements for Marimba* (1965) by Toshimitsu Tanaka (b. 1930); *Time* (1968) by Minoru Miki; *Two Mexican Dances* (1974) by Gordon Stout (b. 1952); *Dream of the Cherry Blossoms* (1984) by Keiko Abe; *Velocities* (1990) by Joseph Schwantner (b. 1943).

Vibraphone

In the mid-1920s, the motorized, aluminum-bar "vibraharp" was introduced by the Chicago, Illinois–based J. C. Deagan Company. Earlier, a rival company, Leedy Manufacturing of Indianapolis, Indiana, had produced the "vibraphone," an adapted version of an existing steel-bar marimba. The design produced by Deagan beat out the rival Leedy adaptation, but the Leedy name "vibraphone" has become the name most often used to identify this unique twentieth-century instrument. Popularized by the great jazz artists of the twentieth century, it became the most recognized instrument of the keyboard percussion family.

As previously discussed, Takemitsu's *Rain Tree* features the vibraphone as does the work of George Crumb discussed in an earlier chapter, but concertos for vibraphone and orchestra were rare during the century. One such concerto by the Argentinian composer Carlo Franci (1927–2019) was published in 1959 but had few performances. Vibraphone solos accompanied by mixed chamber groups were somewhat more prevalent, for example, the popular *Interactions for Vibraphone and Percussion* (1963) written by percussionist John Bergamo (1940–2013) and Siegfried Fink's (1928–2006) *Vibracussion* (1972). Unaccompanied vibraphone solos were, by far, the most common, though nowhere as numerous as those written for marimba.

An early unaccompanied solo work, *Constructions for Vibraphone Solo* (1962), written by the Polish composer and artist Boguslaw Schäffer (1929–2019), reflects both his artistic and compositional skills. In *Constructions*, Schäffer uses standard notation, plus a great variety of original graphic symbols. This work calls for the use of various mallets and beaters—wooden sticks, timpani mallets, jazz brushes, metal beaters, vibe mallets, and fingers. Schäffer explores the sonic possibilities of the vibraphone with a notation that implies extended performance techniques. He also alters its timbre via the use of nontraditional beaters.

The use of sticks and mallets is not the only way to activate the vibraphone. Bowing the instrument produces a sustained sound without the normal attack envelope that occurs when you strike a bar. In 1983, the composer/percussionist Christopher Deane (b. 1957) composed *Mourning Dove Sonnet*, a work requiring great finesse and manual dexterity. The composer notes that the work is "quasi-programmatic"[34] as the piece contains a "literal transcription of a mourning dove song on the exact pitches."[35] Bass bows are used to sound the pitches (notated as up-bow and down-bow) and to produce harmonics by lightly touching the center of the bar that is being bowed. The work also requires "bending the pitch" as described in an earlier chapter, "dead strokes," and other special effects. The lyrical nature present at the work's onset is contrasted with a middle section that is more rhythmic. Here the player mutes the lowest four natural keys (f, g, a, b) to produce "a sound similar to a marimba."[36] A reprise of the opening concludes the work.

One artist who has contributed greatly to the solo vibraphone literature is the American composer Stuart Saunders Smith (b. 1948). Smith began his musical career as a snare drummer. In his teens, he added the drum set and formed a small combo that did more than play dance gigs. "Composing, improvising, and experimenting in free-form as well as in more traditional jazz styles were regular activities for more than five years in his group."[37] Smith attended the Hartt College of Music (BMA cum laude and MM), completing his formal education at the University of Illinois (DMA 1977) where he studied composition with Herbert Brün and Ben Johnston.[38] His compositional output includes transmedia constructs in which "process, not content, is notated."[39] These works are not only for musicians, but can also be realized by actors, dancers, mimes, and so on. In 1970, Smith composed three poems for percussion and narrator that he labels "speech songs." In 1974, Smith began a series of works featuring the vibraphone. His so-called *Links* series includes eleven compositions covering a span of fourteen years ending in 1994 with a work for three vibraphones titled *Links 11*. In the fifth work of the series, *Links 5*, Smith adds three sets of orchestra bells positioned offstage and a set of chimes to be located behind the audience. Together they produce ambient sounds that accompany the primary vibraphone solo. In *Links 6* Smith adds a piano, in *Links 7* a folk singer, and in *Links 8* a flute/listener. The remaining six works are for vibraphone alone.

The first of the series, simply titled *Links*, runs about four minutes in duration. Its notation is traditional, although there are no bar lines. The musical language is tonal, though not in a traditional sense, and its harmonic construct is not serial, but rather implies chordal harmonies. In his detailed analysis of the work, author John P. Welsh breaks down the work into the following sections: A B C (A' B') suggesting "a surface resemblance to traditional four-movement form (as seen, in the sonata)."[40] Welsh considers section A as six phrases. Together they have a jazzlike feel. (Fig. 11.11) The composer stated: "The improvised melodic line found in jazz (especially Free Jazz) is the basis for these solos."[41] Smith's musical syntax, poetic in nature, stems from within himself. It is a unique voice and without parallel in the literature for solo vibraphone.

Other works to consider: *Five Improvisations* (1965) by Koji Takeuchi (b. 1932); *Katalog für einen Vibraphonspieler* (1965) by Werner Heider (b. 1930); *Four Bagatelles* (1970) by Gitta Steiner (1932–1990); *The Red Lion* (1988) by Warren Benson (1924–2005).

MULTIPLE PERCUSSION

In the Western world, the concept of combining dissimilar percussion instruments to create a multiple timbral array to be played by a single performer has its roots in the eighteenth century. It appears that from mid-century on, percussionists in concert bands and theater pit orchestras developed the ability to play both snare drum and bass drum at the same time (double-drumming). With the invention of the bass drum foot pedal around the beginning of the twentieth century, drummers were finally free to add other instruments (cymbals, wood blocks, and more) to their trap set, or drum kit. Milhaud's use of the drum set with a pedal and cymbal attachment in his 1923 work, *La Création du monde*, and later in his 1929–30 *Concerto*, employs these early technical innovations. Of course, Stravinsky's adaptation of the drum set heard in his *Histoire du soldat* (1918) must have influenced other composers as did the percussion scoring in Bartok's *Sonata* (1937). After World War II, orchestral percussionists, like the timpanist, looked for literature that would showcase their talents. There were a number of works written just before and after the war that featured solo percussion with orchestra, namely concertos. Most were often available only in manuscript form and many languished after the excitement of their premiere.

In 1939, the French composer Henri Tomasi (1901–1971) composed the first two movements of his concerto for percussion and orchestra titled *Concert Asiatique*, adding a final movement in 1953, the year of its publication. His compositions for opera (eleven total) and chamber music are well known. His work *Fanfares Liturgiques*, for brass and percussion, is one of the best in the literature. "However, about fifteen concerti, numerous film scores, chamber works, and a considerable body of symphonic music also make up a valuable part of Tomasi's creative work."[42]

Concert Asiatique's opening movement, titled "Invocation and Dance," requires three (or four) kettledrums having a total range of a diminished octave (F sharp to f). The middle movement, with the title "Scherzo for a Night Celebration," features instruments standard to an orchestra percussion section (tam-tam, wood block, triangle, tambourine, snare drum, suspended cymbal) and is performed using the normal techniques common to each. In addition, two tambours *arabes* (single-headed hourglass drums) are required, serving as high and low drum sounds. The last movement, "Finale," is written for both xylophone and vibraphone, the latter used sparingly. "The original xylophone part bears the indication 'octave réelle' (octave as written)."[43] This indication, that the xylophone is to sound as written, takes it out of the standard xylophone range; marimba would be a suitable substitute. Overall, *Concert Asiatique* presented few problems for the solo percussionist. Its technical challenges were well within the ability of most orchestral percussionists of the day. This was true of a number of solo percussion pieces published in the 1950s by the French publisher Alphonse Leduc. Solo works by French composers Serge Baudo (b. 1927), Eugène Bigot (1888–1965), George Delerue (1925–1992), Pierre Dervaux (1917–1992), Maurice Jarre (1924–2009), and others followed a similar compositional plan, separating rather than integrating each instrument into a multiple-percussion array.

In earlier chapters we examined a number of solo unaccompanied multiple-percussion works written after World War II, including those by Cage, Stockhausen, Feldman, Nørgård, and Xenakis. Unlike Tomasi and the composers mentioned above, they presented the solo percussionist with new notations to learn, advanced performance problems to solve, and unique conceptual dilemmas to resolve. Many percussionists met these challenges, thus advancing their technical and conceptual prowess and, by the 1990s, a coterie of star percussion soloists, who were equal to playing concerti of great complexity, emerged on the international scene. The Scottish composer James Macmillan (b. 1959) composed *Veni, Veni, Emmanuel* in 1992, a concerto first performed by the solo percussion artist Evelyn Glennie (b. 1965). *Veni, Veni, Emmanuel* (in English "O Come, O Come, Emmanuel") are the opening words, in Latin, of a medieval text sung as part of Roman Catholic Advent services. In the program notes to the score, the composer states that "all the musical material is drawn from the fifteenth-century French Advent plainchant of the same name."[44] The work itself is approximately twenty-five minutes in duration. Though contrasting sections are obvious, it is performed as one continuous movement. Most of *Veni, Veni, Emmanuel* can be described as spirited, almost frantic at times, with the exception of two more tranquil transitions, marked "Sequence I and II," that divide the concerto into five sections.

The score calls for a full orchestra, winds, brass, strings, and a timpanist. The instrument requirements for the soloist are considerable. (Fig. 11.12) To stage right, an array of thirteen membranophones are joined by two cymbals (one sizzle), wood blocks, cowbells, temple blocks, log drum (two pitches), and six graduated metallophones (either Javanese gongs or cencerros). Across the stage are a five-octave marimba, vibraphone, mark tree, plus large and medium tam-tams. Finally, at the rear of the orchestra, Macmillan positions six tubular chimes, each two inches in diameter. The chimes are used at the work's conclusion where they are joined by the entire orchestra playing assorted bells (or alternatively, 2 pieces of loud clanging metal).

In the opening section, the tempo is fast and the dynamic rarely drops below fortissimo. To begin, Macmillan writes a brief, six-bar vibraphone solo, then focuses on the large multiple-percussion setup that contains thirty-three different sounds. Selecting from the various instruments, he combines two or three for extended rhythmic passages, occasionally riffing across the entire array with wild abandon. At the end of the first section, a transition for orchestra alone allows time for the soloist to move to the keyboard percussion setup. The next section, marked "Gaude, Gaude" (Rejoice, Rejoice) features an extended four-mallet marimba solo. More lyrical than the opening material, with melismatic runs over the entire five octaves, it allows the soloist to display more than athletic prowess while the addition of the mark tree creates a nice ambience. A second orchestral transition returns the soloist to the multiple-percussion array and the final section of the piece. After a brief reprise of the opening material, each member of the orchestra sequentially stops playing and takes up their assigned metallophone. Joined by the soloist on chimes, they combine in a final "roaring" crescendo—intended to sound like all the church bells in Scotland.

The American composer Christopher Rouse (1949–2019) was well known to the percussion community. As a young man, Rouse studied percussion and his technical knowledge of the possibilities of those instruments is evident in his compositions. He wrote a number of percussion ensembles and was known to expand the percussion section when composing works for symphony orchestra. His percussion concerto, *Der gerettete Alberich* from 1997, is dedicated to the Scottish virtuoso Evelyn Glennie and was made possible by a commissioning consortium of world-class orchestras. Rouse, in his program notes, refers to the work as "a fantasy for solo percussion and orchestra on themes of Wagner, with the soloist taking on the 'role' of Alberich,"[45] who is described as a sly and slightly malevolent character. The solo part requires four wood blocks, two log drums (4 pitches), four tom-toms, bongos, timbales, snare drum, a tenor steel drum, marimba, two large guiros, bass drum with pedal, and a drum set. The full orchestra requires three additional percussionists, plus timpani. As in the Macmillan work, the nonpitched percussion instruments are combined into a single setup; the marimba and drum set stand alone. Also, like the Macmillan piece, the music is both tonal and atonal; however, a great deal of the Rouse work is quiet, sometimes ominous-sounding or mischievous, in keeping with the title character.

Before the soloist comes on stage, the orchestra plays a quote from the ending of Richard Wagner's *Götterdämmerung*, the last opera in his cycle *Der Ring des Nibelungen*. Rouse states that the work is not programmatic, but knowledge of leitmotifs used by Wagner, such as horn calls and other musical markers, including the one used for Alberich, will make the work more interesting for the listener.

Like a concerto, the work is in three parts. It begins with a guiro cadenza, a first in the literature, signifying the return of Alberich, who went missing at the end of the *Ring*. (Fig. 11.13) The senza misura solo transitions to a faster tempo, presto, featuring kick drum and wood blocks, then to all the nonpitched percussion, timbales, bongos, and so on, ending at a reprise of the guiro figures. The middle section, marked molto adagio, features the marimba and the tenor pan. Here the mood is quiet, the writing melodic with soft marimba chords placed against high string harmonics. Suddenly, Alberich becomes a rock drummer; the style change is as shocking as is the sudden forte. A transition leads to a bravura section featuring the multiple-percussion setup and includes a brief cadenza. Orchestra and soloist combine to propel the work to a dramatic ending. A solo six-note figure on the guiros gives Alberich the final laugh.

Other works to consider: *7 Fogli, No. 2 "Coeur Pour Batteur"* (1959) by Sylvano Bussotti (b. 1931); *Interieur 1* (1966) by Helmut Lachenmann (b. 1935); *Prison Song* (1971) by Hans Werner Henze (1926–2012); *Thirteen Drums* (1985) by Maki Ishii; *The Anvil Chorus* (1991) by David Lang (b. 1957); *Spider Walk* (1993) by Marta Ptaszynska.

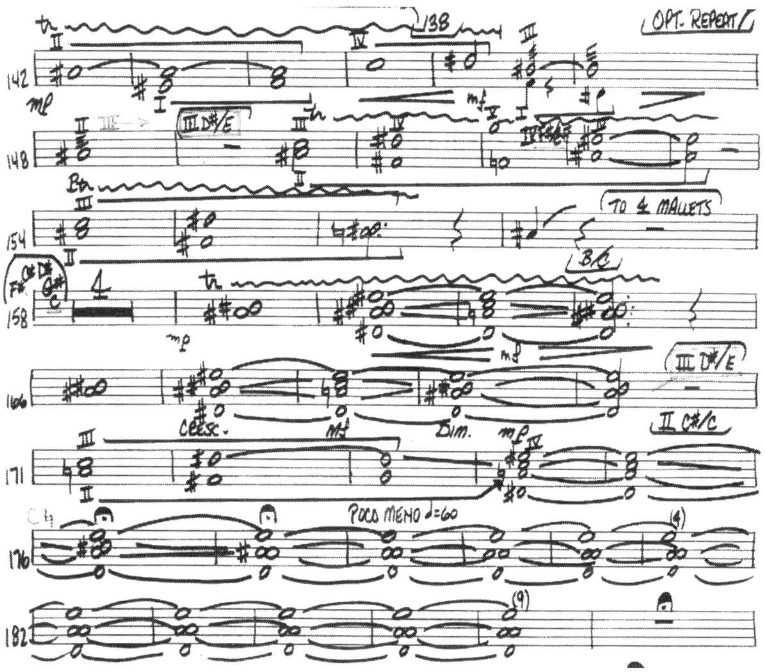

Fig. 11.1 Kraft, *Concerto for Timpani and Orchestra* (solo part, Mvt. III, meas. 142–197). Copyright © 1985 by Theodore Presser Company. All rights reserved. Used with permission.

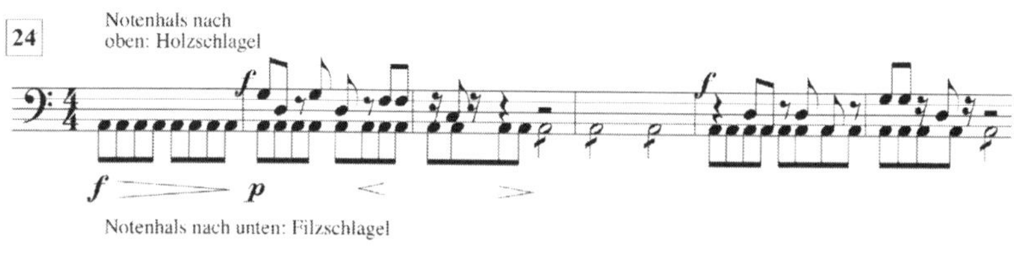

Fig. 11.2 Thärichen, *Konzert für Pauken und Orchester* (solo part, Mvt. I, reh. no. 24)

Fig. 11.3 Carter, *Eight Pieces for Four Timpani* (*Adagio*, p. 9). Copyright © 1968 (renewed) by Associated Music Publishers, Inc. (BMI). International Copyright Secured. All rights reserved. Used by permission.

Fig. 11.4 Hanuš, *Concertino for Timpani and Tape, Opus 69* (meas. 3–18)

Fig. 11.5 Hovhaness, *Fantasy on Japanese Wood Prints* (meas. 1–8)

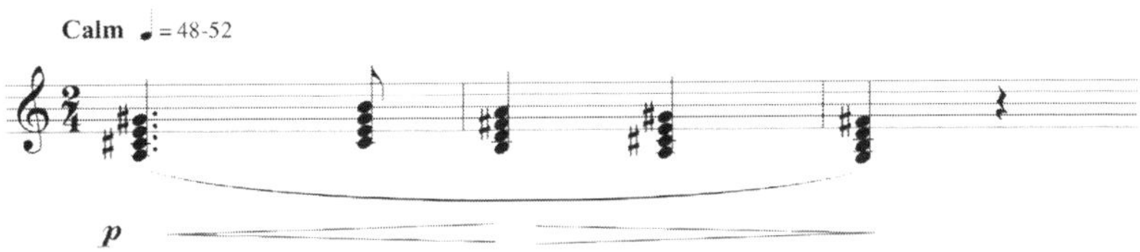

Fig. 11.6 Creston, *Concertino for Marimba* (Mvt. II, meas. 3–5)

Fig. 11.7 Milhaud, *Concerto for Marimba and Vibraphone* (meas. 54–58)

Fig. 11.8 Kurka, *Concerto for Marimba and Orchestra, Op. 34* (excerpt from Mvt. III)

Fig. 11.9 Miyoshi, *Torse III* (Mvt. IV, final two measures)

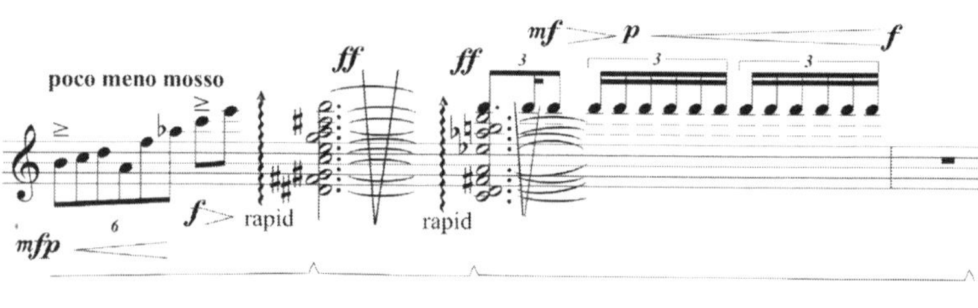

Fig. 11.10 Takemitsu, *Rain Tree* (meas. 126)

Fig. 11.11 Smith, *Links* (opening phrase). Copyright © Sonic Art Editions, c/o Smith Publications, 54 Lent Rd., Sharon, VT 05065. Used by permission.

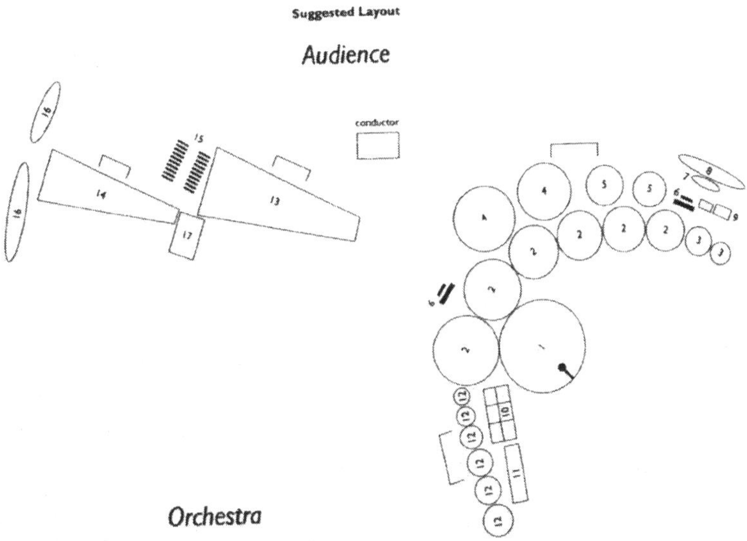

1. Bass drum with pedal
2. 6 tom-toms
3. 2 bongos
4. 2 timbales
5. 2 congas
6. 2 cowbells
7. sizzle cymbal
8. large cymbal
9. 2 wood blocks
10. 6 temple blocks
11. Log drum
12. 6 gongs (Javanese or cencerros)
13. Marimba (5 octave)
14. vibraphone
15. mark tree
16. 2 tam-tams (one large)
17. stick tray
18. 2" bass tubular bells

Fig. 11.12 Macmillan, *Veni, Veni, Emmanuel* (suggested layout)

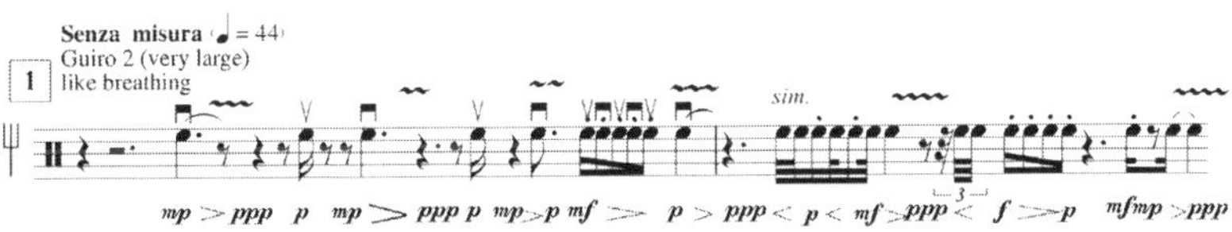

Fig. 11.13 Rouse, *Der gerettete Alberich* (solo guiro, reh. no. 1)

EPILOGUE

The twentieth century is notable for its many technological advances as well as for the global conflicts that disrupted the lives of millions. Both had significant impact on the arts. The invention of the automobile and the airplane captivated the imagination of the Italian Futurists, who used the newly invented radio to propagandize their movement. World wars brought a halt to artistic activities in Europe and Asia, forcing many artists and musicians to seek refuge in the Americas. The tape recorder, invented in the 1930s, served as a critical tool for composers leading to the creation of a new form of music. Civil unrest during the 1960s and 1970s was reflected in a genre of music that encompassed theatrical trappings. Synthesizers and computers were used both to create and to realize musical works for the first time. With or without this new technology and despite global conflicts, twentieth-century composers continued to create. For the first time in the history of Western music, they produced an extensive literature for instruments of the percussion family.

The importance to the percussive arts of the three composers (Stravinsky, Bartók, and Milhaud) highlighted in chapter one cannot be overstated. At this writing, we are in the second decade of the twenty-first century and their genius continues to influence the international music community. Stravinsky's ballet music for *Le Sacre du printemps,* with its shifting metric patterns and driving, percussive rhythms, combined to create a Dionysian frenzy that caused the audience to riot. Both the work and the reaction to it influenced the future of music.

Bartók's compositional approach demonstrated a new sensitivity in orchestrating for percussion. Cymbals and drums were able to do more than "crash" and "boom"—his writing exploited their subtlest nuances. Referencing jazz and the drum set in a number of his compositions, Milhaud brought attention to the solo percussionist and wrote one of the first concertos for marimba. The contributions of these three composers to the art of percussion were seminal, influencing the writings of their contemporaries throughout the century.

The notion that Western percussion instruments alone, grouped into ensembles, could provide a satisfactory artistic experience was first demonstrated during this hundred-year period. Tcherepnin and Shostakovich inserted percussion ensemble movements within larger musical forms, both symphonic and operatic. Although Antheil's attempt at writing a percussion score for an early film failed, his works evoked the same reaction as Stravinsky's *Rite,* causing an international hullabaloo with the New York premiere of his *Ballet mécanique.* He subsequently abandoned that compositional direction, but other composers were not deterred by his failure. Varèse created stirs of his own, redefining music as "organized sound" and composing one of the century's most iconic percussion ensemble works. Although he did not create a school of composition or define a new genre, Varèse stands as one of the period's most important composers, inspiring others who followed. The music of Latin America, Cuba, and Mexico, influenced by European and African cultures, ushered new instruments into the percussion family. The Afro-Cuban rhythms heard in Havana during the 1930s, mixed with classic European forms, were heard in the percussion ensembles of Ardévol and Roldán. Visualizing an imagined music of Mexico, Chávez wrote *Xochipilli,* adding teponaxtle, *huehuetl,* and various rattles and rasps to the percussionist's trap case. His popular *Toccata,* with its skillful construction and use of classic compositional devices, became a model for numerous postwar composers.

Prewar composers on the Atlantic side of the Americas looked to the traditions of European music either to emulate or to rebel against. West Coast composers referenced Asia and the countries of the Pacific Rim where they found new forms, new instruments, and unique rhythmic schemes. The century's most prominent crusader for new music, West Coast composer and pedagogue Henry Cowell, assimilated the musics of East Asia into his own to create original works for dance and percussion. Cowell influenced a generation of young composers through his publishing company, New Music, and his teachings on world musics.

The modern dance movement was born in the twentieth century in reaction to classical ballet. With a desire to make dance emotive rather than decorative, modern dance pioneers, including Ruth St. Denis (1879–1968), Ted Shawn (1891–1972), Doris Humphrey, Charles Weidman (1901–1975), and others, formed dance troupes, teaching, performing, and touring to bring this new dance aesthetic to the interested public. In their studios, percussion began to replace the ubiquitous piano and composers like Cowell, Beyer, Green, Reigger, and others wrote percussion music for their dance concerts and recitals. On the West Coast of the United States, Cage and Harrison joined forces to write percussion ensembles that included both traditional instruments and exotic sound sources salvaged from junkyards or found in local curiosity shops. Cage created the first professional percussion ensemble. Both composers realized that their music could stand alone. Together they initiated a series of percussion ensemble concerts programming their own music as well as that of other West Coast composers. Cage brought this new repertoire to Chicago and later to New York, where he returned to accompany dance and began a life-long association with the Merce Cunningham Dance Company as its music director. Cage, like Varèse, was to become more than a composer, redefining the intent of music, removing its communicative powers, and equating all sounds, including noise, as equal: "He upended long-held conventions about the listening process and prodded us to re-evaluate how we define not only music but the entire experience of encountering art."[1]

The Second World War was truly global. The destruction in Asian and European countries was horrific. Fortunately, the Americas were largely untouched. With its economic and military might, the United States helped secure victory over the Axis nations and, in so doing, grew to be the world's strongest nation. The United States also benefited from the many prominent scientists and artists who immigrated to its shores in an effort to avoid conflicts in their home countries. Composers like Stravinsky, Varèse, Bartók, Schoenberg, and Milhaud fled Europe for the safety of the United States where they continued to teach and compose. Following World War II, the GIs returned home to the States to resume their lives; many enrolled in colleges and universities hoping to gain skills and find jobs upon graduation. Millions were able to do so with the support of the GI Bill. Their educational efforts had far-reaching implications for the future economic growth of the country and for the development of higher education. Various college disciplines found it necessary to adjust their curricula to satisfy the needs of these new students and to employ additional faculty to teach them. Rarely has government legislative action had such a positive impact on the U.S. educational system.

In the field of applied music, percussion was added to the curricula of music schools and departments. Educators, like Paul Price at the University of Illinois, pioneered a new approach to teaching percussion. Students were expected to become technically proficient in more than one area of percussion. As before, students played in the school's bands and orchestras, but also gained musicianship by performing in chamber music ensembles comprised solely of instruments of the percussion family. Composers were attracted to this novel musical medium and, realizing its potential to express their artistic visions, began to compose a new kind of music. In this well-trained, college-educated group of percussionists, composers found excellent musicians willing to commission and to perform their works.

The small body of solo and ensemble works for percussion written before the war was rediscovered by the percussion community. The prewar works of Cage, Harrison, Chávez, and others became part of the fast-growing repertoire for solo and ensemble percussion. As Europe recovered from the war's devastation, composers from France, Italy, and Germany contributed new works to the canon as well. Written as a test piece for a solo competition, Stockhausen's multiple-percussion work *Zyklus* caught the attention of the avant-garde, who reacted to its graphic notation and mobile form by emulating it. Statistically organized, incorporating both randomness and serialization, *Zyklus* became a model for numerous other unaccompanied percussion solos. Berio's *Circles*, for soprano, harp, and two multiple percussionists, each with a larger array than called for in *Zyklus*, introduced yet other new forms of notation. Berio eschewed serialism, letting the text dictate the form and allowing the players a degree of improvisation. The American composer, Wuorinen embraced serialism and applied its discipline to a number of his mature works for percussion, both solo and ensemble. His *Janissary Music* for solo percussion challenged both the musical and athletic abilities of the percussionist. One of Argentina's greatest composers, Ginastera, applied serial techniques to create a masterpiece for percussion ensemble. His *Cantata para América mágica* used volumes of both standard and Latin percussion instruments to color an emotional text sung by a dramatic soprano. Using the mathematical skills learned as a student of architecture, the Greek composer Xenakis brought new rhythmical structures to the literature for percussion, creating both solo and ensemble works. The influential French composer Boulez castigated Schoenberg and his dodecaphony as he championed a new, more dynamic serialism, one that organized not only pitch, but every other musical parameter. His views held sway over the European avant-garde until the 1950s, when Cage performed at both the Donaueschinger Musiktage and Darmstadt's summer music courses. Boulez reacted. "In 1958, Cage came to Europe with a bag full of tricks," he complained.[2] In Cage's "bag" was "indeterminacy" and it made a significant impact on a number of composers worldwide. Some thought that the music Cage produced using chance methods sounded similar to the works of the serialists, but then again Cage's focus on the quality and importance of a single sound, that "any sound can be a musical sound," helped free composers from the restrictions of traditional notation. Consequently, they found new ways to visually illustrate complex musical ideas, using original graphic notations. Feldman's *The King of Denmark,* notated on graph paper, excised the percussive attack heard when striking an instrument by using fingers instead of sticks. In so doing, the piece brought focus to percussion's resonant timbres and to Cage's idea that a single sound could stand alone. In deciphering new graphic symbols and complex structures, percussionists became partners in the creative process, working hand in hand with composers to produce a definitive performance.

The technological advances of the twentieth century had a significant impact on music and the percussive arts. Radio, phonograph, tape and video recorders, synthesizers, and computers, to name a few, were invented during this time. In postwar Europe, state-owned radio stations supported the arts, not only by broadcasting music, but also by creating research studios dedicated to exploring the possibilities of electronic music. Earlier, composers like Cage and Varèse had prophesied the medium's creation, contributing initial works to the genre. As the technology became more sophisticated, composers Stockhausen, Davidovsky, and others wrote works, both solo and ensemble, that brought the combination of tape and percussion to a higher level. Late in the century, the computer opened a Pandora's box of possibilities as this machine was able to combine and manipulate percussion and electronic sounds in "real time."

The twentieth century witnessed worldwide social unrest in the 1960s and 1970s and composers responded to the times accordingly. They began to exploit the inherent theatricality in live musical performance by composing works that added many elements common to the theater, such as lighting, action, dance, costumes, social commentary, and more. Early on, the maverick composer Harry Partch looked to the ancient Greeks to find a tuning system that would satisfy his aesthetic needs. Essential to his concept of music-theater were instruments that not only sounded good, but were also visually engaging. Consequently, he constructed a new instrumentarium sculpted in wood that included an entire keyboard percussion family. His student Ben Johnston's work, *Knocking Piece,* viewed by many at the time as an attack on the establishment, explored the sonorities of the grand piano without using the keyboard. Opening with a circus tune, Kagel's *Dressur* is an elaborately staged work for a trio of percussionists that "strives to rediscover what has been lost in Western classical music: the visual and kinetic nature of performance, the physicality of music-making, the bodily presence of the performers, the three-dimensional space of the stage, the spectacle of stage events."[3] His work helped to define the genre. Ritual was a feature of many works during this period. Stockhausen, in his *Musik im Bauch,* suspended a giant, birdlike figure center stage that is attacked and beaten by three switch-wielding percussionists, who eventually disembowel it to remove the music therein. A cry for peace is heard in the work of Drouet as he quotes classic literature in his *Variations sur un texte de Victor Hugo,* which demands vocalization and dance skills as well as technical finesse. It seemed inevitable that the music-theater genre would produce an opera, albeit an unconventional one. Udow's *The Shattered Mirror* brings all the trappings of opera to the stage. His antiwar sextet, *Understanding,* reflects the anger and rebellion of the younger generation in the 1970s.

Timbre delineates one musical instrument from another. String, brass, and reed instruments have similar overtones and can be heard as a group, but the percussion group incorporates many dissimilar instruments with overtones that vary widely. Its group is defined as one whose sound is produced when struck. We have seen that there are many ways to activate a percussion instrument utilizing different mallets and different actions—bowing, rubbing, shaking, and so on. Given the multitude of instruments, the resultant timbral possibilities seem endless. Composers like Crumb, Serocki, and Ptaszynska made timbre a major element in the construction of their works for percussion. For Serocki, moving various timbres through space, over and around the listener, was an important part of his percussion sextet. Crumb had an ear for the subtlest of percussion nuances. Bowing tam-tams and bending vibraphone pitches, he created atmospheres that surround us with resonant clouds of complex timbres. Ptaszynska found her inspiration in graphic works of art and translated their imagery and color into exciting compositions for percussion.

Repetition is one of the unifying factors of traditional Western music. Variation, rondo, and sonata allegro forms use motifs that return and are recognized by the listener. In serial and aleatoric works, such unifying figures occur at a rapid pace and, often, the listener is left behind. The decade of the 1960s gave us a new genre, minimalism, in which change occurs at a slow pace and allows the listener to hear its structure slowly unfold. This new music refuted Stockhausen's serialism and Cage's indeterminacy. Its affinity with the constant pulse found in popular music engaged a new, younger audience. Steve Reich's *Drumming* is truly one of the genre's masterworks. In it, Reich empirically explored the acoustical phenomena of resultant tones and interference tones and used amplification to allow the phenomena to be more easily heard.[4] He then formed his own percussion ensemble to ensure his music's authentic reproduction. Of the minimalist composers of the 1960s, only Young continued to work within its strictures, though minimalism influenced many in the next thirty years.

New concertos that featured percussion and orchestra were extremely rare in the early years of the twentieth century, though composers Milhaud, Creston, and Tomasi provided excellent examples. With the increased amount of skilled percussion players following World War II, unaccompanied solo works were written in exponential numbers and the idea of an unaccompanied solo percussion recital was born. Eventually, concertos for orchestra and timpani (or keyboard percussion instruments, or multiple-percussion players) were commissioned by and for the new virtuoso percussionists. The percussionist was relocated to the front of the orchestra with greater frequency.

In 1967, Leonard B. Meyer wrote that the arts had entered a period in which a multiplicity of styles and techniques, attitudes and ideologies, would coexist for a considerable period of time.[5] The preceding chapters trace the evolution of a literature for percussion, a century-long explosion of creativity by the leading composers of the twentieth century. Their compositional skills, inquisitive natures, and willingness to reevaluate the meaning and intent of music and to embrace new ideologies helped create a number of identifiable genres. Works written by the composers I have highlighted, as well as many others, helped advance the percussive arts to a new level, one equal to that of other instrumental groups.

What will the twenty-first century bring? We have already seen that some of the works examined herein embraced more than one genre, and that many composers synthesized various styles to create new hybrid art forms. The elements of theater will always be important to the percussive arts, which are, by nature, both tactile and visual. With the aid of the computer, composers can now generate unique, complex ways to organize sounds as well as ways to disorganize them. The postmillennial generation was born into technology created by the past century. Will it embrace or reject the past? Only time will tell. "It is worth one last reminder that all 'style periods' are plural, and that the dominance of trends is never as absolute or obvious as historical accounts inevitably make them seem."[6]

NOTES

INTRODUCTION

1. Ross, *The Rest Is Noise,* xi.

2. Broyles, *Mavericks and Other Traditions in American Music,* 7.

3. Broyles, *Mavericks and Other Traditions in American Music,* 93.

4. Howard E. Smither, "Rhythm," in *Dictionary of Contemporary Music,* edited by John Vinton (New York: E. P. Dutton, 1974), 618.

5. Crawford, *America's Musical Life,* 690.

CHAPTER 1. ORIGINS

1. Kostelanetz, *Dictionary of the Avant-Gardes,* 54.

2. Barzun, *From Dawn to Decadence,* 718.

3. Ernst, *The Evolution of Electronic Music,* xxx.

4. Knaack, *The Bride Stripped Bare by Her Bachelors, Even. Erratum Musical* by Marcel Duchamp, liner notes.

5. Broyles, *Mavericks and Other Traditions in American Music,* 145.

6. Tisdall and Bozzolla, *Futurism,* 119.

7. Broyles, *Mavericks and Other Traditions in American Music,* 145.

8. Copland, *Our New Music,* 65.

9. "Stravinsky," in *Baker's Biographical Dictionary of Musicians,* 8th ed., edited by N. Slonimsky (New York: Schirmer, 1992), 1807.

10. "Stravinsky," 1807.

11. Stravinsky, *Histoire du soldat,* score note.

12. Kraft, *Notes*, 214.
13. Kraft, *Notes*, 214.
14. Kraft, *Notes*, 213.
15. Morgan, *Twentieth-Century Music*, 169.
16. Lang, "A Journey to the Source on *L'Histoire du Soldat*," 52.
17. Austin, *Music in the 20th Century*, 263.
18. Ross, *The Rest Is Noise*, 104.
19. Stevens, *Life and Music of Béla Bartók*, 56.
20. Stevens, *Life and Music of Béla Bartók*, 213.
21. Bartók, *Sonata for Two Pianos and Percussion*, score instruction page.
22. Ernö Lendvai, *Béla Bartók: An Analysis of His Music*, 95.
23. Stevens, *Life and Music of Béla Bartók*, 215.
24. Stevens, *Life and Music of Béla Bartók*, 215.
25. Stevens, *Life and Music of Béla Bartók*, 218.
26. Horowitz, *Artists in Exile*, 118.
27. Mawer, *Darius Milhaud*, 9.
28. Milhaud, *Notes without Music*, 110.
29. Mawer, *Darius Milhaud*, 117.
30. Milhaud, *Notes without Music*, 118.
31. Milhaud, *Notes without Music*, 137.
32. Mawer, *Darius Milhaud*, 146.
33. Rosen, "The Milhaud Concerto pour batterie et petit orchestre," 27.
34. Lisnik, "Darius Milhaud's Concerto for Percussion," 64.
35. Mawer, *Darius Milhaud*, 9.

CHAPTER 2. AN EMERGING LITERATURE FOR PERCUSSION ENSEMBLE

1. Qtd. in Ross, *The Rest Is Noise*, 53.
2. Cope, *New Directions in Music*, 21.
3. Price, "The Exciting World of Percussion," 44.
4. Phillip Ramey, *Alexander Tcherepnin*, accessed April 15, 2017, http://www.tcherepnin.com/alex/bio_alex.htm, 3.
5. Qtd. in Korabelnikova, *Alexander Tcherepnin*, 130.
6. Arias, "Alexander Tcherepnin," 185.
7. Qtd. in Wilson, *Shostakovich: A Life Remembered*, 85.
8. Antheil, *Bad Boy of Music*, 138.
9. Whitesitt, *The Life and Music of George Antheil*, 106.
10. Whitesitt, *The Life and Music of George Antheil*, 106.
11. Whitesitt, *The Life and Music of George Antheil*, 25.
12. Antheil, *Bad Boy of Music*, 192.
13. Whitesitt, *Life and Music of George Antheil*, 108.
14. Antheil, *Bad Boy of Music*, 140.
15. Rich, *American Pioneers*, 77.

16. Schuller, "Conversation with Edgard Varèse," 32.
17. Schuller, "Conversation with Edgard Varèse," 35.
18. Salzman, *Twentieth-Century Music*, 134.
19. Feisst, "Varèse and His New York Choruses," 257.
20. Edgard Varèse, *Amériques*, score notes by Chou Wen-Chung, vi.
21. MacDonald, *Varèse: Astronomer in Sound*, 110.
22. Louise Varèse, *Varèse: A Looking-Glass Diary*, 1:150.
23. Rosen, "*Amériques* by Varèse," 44.
24. Root, "The Performance Guilds of Edgard Varèse," 57.
25. Felix Meyer, "'The Exhilarating Atmosphere of Struggle,'" 86.
26. Louise Varèse, *Varèse: A Looking-Glass Diary*, 1:191.
27. Horowitz, *Classical Music in America*, 453.
28. Louise Varèse, *Varèse: A Looking-Glass Diary*, 1:191.
29. Lichtenhahn, "'A New Primitiveness,'" 193.
30. Schick, *The Percussionist's Art*, 56.
31. Letter to the author, April 13, 1972.
32. Qtd. in Wen-chung, "*Ionisation*: The Function of Timbre in its Formal and Temporal Organization," 74.
33. Slonimsky, *Music since 1900*, 340.
34. François, "*Organization of Scattered Timbral Qualities*," 48–79. Wen-chung, "*Ionisation*: The Function of Timbre in its Formal and Temporal Organization," 27–74.
35. Gann, "'Magnificent—in a Mysterious Way,'" 427.
36. Edgard Varèse, "The Liberation of Sound," 202.
37. De la Motte-Haber, "Blurred Traces,"40.
38. Cowell, "Roldán and Caturla of Cuba," 98.
39. Carpentier, *Music in Cuba*, 275.
40. Stallings, "Collective Difference," 59.
41. Root, "The Performance Guilds of Edgard Varese," 31.
42. Review (1954) by the *Chicago Daily News* music critic Roger Dettmer, who remarked: "Best among these is the Illini presentation. Not only is this student enterprise superbly recorded and played with proper abandon, but it offers four other percussion works as a bonus including Edgard Varèse's classic *Ionisation* and Lou Harrison's haunting *Canticle No. 3*." "Recommended."
43. Parker, *Carlos Chávez*, 51.
44. Parker, *Carlos Chávez*, 51.
45. Chávez, *Tambuco*, score note by composer.

CHAPTER 3. HENRY COWELL AND THE WEST COAST DANCE SCENE

1. Slonimsky, "Henry Cowell," 58.
2. Saylor, Lichtenwanger, and Wright, "Henry Cowell," 521.
3. Broadcast Music, Inc. (BMI), *Henry Cowell*, commemorative booklet in honor of fifty years as a composer (1962), 8.

4. Sachs, *Henry Cowell: A Man Made of Music*, 224.
5. Mead, *Henry Cowell's New Music*, 188.
6. Marcuse, *Musical Instruments*, 264.
7. Gordon, "Drums along the Pacific," 27.
8. Cage, *Silence: Lectures and Writings*, 71.
9. Sydney Cowell, Note to author, October 1, 1975.
10. Beal, "How Johanna Beyer Spent Her Days."
11. Kennedy and Polansky, "'Total Eclipse,'" 726.
12. Coulter, "Forgotten Percussion Works: Johanna Magdalena Beyer," 9.
13. Blatter, *Instrumentation/Orchestration*, 179.
14. Stone, *Music Notation in the Twentieth Century*, 220.
15. Qtd. in Mead, *Henry Cowell's New Music*, 336.
16. Mead, *Henry Cowell's New Music*, 336.
17. R. Vise, "Ray Green," 4.
18. R. Vise, "Ray Green," 14.
19. Humphrey, *Dance Rhythms*, score.
20. Cohen, ed., *Doris Humphrey: An Artist First*, 132.
21. Gillespie and Young, "William Russell: An American Original," 41.
22. Qtd. in Gillespie and Young, "William Russell: An American Original," 45.
23. Craycraft, "William Russell's Percussion Music," 26.
24. Gillespie and Young, "William Russell: An American Original," 45.
25. John Kennedy and Charles Wood, "Made in America: The Music of William Russell," Program note, Florence Gould Hall, New York City, February 24, 1990.
26. Berman, "Gerald Strang: Composer, Educator, Acoustician," 2.
27. Berman, "Gerald Strang: Composer, Educator, Acoustician," 10.
28. Berman, "Gerald Strang: Composer, Educator, Acoustician," 4.
29. Strang, *Percussion Music*, score note.
30. Sachs, *Henry Cowell: A Man Made of Music*, 365.
31. Miller, "The Art of Noise," 252.
32. Miller and Lieberman, Lou Harrison: *Composing a World*, 11.
33. Qtd. in Sachs, *Henry Cowell: A Man Made of Music*, 265.
34. Miller and Lieberman, *Lou Harrison: Composing a World*, 10.
35. Baker, "The Percussion Ensemble Music of Lou Harrison," 75.
36. Miller, "The Art of Noise," 248.
37. Ravenscroft, "Working Out the 'Is-Tos and As-Tos,'" 25–43.
38. Ravenscroft, "Working Out the 'Is-Tos and As-Tos,'" 42.
39. Miller, "Cultural Intersections," 47.
40. Miller, "Cultural Intersections," 63.
41. Cage, *Silence: Lectures and Writings*, 86.
42. Tomkins, *The Bride and the Bachelors*, 93.
43. Henry Cowell, "Drums along the Pacific," 46–47.

CHAPTER 4. POST WORLD WAR II—AMERICA RISING

1. Humes, *Over Here*, 88.

2. Colgrass, *Michael Colgrass: Adventures of an American Composer*, 53.

3. Michael Colgrass and Phillip Ramey, Excerpt from program notes written for the New York Philharmonic Orchestra premiere of *Déjà vu*, October 1977.

4. Colgrass, *Michael Colgrass: Adventures of an American Composer*, 218.

5. Colgrass, "Small Essay on My Early Percussion Music," 70.

6. Thomas Siwe, "Interview with Michael Colgrass," September 21, 2009, Toronto, Canada.

7. Peters, "Treatise on Percussion."

8. Hovhaness, "The Alan Hovhaness Website."

9. Oliver, "Hovhaness: In and Out of Our Time," 42.

10. Brant, Interview by Cole Gagne and Tracy Caras, 54.

11. Brant, Program notes for the premiere of *Symphony for Percussion*.

12. William Kraft, Email to the author, March 3, 2015.

13. Judt, *Postwar*, 198.

14. Barraud, "France," 250.

15. Kelly, "Jolivet."

16. Rae, "Marius Constant."

17. Rae, *The Music of Maurice Ohana*, 17.

18. Rae, *The Music of Maurice Ohana*, 130.

19. Rae, *The Music of Maurice Ohana*, 23.

20. Rae, *The Music of Maurice Ohana*, 270.

21. Qtd. in Rae, *The Music of Maurice Ohana*, 84.

CHAPTER 5. SERIALISM

1. Beal, *New Music, New Allies*, 11.

2. Pauli, "Austria and Germany," 37.

3. Krenek, "Serialism," 670.

4. Wörner, *Stockhausen: Life and Work*, 78.

5. Karlheinz Stockhausen, Booklet included with *Zyklus-Refrain-Kontakte*, CD6 (Kürten: Stockhausen-Verlag, 1993).

6. Stockhausen, Booklet, 108.

7. Maconie, *Works of Karlheinz Stockhausen*, 112.

8. Maconie, *Works of Karlheinz Stockhausen*, 112.

9. Schrader, *Introduction to Electro-Acoustic Music*, 82.

10. Judt, *Postwar*, 256.

11. Osmond-Smith, *Berio*, 11.

12. Beck, ed., *Encyclopedia of Percussion*, 56.

13. O'Neill, "Recent Trends in Percussion Notation," 31.

14. Jones, "Text and Music in Luciano Berio's *Circles*," 108.

15. Sekhon, "Percussion Composition," 12.

16. O'Neill, "Recent Trends in Percussion Notation," 27.

17. Wuorinen, Interview, 392.

18. Wuorinen, Interview, 393–394.

19. Schwartz-Kates, "Alberto Ginastera," *Grove Music Online.*

20. Eyler, "Cantata para América Mágica," 30.

21. Eyler, "Cantata para América Mágica," 30.

22. Alberto Ginastera, "Cantata para América Mágica," unsigned program note, Los Angeles Philharmonic, March 25, 2008, http://www.laphil.com/philpedia/music/cantata-para-america-magica-alberto-ginastera, accessed December 3, 2018.

23. Eyler, "Cantata para América Mágica," 30.

24. Flint, "Metabolae, Arborescences, and the Reconstruction of Time in Iannis Xenakis' *Psappha*," 221.

25. Ross, "Waveforms," 78.

26. Harley, *Xenakis: His Life in Music*, 46.

27. Harley, *Xenakis: His Life in Music*, 64.

28. Harley, *Xenakis: His Life in Music*, 64.

29. Sekhon, "Percussion Composition," 45.

30. Harley, *Xenakis: His Life in Music*, 115.

31. Emmerson, "Xenakis," 24.

32. Harley, *Xenakis: His Life in Music*, 94.

33. Emmerson, "Xenakis," 24.

34. Harley, *Xenakis: His Life in Music*, 97.

CHAPTER 6. CHANCE AND INDETERMINACY IN MUSIC

1. Wörner, *Stockhausen: Life and Work*, 106.

2. Donal Henahan, "John Cage: Disorder as a Goal in Life," *Chicago Tribune Book World*, October 18, 1981.

3. Pritchett, "John Cage," 797.

4. Tomkins, *The Bride and the Bachelors*, 100.

5. Kerson Huang and Rosemary Huang, *I Ching* (New York: Workman Publishing, 1987), 64.

6. Nicholls, "Toward Infinity," 106.

7. Cage, *27′ 10.554″, for a Percussionist*, score.

8. Cage, *27′ 10.554″, for a Percussionist*, score.

9. Cage, *Child of Tree*, score.

10. Shultis, "The Process of Discovery," 570.

11. Cage, *Child of Tree*, score.

12. Cage, *Child of Tree*, score.

13. Allan Kozinn, "John Cage, 79, a Minimalist of Musical Prolificacy, Dies," *New York Times*, August 13, 1992.

14. Johnson, "Morton Feldman."
15. Williams, "An Interview with Morton Feldman," 4, 5, 6.
16. Johnson, "Morton Feldman."
17. Sekhon, "Percussion Composition," 56.
18. Feldman, *The King of Denmark*, score instruction page.
19. Salzman, *Twentieth-Century Music*, 156.
20. Salzman and Desi, *The New Music Theater*, 152.
21. Lichtenfeld and Kager, "Roman Haubenstock-Ramati."
22. Chandra, ed., *When Music Resists Meaning*, 285.
23. Siwe, "An Interview with Herbert Brün," 8.
24. Chandra, *When Music Resists Meaning*, 208.
25. Brün, *Stalks and Trees and Drops and Clouds*, performance notes.
26. Brün, *Stalks and Trees and Drops and Clouds*, performance notes.
27. Brün, *Stalks and Trees and Drops and Clouds*, performance notes.
28. Otte, "At Loose Ends with Anticommunication," 41.

CHAPTER 7. ELECTRONIC MUSIC

1. Luening, "Origins," 2.
2. Griffiths, *Modern Music*, 31.
3. Holmes, *Electronic and Experimental Music*, 66.
4. Holmes, *Electronic and Experimental Music*, 103.
5. Mumma, "Live-Electronic Music," 292.
6. Davis, "Electronic Music," 215.
7. Shreffler, "Varèse and the Technological Sublime," 291.
8. Edgard Varèse, "The Liberation of Sound," 200.
9. Chandra, ed., *When Music Resists Meaning*, 164.
10. Boulez, "Catalogue 154," 334.
11. Schrader, *Introduction to Electro-Acoustic Music*, 163.
12. Ciamaga, "The Tape Studio," 113.
13. Wörner, *Stockhausen: Life and Work*, 54.
14. Stockhausen, *Mikrophonie I*, score, 11.
15. Ernst, *The Evolution of Electronic Music*, 166.
16. Stockhausen, *Mikrophonie I*, 9.
17. Zahler, "Mario Davidovsky."
18. Zahler, "Mario Davidovsky."
19. Schrader, *Introduction to Electro-Acoustic Music*, 165.
20. Salzman, *Twentieth-Century Music*, 140.
21. Holmes, *Electronic and Experimental Music*, 37.
22. Holmes, *Electronic and Experimental Music*, 131.
23. Steven Everett, email to the author, January 13, 2016.
24. Steven Everett, email to the author, January 13, 2016.
25. Steven Everett, email to the author, January 13, 2016.
26. Crawford, *America's Musical Life*, 702.

CHAPTER 8. MUSIC-THEATER

1. Salzman and Desi, *New Music Theater,* 5.
2. Introduction to Partch, *Bitter Music,* xviii.
3. Partch, *Genesis of a Music,* vii.
4. Partch, *Genesis of a Music,* vii.
5. Partch, *Genesis of a Music,* 7.
6. Granade, *Harry Partch, Hobo Composer,* 277.
7. Partch, *Genesis of a Music,* 6.
8. Partch, *Genesis of a Music,* 324.
9. Partch, *Genesis of a Music,* xviii.
10. Partch, *Genesis of a Music,* 276.
11. Partch, *Genesis of a Music,* 296.
12. Partch, *Genesis of a Music,* 350.
13. Partch, *Genesis of a Music,* 321.
14. Partch, *Genesis of a Music,* 321.
15. Partch, *Genesis of a Music,* 321–322.
16. Residencies included: University of Wisconsin, Madison (1944–1947); Mills College (1951–1952); University of Illinois, Urbana–Champaign (1956–1957 and 1959–1962).
17. Partch, *Bitter Music,* xx.
18. Johnston, an interview by Cole Gagne and Tracy Caras, 254.
19. Johnston, "The Genesis of *Knocking Piece,*" 25–31.
20. Johnston, "The Genesis of *Knocking Piece,*" 27.
21. Johnston, "The Genesis of *Knocking Piece,*" 28.
22. Johnston, "The Genesis of *Knocking Piece,*" 28–29.
23. Attinello, "Mauricio Kagel."
24. Heile, *The Music of Mauricio Kagel,* 14–15.
25. Heile, *The Music of Mauricio Kagel,* 16.
26. Attinello, "Mauricio Kagel."
27. Heile, *The Music of Mauricio Kagel,* 47.
28. Heile, *The Music of Mauricio Kagel,* 71.
29. Heile, *The Music of Mauricio Kagel,* 37.
30. Heile, *The Music of Mauricio Kagel,* 33.
31. Salzman and Desi, *New Music Theater,* 147.
32. Stockhausen, *Musik im Bauch,* score, xix.
33. Maconie, *The Works of Karlheinz Stockhausen,* 245–246.
34. Victor Hugo, *Les Misérables* (New York: Signet Classics, 2013), 1187.
35. Huang, "Percussion Theater," 140.
36. Udow, *Understanding,* score note.
37. Benjamin Toth, Unpublished interview with Michael Udow, 1985.

CHAPTER 9. SONORISM

1. Shultis, "No Ear for Music," 91.

2. Tompkins, *Composing the Party Line*, 4.
3. Thomas, "Serocki."
4. Steinitz, "George Crumb."
5. Crumb, *Music for a Summer Evening*, liner notes.
6. Crumb, *Music for a Summer Evening*, liner notes.
7. Donal Henahan, "George Crumb," *New York Times Magazine*, May 11, 1975, 59.
8. Crumb, *Music for a Summer Evening*, liner notes.
9. Taruskin, *Music in the Late Twentieth Century*, 423–424.
10. Marta Ptaszynska, Excerpts from the Paderewski Lecture, October 14, 2005, Los Angeles, http//www.martaptaszynska.com.
11. Ptaszynska, Excerpts from the Paderewski Lecture.
12. Ptaszynska, *Siderals*, score.
13. Ptaszynska, *Siderals*, score.

CHAPTER 10. MINIMALISM

1. Ross, *The Rest Is Noise*, 492.
2. Riley, Interview with Duckworth, 266.
3. Reich, Interview with Duckworth, 296.
4. Riley, Interview with Duckworth, 272.
5. Reich, Interview with Duckworth, 294.
6. Reich, Interview with Cole Gagne and Tracy Caras, 311.
7. Hoek, *Steve Reich: A Bio-Bibliography*, 10.
8. Reich, *Drumming*, score performance notes.
9. Reich, *Drumming*, score performance notes.
10. Steve Reich, "Music as a Gradual Process," in *Anti-Illusion: Procedures/Materials*, exhibition catalogue (New York: Whitney Museum of American Art, 1969), 56–57.
11. Reich, "Music as Gradual Process," 35.
12. Kam, "Repetition and the Drift towards Constant Focus," 14.
13. Reich, "Music as a Gradual Process," 35.
14. Reich, "Music as a Gradual Process," 35.
15. Reich, "Music as a Gradual Process," 36.
16. Reich, "Thoughts on Percussion and Rhythm," 177.
17. Strickland, "Philip Glass."
18. Taruskin, *Music in the Late Twentieth Century*, 389.
19. Glass, Interview with Duckworth, 330.
20. Beyer, *The Voice of Music*, 124.
21. Hansen, "Waves, Hierarchies, Interferences," 107.
22. Nørgård, *Waves*, 1.
23. Hansen, "Waves, Hierarchies, Interferences," 110.
24. Polansky and Winter, "James Tenney."
25. Tenney, *Having Never Written a Note for Percussion*, score.
26. Knapp, "Hocket," 378.
27. Taruskin, *Music in the Late Twentieth Century*, 396.

CHAPTER II. THE SOLO PERCUSSIONIST—CENTER STAGE

1. Schick, *The Percussionist's Art*, xi.

2. Bump, "Genesis and Early Development of a Literature for Solo Timpani," 72–73.

3. See chapter 4 for Kraft's biography.

4. Kraft, *Concerto for Timpani and Orchestra*, note by the composer.

5. The NACWPI was founded at the University of Michigan in 1951; PAS published *The Percussionist* beginning in 1963.

6. Qtd. in Patrick Wilson, "Elliott Carter: *Eight Pieces for Four Timpani*," 65.

7. Williams, "Elliot Carter's 'Eight Pieces for Timpani'—The 1966 Revisions,"14.

8. Altmire, "Time Travel," 56.

9. Taruskin, *Music in the Late Twentieth Century*, 275.

10. Altmire, "Time Travel," 78.

11. Hanuš, *Concertino for Timpani and Tape*, inside cover.

12. Cahn, "The Xylophone in Acoustic Recordings," 134.

13. Cahn, "The Xylophone in Acoustic Recordings," 134.

14. Cahn, "The Xylophone in Acoustic Recordings," 135.

15. Goto, "Yoichi Hiraoka," 14.

16. Hovhaness, *Fantasy on Japanese Wood Prints*, inside cover.

17. Hovhaness, *Fantasy on Japanese Wood Prints*, inside cover.

18. Kastner, "The Emergence and Evolution of a Generalized Marimba Technique," 9.

19. Eyler, "The History and Development of the Marimba Ensemble," 96.

20. Kastner, "The Emergence and Evolution of a Generalized Marimba Technique," 15.

21. Fink, "An Interview with Jack Connor, Marimba Virtuoso," 26.

22. Kastner, "Creston, Milhaud, Kurka," 84.

23. Kastner, "Creston, Milhaud, Kurka," 84.

24. Chenoweth, "Pioneering the Marimba," 2.

25. Strain, "Vida Chenoweth," 8.

26. Kastner, "Creston, Milhaud, Kurka," 85.

27. Jay Harrison, Review of Kurka's "Marimba Concerto," *New York Herald Tribune*, November 12, 1959.

28. Strain, "Vida Chenoweth," 8.

29. Wade, *Composing Japanese Musical Modernity*, 213.

30. Kanazawa, "Japan: Music in the Period of Westernization," 885.

31. Holm, "The Common Voice from Japan," 40.

32. Yasuko Claremont, *The Novels of Oe Kenzaburo* (London: Routledge, 2009), 99.

33. Takemitsu, *Rain Tree*, score, 5.

34. Deane, *Mourning Dove Sonnet*, score.

35. Deane, *Mourning Dove Sonnet*, score.

36. Deane, *Mourning Dove Sonnet*, score.

37. Welsh, *The Music of Stuart Saunders Smith*, xxvii.

38. Welsh, *The Music of Stuart Saunders Smith*, xxvii.

39. Welsh, *The Music of Stuart Saunders Smith*, xxxv.
40. Welsh, *The Music of Stuart Saunders Smith*, 240.
41. Qtd. in Welsh, *The Music of Stuart Saunders Smith*, 244.
42. Lesnik, "Henri Tomasi: *Concert Asiatique*," 62.
43. Lesnik, "Henri Tomasi: *Concert Asiatique*," 64.
44. Macmillan, *Veni, Veni, Emmanuel*, score.
45. Rouse, *Der gerettete Alberich*, score.

EPILOGUE

1. John Adams, "The Zen of Silence," Review of *Begin Again: A Biography of John Cage*, by Kenneth Silverman, *New York Times Book Review*, November 21, 2010, 17.
2. Qtd. in Brown, *Chance and Circumstance*, 224.
3. Heile, *The Music of Mauricio Kagel*, 37.
4. Duckworth, *Talking Music*, 304.
5. Leonard B. Meyer, *Music, the Arts, and Ideas*.
6. Taruskin, *Music in the Late Twentieth Century*, 473.

BIBLIOGRAPHY

Aguilar, Gustavo. "Not Knowing, the Cart Got in Front." In *The Modern Percussion Revolution: Journeys of the Progressive Artist,* edited by Kevin Lewis and Gustavo Aguilar, 3–17. New York: Routledge, 2014.

Altmire, Matthew D. "Time Travel: Musical Metrics in Elliott Carter's *Eight Pieces for Four Timpani.*" DMA thesis, UCLA, 2013.

Antheil, George. *Bad Boy of Music.* Garden City, NY: Doubleday, Doran, and Company, 1945. Reprint. New York: Da Capo Press, 1981.

Arias, Enrique Alberto. "Alexander Tcherepnin." In *The New Grove Dictionary of Music and Musicians,* edited by Stanley Sadie and John Tyrrell, Vol. 25: 186–187. 2nd ed. London: Macmillan, 2001.

Arias, Enrique Alberto. "The Symphonies of Alexander Tcherepnin." *Tempo* 158 (1986): 23–31.

Attinello, Paul. "Mauricio Kagel." In *Grove Music Online,* edited by Deane Root. Accessed August 10, 2017. http://www.oxfordmusiconline.com.

Austin, William W. *Music in the 20th Century: From Debussy through Stravinsky.* New York: W. W. Norton, 1966.

Baker, Don Russell. "The Percussion Ensemble Music of Lou Harrison: 1939–1942." DMA thesis, University of Illinois at Urbana-Champaign, 1985.

Bandur, Markus. *Aesthetics of Total Serialism.* Basel: Birkhäuser, 2001.

Barraud, Henry. "France." In *Dictionary of Contemporary Music,* edited by John Vinton. New York: E. P. Dutton, 1974.

Barzun, Jacques. *From Dawn to Decadence.* New York: HarperCollins, 2000.

Beal, Amy C. "How Johanna Beyer Spent Her Days." Web-published essay draft (2007; rev. 2011): 1–46: http://music.ucsc.edu/faculty/amy-beal.

Beal, Amy C. *New Music, New Allies.* Berkeley: University of California Press, 2006.

Beck, John, ed. *Encyclopedia of Percussion.* New York: Garland Publications, 1995.

Bennett, Mark Stephen. "A Brief History of Minimalism: Its Aesthetic Concepts and Origins and a Detailed Analysis of Steve Reich's *The Desert Music.*" DMA thesis, University of Illinois at Urbana–Champaign, 1993.

Berman, Mitchell Alan. "Gerald Strang: Composer, Educator, Acoustician." Master's thesis, California State University, Long Beach, 1977.

Bernard, Jonathan W. *The Music of Edgard Varèse.* New Haven: Yale University Press, 1987.

Bernard, Jonathan W. "Varèse's Space, Varèse's Time." In *Edgard Varèse: Composer, Sound Sculptor, Visionary,* edited by Felix Meyer and Heidy Zimmermann, 149–155. Woodbridge, UK: Boydell Press, 2006.

Beyer, Anders. *The Voice of Music: Conversations with Composers of Our Time.* Edited and translated by Jean Christensen and Anders Beyer. Aldershot, UK: Ashgate Publishing, 2000.

Blades, James. *Percussion Instruments and Their History.* New York: Praeger, 1970.

Blatter, Alfred. *Instrumentation/Orchestration.* New York: Longman, 1980.

Borio, Gianmario. "A Strange Phenomenon: Varèse's Influence on the European Avant-Garde." In *Edgard Varèse: Composer, Sound Sculptor, Visionary,* edited by Felix Meyer and Heidy Zimmermann, 361–370. Woodbridge, UK: Boydell Press, 2006.

Boulez, Pierre. "Catalogue 154." In *Edgard Varèse: Composer, Sound Sculptor, Visionary,* edited by Felix Meyer and Heidy Zimmermann, 334. Woodbridge, UK: Boydell Press, 2006.

Boulez, Pierre. "Utopia and Reality." In *Edgard Varèse: Composer, Sound Sculptor, Visionary,* edited by Felix Meyer and Heidy Zimmermann, 470–471. Woodbridge, UK: Boydell Press, 2006.

Brant, Henry. Interview with Cole Gagne and Tracy Caras. In *Soundpieces: Interviews with American Composers,* 53–68. Metuchen, NJ: Scarecrow Press, 1982.

Brant, Henry. Program notes for the premiere of *Symphony for Percussion.* Lincoln Hall, Urbana, Illinois, University of Illinois Percussion Ensemble, Paul Price, conductor, March 13, 1956. UIUC Music Library archives (780.73 ILIM).

Brown, Carolyn. *Chance and Circumstance: Twenty Years with Cage and Cunningham.* New York: Alfred A. Knopf, 2007.

Broyles, Michael. *Mavericks and Other Traditions in American Music.* New Haven: Yale University Press, 2004.

Bump, Michael R. "The Genesis and Early Development of a Literature for Solo Timpani through the Early Nineteenth Century." DMA research project, University of Illinois at Urbana–Champaign, 2001.

Cage, John. *Silence: Lectures and Writings.* Middletown, CT: Wesleyan University Press, 1961.

Cahn, William L. "The Xylophone in Acoustic Recordings (1877–1929)." *Percussionist* 16, no. 3 (Spring/Summer 1979): 133–152.

Carpentier, Alejo. *Music in Cuba.* Minneapolis: University of Minnesota Press, 2001.

Chandra, Arun, ed. *When Music Resists Meaning: The Major Writings of Herbert Brün.* Middletown, CT: Wesleyan University Press, 2004.

Chávez, Carlos. *Toward a New Music.* New York: Da Capo Press, 1975.

Chenoweth, Vida. "Pioneering the Marimba." *Percussive Notes* 3, no. 2 (December 1964): 1–3.

Childs, Barney. "Indeterminancy." In *Dictionary of Contemporary Music,* edited by John Vinton, 336–339. New York: E. P. Dutton, 1974.

Ciamaga, Gustav. "The Tape Studio." In *The Development and Practice of Electronic Music,* edited by Jon H. Appleton and Ronald C. Perera, 68–137. Englewood Cliffs, NJ: Prentice-Hall, 1975.

Clarkson, Austin. "The Varèse Effect: New York City in the 1950s and 60s." In *Edgard Varèse: Composer, Sound Sculptor, Visionary,* edited by Felix Meyer and Heidy Zimmermann, 371–381. Woodbridge, UK: Boydell Press, 2006.

Cohen, Selma Jeanne, ed. *Doris Humphrey: An Artist First.* Pennington, NJ: Princeton Book Co., 1972.

Colgrass, Michael. *Michael Colgrass: Adventures of an American Composer.* Galesville, MD: Meredith Music Publications, 2010.

Colgrass, Michael. "Small Essay on My Early Percussion Music." *Percussive Notes* 34, no. 4 (August 1996): 70–72.

Collaer, Paul. *Darius Milhaud.* San Francisco: San Francisco Press, 1988.

Conklin, M. Christine. "An Annotated Catalogue of Published Marimba Concertos in the United States from 1940–2000." DMA thesis, University of Oklahoma, 2004.

Cope, David H. *New Directions in Music.* 5th ed. Dubuque, IA: Wm. C. Brown, 1989.

Copland, Aaron. "America's Young Men of Promise." *Modern Music* 3, no. 3 (March–April 1926): 13–20.

Copland, Aaron. *Our New Music.* New York: McGraw-Hill, 1941.

Coulter, Ron. "Forgotten Percussion Works: Johanna Magdalena Beyer." *Percussive Notes Online Research Edition* 1, no. 1(December 2016): 5–23.

Cowell, Henry. "Drums along the Pacific." *Modern Music* 18, no. 1 (November–December 1940): 46–49.

Cowell, Henry. "Roldán and Caturla of Cuba." *Modern Music* 18, no. 2 (1941): 98–99.

Crawford, Richard. *America's Musical Life: A History.* New York: W. W. Norton, 2001.

Craycraft, Jeremy L. "William Russell's Percussion Music, 1931–1940." DMA thesis, University of Cincinnati, 2011.

Crumb, George. *Music for a Summer Evening (Makrokosmos I & II).* Nonesuch H-71311 (1975), liner notes.

Daehlin, Vera. "Clair Omar Musser." *Percussive Notes* 37, no. 2 (April 1999): 6–17.

Danuser, Hermann. "The Varèse Myth." In *Edgard Varèse: Composer, Sound Sculptor, Visionary,* edited by Felix Meyer and Heidy Zimmermann, 418–425. Woodbridge, UK: Boydell Press. 2006.

Davis, Hugh. "Electronic Music: History and Development." In *Dictionary of Contemporary Music,* edited by John Vinton, 212–216. New York: E. P. Dutton, 1974.

De la Motte-Haber, Helga. "Blurred Traces: Varèse's Years in Berlin." In *Edgard Varèse: Composer, Sound Sculptor, Visionary*, edited by Felix Meyer and Heidy Zimmermann, 35–43. Woodbridge, UK: Boydell Press. 2006.

DeLio, Thomas. *Circumscribing the Open Universe.* Lanham, MD: University Press of America, 1984.

Dodge, Stephen W. "The Concerto pour batterie et petit orchestre." *Percussive Notes* 17, no. 3 (Spring–Summer 1979): 58–59.

Emmerson, Simon. "Xenakis," *Music and Musicians* 24, no. 9 (May 1976): 24–26.

Ernst, David. *The Evolution of Electronic Music.* New York: Schirmer Books, 1977.

Eyler, David P. "Cantata para América Mágica." *Percussive Notes* 17, no. 1 (Fall 1978): 30–31.

Eyler, David P. "The History and Development of the Marimba Ensemble in the United States and Its Current Status in College and University Percussion Programs." DMA thesis, Louisiana State University, 1985.

Feisst, Sabine. "Varèse and His New York Choruses." In *Edgard Varèse: Composer, Sound Sculptor, Visionary*, edited by Felix Meyer and Heidy Zimmermann, 257–263. Woodbridge, UK: Boydell Press. 2006.

Fink, Ron. "An Interview with Jack Connor, Marimba Virtuoso." *Percussive Notes* 16, no. 2 (Winter 1978): 26–27.

Flint, Ellen Rennie. "Metabolae, Arborescences, and the Reconstruction of Time in Iannis Xenakis' *Psappha.*" *Contemporary Music Review* 7 (1993): 221–248.

François, Jean-Charles. "Organization of Scattered Timbral Qualities: A Look at Edgard Varèse's *Ionisation.*" *Perspectives of New Music* 29, no. 1 (Winter 1991): 48–79.

Gann, Kyle. "'Magnificent in a Mysterious Way': Varèse's Impact on American Music." In *Edgard Varèse: Composer, Sound Sculptor, Visionary*, edited by Felix Meyer and Heidy Zimmermann, 426–432. Woodbridge, UK: Boydell Press, 2006.

Gann, Kyle. *No Such Thing as Silence*. New Haven: Yale University Press, 2010.

Gillespie, Dan, and Donel Young. "William Russell: An American Original." *Ear Magazine of New Music* 15, no. 5 (June 1990): 40–45.

Glass, Philip. Interview with William Duckworth. In *Talking Music*, 318–342. New York: Schirmer Books, 1995.

Gordon, Ingrid Crete. "Drums along the Pacific: The Influence of Asian Music on the Early Percussion Ensemble Music of Henry Cowell, John Cage, and Lou Harrison." DMA thesis, University of Illinois at Urbana–Champaign, 2000.

Goto, Akiko Iino. "Yoichi Hiraoka: His Artistic Life and His Influence on the Art of Xylophone Performance." DMA thesis, University of North Texas, 2013.

Granade, S. Andrew. *Harry Partch, Hobo Composer.* Rochester, NY: University of Rochester Press, 2014.

Grant, M. J. *Serial Music, Serial Aesthetics*. Cambridge: Cambridge University Press, 2001.

Griffiths, Paul. *Modern Music: The Avant Garde since 1945*. New York: George Braziller, 1981.

Hall, John Richard. "Development of the Percussion Ensemble through the Contributions of the Latin American Composers Amadeo Roldán, José Ardévol, Carlos Chávez, and Alberto Ginastera." DMA thesis, Ohio State University, 2008.

Hansen, Ivan. "Waves, Hierarchies, Interferences: Per Nørgård and Percussion Music." In *The Music of Per Nørgård: Fourteen Interpretive Essays*, edited by Anders Beyer, 107–125. Aldershot, UK: Scolar Press, 1996.

Harley, James. *Xenakis: His Life In Music.* New York: Routledge, 2004.

Harley, Maria Anna. "An American in Space: Henry Brant's 'Spatial Music.'" *American Music* 15, no. 1 (Spring 1997): 70–92.

Harrison, Lou. *Lou Harrison's Music Primer.* New York: C. F. Peters, 1971.

Heile, Björn. *The Music of Mauricio Kagel.* Aldershot, UK: Ashgate Publishing, 2006.

Hitchcock, Wiley. "Henry Cowell's Ostinato Pianissimo." *Musical Quarterly* 70, no. 1 (Winter 1984): 23–44.

Hoek, D. J. *Steve Reich: A Bio-Bibliography.* Westport, CT: Greenwood Press, 2002.

Holm, Matthew. "The Common Voice from Japan: A Performance Guide and Examination of the Three Unaccompanied Pieces Performed by Keiko Abe on October 4th, 1968." DMA research paper, Arizona State University, 2016.

Holmes, Thom. *Electronic and Experimental Music.* 5th ed. New York: Routledge, 2016.

Horowitz, Joseph. *Artists in Exile: How Refugees from Twentieth-Century War and Revolution Transformed the American Performing Arts.* New York: HarperCollins, 2008.

Horowitz, Joseph. *Classical Music in America: A History of Its Rise and Fall.* New York: W. W. Norton, 2005.

Hovhaness, Alan. "The Alan Hovhaness Website." Accessed December 6, 2017. http://www.hovhaness.com.

Huang, Aiyun. "Percussion Theater." In *The Cambridge Companion to Percussion*, edited by R. Hartenberger, 128–142. Cambridge: Cambridge University Press, 2016.

Humes, Edward. *Over Here: How the G.I. Bill Transformed the American Dream.* Orlando, FL: Harcourt, 2006.

Johnson, Steven. "Morton Feldman." In *Grove Music Online*, edited by Deane Root. Accessed August 10, 2017. http://www.oxfordmusiconline.com.

Johnston, Ben. "The Genesis of *Knocking Piece*." *Percussive Notes Research Edition* 21, no. 3 (March 1983): 25–31.

Johnston, Ben. "Harry Partch." In *Dictionary of Contemporary Music*, edited by John Vinton, 555–556. New York: E. P. Dutton, 1974.

Johnston, Ben. Interview by Cole Gagne and Tracy Caras. In *Soundpieces: Interviews with American Composers*, 249–267. Metuchen, NJ: Scarecrow Press, 1982.

Jones, David Evan. "Text and Music in Luciano Berio's *Circles*." *Ex Tempore* 4, no. 2 (1987): 108–114.

Judt, Tony. *Postwar: A History of Europe since 1945.* New York: Penguin Press, 2005.

Kam, Dennis Koon Ming. "Repetition and the Drift towards Constant Focus in the Pattern-Pulse Works of Terry Riley and Steve Reich." DMA thesis, University of Illinois at Urbana–Champaign, 1974.

Kanazawa, Masakata. "Japan: Music in the Period of Westernization." In *The New Grove Dictionary of Music and Musicians*, edited by Stanley Sadie and John Tyrrell, Vol. 12, 884–890. 2nd ed. London: Macmillan, 2001.

Kastner, Kathleen S. "Creston, Milhaud, Kurka: An Examination of the Marimba Concerti." *Percussive Notes*, 32, no. 4 (August 1994): 83–87.

Kastner, Kathleen S. "The Emergence and Evolution of a Generalized Marimba Technique." DMA thesis, University of Illinois at Urbana–Champaign, 1989.

Kelly, Barbara L. "André Jolivet." In *Grove Music Online*, edited by Deane Root. Accessed December 3, 2017. http://www.oxfordmusiconline.com.

Kennedy, John, and Larry Polansky. "'Total Eclipse': The Music of Johanna M. Beyer: An Introduction and Preliminary Annotated Checklist." *Musical Quarterly* 80, no. 4 (Winter 1996): 719–778.

Kernan, Thomas J. "What of the Performers?" In *The Modern Percussion Revolution: Journeys of the Progressive Artist*, edited by Kevin Lewis and Gustavo Aguilar, 18–37. New York: Routledge, 2014.

Knaack, Donald. *The Bride Stripped Bare by Her Bachelors, Even. Erratum Musical* by Marcel Duchamp. Finnadar Records, SR9017, 1977, liner notes.

Knapp, Janet. "Hocket." In *The New Harvard Dictionary of Music*, edited by Don Michael Randall, 378–379. Cambridge, MA: Belknap Press of Harvard University Press, 1986.

Korabelnikova, Ludmila. *Alexander Tcherepnin: The Saga of a Russian Emigré Composer.* Bloomington: Indiana University Press, 2008.

Kostelanetz, Richard. *Dictionary of the Avant-Gardes.* Chicago: A Cappella Books, 1993.

Kramer, Jonathan D. "Stockhausen." In *Dictionary of Contemporary Music*, edited by John Vinton, 709–711. New York: E. P. Dutton, 1974.

Kraft, William. "Igor Stravinsky." *Notes*, 2nd ser., 46, no. 1 (September 1989): 212–216.

Krenek, Ernst. "Serialism." In *Dictionary of Contemporary Music*, edited by John Vinton, 670–674. New York: E. P. Dutton, 1974.

Kropfinger, Klaus. "You Never Took the Simple Path." In *Edgard Varèse: Composer, Sound Sculptor, Visionary*, edited by Felix Meyer and Heidy Zimmermann, 156–163. Woodbridge, UK: Boydell Press, 2006.

Lang, Morris. "A Journey to the Source on *L'Histoire du Soldat*." *Percussionist* 12, no. 2 (Winter 1975): 50–54.

Lendvai, Ernö. *Béla Bartók: An Analysis of His Music.* London: Kahn and Averill, 2009.

Lesnik, Igor. "Darius Milhaud's Concerto for Percussion." *Percussive Notes* 35, no. 2 (April 1997): 64–67.

Lesnik, Igor. "Henri Tomasi: *Concert Asiatique*." *Percussive Notes* 34, no. 6 (December 1996): 62–65.

Lichtenfeld, Monika, and Reinhard Kager. "Roman Haubenstock-Ramati." *Grove Music Online*, edited by Deane Root. Accessed April 15, 2017. http://www.oxfordmusiconline.com.

Lichtenhahn, Ernst. "'A New Primitiveness': Varèse's *Ecuatorial* in Its Parisian Surroundings." In *Edgard Varèse: Composer, Sound Sculptor, Visionary*, edited by Felix Meyer and Heidy Zimmermann, 193–201. Woodbridge, UK: Boydell Press, 2006.

Luening, Otto. "Origins." In *The Development and Practice of Electronic Music*, edited by Jon H. Appleton and Ronald C. Perera, 1–21. Englewood Cliffs, NJ: Prentice-Hall, 1975.

MacDonald, Malcolm. *Varèse: Astronomer in Sound.* London: Kahn and Averill, 2006.

Maconie, Robin. *The Works of Karlheinz Stockhausen.* Oxford: Clarendon Press, 1990.

Marcuse, Sibyl. *Musical Instruments: A Comprehensive Dictionary.* New York: Doubleday, 1964.

Mawer, Deborah. *Darius Milhaud: Modality and Structure in Music of the 1920s.* Aldershot, UK: Scolar Press, 1997.

Mead, Rita H. *Henry Cowell's New Music, 1925–1936: The Society, the Music Editions, and the Recordings.* Ann Arbor: UMI Research Press, 1981.

Meyer, Felix. "'The Exhilarating Atmosphere of Struggle': Varèse as a Communicator of Modern Music in the 1920s." In *Edgard Varèse: Composer, Sound Sculptor, Visionary,* edited by Felix Meyer and Heidy Zimmermann, 82–91. Woodbridge, UK: Boydell Press, 2006.

Meyer, Leonard B. *Music, the Arts, and Ideas: Patterns and Predictions in Twentieth Century Culture.* Chicago: University of Chicago Press, 1967.

Milhaud, Darius. *Notes without Music: An Autobiography.* New York: Alfred A. Knopf, 1953.

Miller, Leta E. "The Art of Noise: John Cage, Lou Harrison, and the West Coast Percussion Ensemble." In *Perspectives on American Music, 1900–1950,* edited by Michael Saffle, 215–263. New York: Garland Publishing, 2000.

Miller, Leta E. "Cultural Intersections: John Cage in Seattle (1938–1940)." In *John Cage: Music, Philosophy, and Intention, 1933–1950,* edited by David W. Patterson, 47–82. New York: Routledge, 2002.

Miller, Leta E. "Henry Cowell and John Cage: Intersections and Influences, 1933–1941." *Journal of the American Musicological Society* 59, no. 1 (Spring 2006): 47–111.

Miller, Leta E., and Fredric Lieberman. *Lou Harrison: Composing a World.* New York: Oxford University Press, 1998.

Morgan, Robert D. *Twentieth-Century Music: A History of Musical Style in Modern Europe and America.* New York: W. W. Norton, 1991.

Mumma, Gordon. "Live-Electronic Music." In *The Development and Practice of Electronic Music,* edited by Jon H. Appleton and Ronald C. Perera, 286–335. Englewood Cliffs, NJ: Prentice-Hall, 1975.

Myers, Rollo. *Modern French Music: From Fauré to Boulez.* New York: Praeger Publishers, 1971.

Nicholls, David. "Toward Infinity: Cage in the 1950s and 1960s." In *The Cambridge Companion to John Cage,* edited by David Nicholls, 100–108. Cambridge: Cambridge University Press, 2002.

Oja, Carol J. *Making Music Modern: New York in the 1920s.* New York: Oxford University Press, 2000.

Oliver, Daniel. "Hovhaness: In and Out of Our Time." *Saturday Review of Literature,* February 22, 1958, 42–43.

O'Neill, John C. "Recent Trends in Percussion Notation." *Percussive Notes Research Edition* 18, no. 1 (Fall 1980): 20–55.

Orovio, Helio. *Cuban Music from A to Z.* Durham, NC: Duke University Press, 2004.

Osmond-Smith, David. *Berio.* New York: Oxford University Press, 1991.

Otte, Allen. "At Loose Ends with Anticommunication." In *The Modern Percussion Revolution: Journeys of the Progressive Artist,* edited by Kevin Lewis and Gustavo Aguilar, 38–44. New York: Routledge, 2014.

Parker, Robert L. *Carlos Chávez: Mexico's Modern-Day Orpheus.* Boston: Twayne Publishers, 1983.

Partch, Harry. *Bitter Music: Collected Journals, Essays, Introductions, and Librettos.* Edited with an introduction by Thomas McGeary. Urbana–Champaign: University of Illinois Press, 1991.

Partch, Harry. *Genesis of a Music: An Account of a Creative Work, Its Roots, and Its Fulfillments.* 2nd ed. New York: Da Capo Press, 1974.

Patterson, David W. *John Cage: Music, Philosophy, and Intention, 1933–1950.* New York: Routledge Publishing, 2002.

Pauli, Hansjörg. "Austria and Germany." In *Dictionary of Contemporary Music,* edited by John Vinton, translated by James Rogers, 33–41. New York: E. P. Dutton, 1974.

Peters, Gordon B. "Treatise on Percussion." MA thesis, Eastman School of Music of the University of Rochester, 1962.

Polansky, Larry, and Michael Winter. "James Tenney." In *Grove Music Online,* edited by Deane Root. Accessed August 10, 2017. http://www.oxfordmusiconline.com.

Price, Paul. "The Emancipation of Percussion." *Music Journal* 17, no. 7 (October 1959): 26.

Price, Paul. "The Exciting World of Percussion." *Hi-Fi Stereo Review* 6, no. 4 (April 1961): 44–48.

Pritchett, James. "John Cage." In *The New Grove Dictionary of Music and Musicians,* edited by Stanley Sadie and John Tyrrell, Vol. 4, 796–804. 2nd ed. London: Macmillan, 2001.

Pritchett, James. *The Music of John Cage.* Cambridge: Cambridge University Press, 1993.

Rae, Caroline. "Marius Constant." In *Grove Music Online,* edited by Deane Root. Accessed April 15, 2017. http://www.oxfordmusiconline.com.

Rae, Caroline. *The Music of Maurice Ohana.* Aldershot, UK: Ashgate, 2000.

Rathert, Wolfgang. "Worlds without End: *Amériques.*" In *Edgard Varèse: Composer, Sound Sculptor, Visionary,* edited by Felix Meyer and Heidy Zimmermann, 132–141. Woodbridge, UK: Boydell Press, 2006.

Ravenscroft, Brenda. "Working Out the 'Is-Tos and As-Tos': Lou Harrison's *Fugue for Percussion.*" *Perspectives of New Music* 38, no. 1 (Winter 2000): 25–43.

Reich, Steve. Interview with Cole Gagne and Tracy Caras. In *Soundpieces: Interviews with American Composers,* 306–317. Metuchen, NJ: Scarecrow Press, 1982.

Reich, Steve. Interview with William Duckworth. In *Talking Music,* 290–317. New York: Schirmer Books, 1995.

Reich, Steve. "Music as a Gradual Process." In *Writings on Music, 1965–2000,* edited by Paul Hillier, 34–36. New York: Oxford University Press, 2002.

Reich, Steve. "Thoughts on Percussion and Rhythm." In *The Cambridge Companion to Percussion,* edited by Russell Hartenberger, 173–183. Cambridge: Cambridge University Press, 2016.

Rich, Alan. *American Pioneers: Ives to Cage and Beyond.* London: Phaidon Press, 1995.

Riley, Terry. Interview with William Duckworth. In *Talking Music,* 266–289. New York: Schirmer Books, 1995.

Root, Deane Leslie. "The Performance Guilds of Edgard Varèse." MM thesis, University of Illinois Urbana–Champaign, 1971.

Rosen, Michael. "*Amériques* by Varèse." *Percussive Notes* 52, no. 6 (November 2014): 44–45.

Rosen, Michael. "The Milhaud Concerto pour batterie et petit orchestre." *Percussive Notes* 25, no. 2 (Winter 1987): 27–28.

Ross, Alex. *The Rest Is Noise: Listening to the Twentieth Century.* New York: Farrar, Straus and Giroux, 2007.

Ross, Alex. "Waveforms." *The New Yorker,* March 1, 2010, 78.

Rouse, Christopher. *Der gerettete Alberich.* www.christopherrouse.com.

Sachs, Joel. *Henry Cowell: A Man Made of Music.* New York: Oxford University Press, 2012.

Salzman, Eric. "Mixed Media." In *Dictionary of Contemporary Music,* edited by John Vinton, 489–492. New York: E. P. Dutton, 1974.

Salzman, Eric. *Twentieth-Century Music: An Introduction.* 2nd ed. Englewood Cliffs, NJ: Prentice-Hall, 1974.

Salzman, Eric, and Thomas Desi. *The New Music Theater: Seeing the Voice, Hearing the Body.* New York: Oxford University Press, 2008.

Saylor, Bruce, William Lichtenwanger, and Elizabeth A. Wright. "Henry Cowell." In *The New Grove Dictionary of American Music,* edited by H. Wiley Hitchcock, Vol. 1, 521–529. London: Macmillan, 1986.

Schick, Steven. *The Percussionist's Art: Same Bed, Different Dreams.* Rochester, NY: University of Rochester Press, 2006.

Schrader, Barry. *Introduction to Electro-Acoustic Music.* Englewood Cliffs, NJ: Prentice-Hall, 1982.

Schuller, Gunther. "Conversation with Edgard Varèse." *Perspectives of New Music* 3, no. 2 (1965): 32–37.

Schwartz-Kates, Deborah. "Alberto Ginastera." *In Grove Music Online,* edited by Deane Root. Accessed August 10, 2017. http://www.oxfordmusiconline.com.

Schwarz, K. Robert. "Steve Reich: Music as a Gradual Process, Part 1." *Perspectives of New Music* 19, no. 1–2 (Autumn 1980–Summer 1981): 373–392.

Sekhon, Baljinder Singh, II. "Percussion Composition: Genres and Compositional Techniques." PhD thesis, University of Rochester, 2013.

Shreffler, Anne C. "Varèse and the Technological Sublime; or, How *Ionisation* Went Nuclear." In *Edgard Varèse: Composer, Sound Sculptor, Visionary,* edited by Felix Meyer and Heidy Zimmermann, 290–297. Woodbridge, UK: Boydell Press, 2006.

Shultis, Christopher. "No Ear for Music: Timbre in the Early Percussion Music of John Cage." In *John Cage: Music, Philosophy, and Intention, 1933–1950,* edited by David W. Patterson, 83–104. New York: Routledge, 2002.

Shultis, Christopher. "The Process of Discovery: Interpreting *Child of Tree.*" *Contemporary Music Review* 33, nos. 5–6 (2014): 570–579.

Shultis, Christopher. *Silencing the Sounded Self: John Cage and the American Experimental Tradition.* Hanover, NH: University Press of New England, 2013.

Siwe, Thomas. "An Interview with Herbert Brün." *Percussive Notes Research Edition,* 22, no. 3 (1984): 1–12.

Siwe, Thomas. "Lou Harrison at the University of Illinois," *Percussive Notes* 18, no. 2 (1980): 30–33, 57–62.

Slonimsky, Nicolas. *Music of Latin America.* New York: Da Capo Press, 1972.

Slonimsky, Nicolas. *Music since 1900.* 3rd ed. New York: Coleman-Ross Company, 1949.

Slonimsky, Nicolas. *Perfect Pitch: A Life Story.* Oxford: Oxford University Press, 1988.

Stallings, Stephani N. "Collective Difference: The Pan-American Association of Composers and Pan-American Ideology in Music, 1925–1945." PhD thesis, Florida State University, 2009.

Steenhuisen, Paul. *Sonic Mosaics: Conversations with Composers.* Edmonton: University of Alberta Press, 2009.

Steinitz, Richard. "George Crumb." In *Grove Music Online,* edited by Deane Root. Accessed August 10, 2017. http://www.oxfordmusiconline.com.

Stenzl, Jürg. "Daily Life, Slavishly Imitated." In *Edgard Varèse: Composer, Sound Sculptor, Visionary,* edited by Felix Meyer and Heidy Zimmermann, 142–148. Woodbridge, UK: Boydell Press, 2006.

Stevens, Halsey. *The Life and Music of Béla Bartók.* Rev. ed. London: Oxford University Press, 1964. Page references are to the 1975 reprint edition.

Stone, Kurt. *Music Notation in the Twentieth Century: A Practical Guidebook.* New York: W. W. Norton, 1980.

Strain, James A. "Vida Chenoweth." *Percussive Notes* 32, no. 6 (December 1994): 8–9.

Strickland, Edward. "Philip Glass." In *Grove Music Online,* edited by Deane Root. Accessed December 3, 2017. http://www.oxfordmusiconline.com.

Taruskin, Richard. *Music in the Late Twentieth Century.* New York: Oxford University Press, 2010.

Taruskin, Richard. "No Ear for Music: The Scary Purity of John Cage." *The New Republic,* March 15, 1993, 26–35.

Thomas, Adrian. "Serocki." In *Grove Music Online,* edited by Deane Root. Accessed December 12, 2017. http://www.oxfordmusiconline.com.

Tisdall, Caroline, and Angelo Bozzolla. *Futurism.* New York: Oxford University Press, 1978.

Tomkins, Calvin. *The Bride and the Bachelors: Five Masters of the Avant Garde.* New York: Penguin Books, 1968.

Tompkins, David G. *Composing the Party Line: Music and Politics in Early Cold War Poland and East Germany.* West Lafayette, IN: Purdue University Press, 2013.

Varèse, Edgard. "The Liberation of Sound." In *Contemporary Composers on Contemporary Music,* edited by Elliott Schwartz and Barney Childs, 195–208. New York: Holt, Rinehart, and Winston, 1967.

Varèse, Louise. *Varèse: A Looking-Glass Diary,* Vol. 1: *1883–1928.* New York: W. W. Norton, 1972.

Varga, Bálint András. *Conversations with Iannis Xenakis.* London: Faber and Faber, 1996.

Vise, Sidney R. "Ray Green: His Life and Stylistic Elements of His Music from 1935–1962." DMA thesis, University of Missouri–Kansas City, 1975.

Vlad, Roman. *Stravinsky.* 2nd ed. London: Oxford University Press, 1967.

Von Glahn, Denise. "'Empty Spaces': The Conceptual Origins of *Déserts*." In *Edgard Varèse: Composer, Sound Sculptor, Visionary,* edited by Felix Meyer and Heidy Zimmermann, 298–308. Woodbridge, UK: Boydell Press, 2006.

Wade, Bonnie C. *Composing Japanese Musical Modernity.* Chicago: University of Chicago Press, 2014.

Welsh, John P. *The Music of Stuart Saunders Smith.* Westport, CT: Greenwood Press, 1995.

Welsh, John P. "The Secret Structure in Morton Feldman's *The King of Denmark* (1964) Part One." *Percussive Notes* 46, no. 2 (April 2008): 34–43.

Wen-chung, Chou. "*Ionisation*: The Function of Timbre in Its Formal and Temporal Organization." In *The New Worlds of Edgard Varèse: A Symposium,* edited by Sherman Van Solkema, 27–74. New York: Brooklyn College Institute for Studies in American Music, 1979.

Whitesitt, Linda. *The Life and Music of George Antheil, 1900–1959.* Ann Arbor: UMI Research Press, 1983.

Williams, Jan. "Elliott Carter's 'Eight Pieces for Timpani' The 1966 Revisions." *Percussive Notes* 38, no. 6 (December 2000): 8–17.

Williams, Jan. "An Interview with Morton Feldman." *Percussive Notes Research Edition* 21, no. 6 (September 1983): 4–14.

Wilson, Elizabeth. *Shostakovich: A Life Remembered.* London: Faber and Faber, 2006.

Wilson, Patrick. "Elliot Carter: *Eight Pieces for Four Timpani.*" *Percussive Notes* 23, no. 1 (October 1984): 63–65.

Wörner, Karl H. *Stockhausen: Life and Work.* Berkeley: University of California Press, 1973.

Wuorinen, Charles. Interview with Cole Gagne and Tracy Caras. In *Soundpieces: Interviews with American Composers,* 384–400. Metuchen, NJ: Scarecrow Press, 1982.

Zahler, Noel B. "Mario Davidovsky." In *Grove Music Online,* edited by Deane Root. Accessed July 11, 2017. http://www.oxfordmusiconline.com.

SCORES

Antheil, George. *Ballet mécanique*. Delaware Gap, PA: Templeton Pub., 1959.
Ardévol, José. *Estudio en forma de preludio y fuga*. Edwin A. Fleisher Music Collection, Free Library of Philadelphia.
Bartók, Béla. *Miraculous Mandarin*. New York: Boosey & Hawkes, 1955.
———. *Piano Concerto No. 1*. New York: Boosey & Hawkes, 1954.
———. *Sonata for Two Pianos and Percussion*. London: Boosey & Hawkes, 1942.
Berio, Luciano. *Circles*. London: Universal Edition, 1961.
Beyer, Johanna M. *IV*. 1936. Reprint. Sharon, VT: Smith Publications.
———. *Percussion Suite*. Lebanon, NH: Frog Peak Music, 2010.
———. *Three Movements for Percussion*. Lebanon, NH: Frog Peak Music, 2005.
Brant, Henry. *Symphony for Percussion*. King of Prussia, PA: Presser, 1952.
Brün, Herbert. *Stalks and Trees and Drops and Clouds*. Sharon, VT: Smith Publications, 1975.
Cage, John. *27′ 10.554″ for a Percussionist*. New York: Henmar Press, 1960.
———. *Child of Tree*. New York: Henmar Press, 1975.
———. *First Construction (in Metal)*. New York: C. F. Peters, 1962.
———. *Imaginary Landscape No. 3*. New York: Henmar Press, 1961.
Carter, Elliott. *Eight Pieces for Four Timpani*. New York: Associated Music Publishers, 1968.
Chávez, Carlos. *Tambuco*. New York: Mills Music, 1967.
———. *Toccata para instrumentos de percusión*. New York: Mills Music, 1954.
———. *Xochipilli*. New York: Mills Music, 1964.

Colgrass, Michael. *Chamber Piece for Percussion Quintet*. New York: Music for Percussion, 1962.
———. *Déjà vu*. New York: Carl Fischer, 1978.
———. *Hammer and Bow*. New York: Carl Fischer, 1999.
———. *Variations for Four Drums and Viola*. Indianapolis: Colla Voce Music, 1959.
Constant, Marius. *14 Stations*. Paris: Editions Salabert, 1971.
Cowell, Henry. *Ostinato Pianissimo*. San Francisco: New Music Editions, 1936.
———. *Pulse*. New York: Music for Percussion, 1971.
Creston, Paul. *Concertino for Marimba*. New York: G. Schirmer, 1949.
Crumb, George. *Makrokosmos III, Music for a Summer Evening*. New York: C. F. Peters, 1974.
Davidovsky, Mario. *Synchronism No. 5*. New York: Edward B. Marks, 1974.
Davidson, Harold G. *Auto Accident*. San Francisco: New Music Editions, 1936.
Deane, Christopher. *Mourning Dove Sonnet*. N.p.: Contemporary Music Project, 1983.
Drouet, Jean-Pierre. *Variations sur un texte de Victor Hugo*. Unpublished.
Everett, Steve. *Quiet Silence*. Unpublished.
Feldman, Morton. *The King of Denmark*. New York: C. F. Peters, 1965.
Ginastera, Alberto. *Cantata para América mágica*. London: Boosey & Hawkes, 1961.
Glass, Philip. *Prelude to End Game*. New York: Dunvagen Music Publisher, 1984.
Green, Ray. *Three Inventories of Casey Jones*. San Francisco: New Music Editions, 1936.
Hanuš, Jan. *Concertino for Timpani and Tape*. Hastings-on-Hudson, NY: General Music Pub., 1973.
Harrison, Lou. *Canticle No. 3*. New York: Music for Percussion, 1960.
———. *Fugue for Percussion*. New York: Music for Percussion, 1962.
Haubenstock-Ramati, Roman. *Liaisons*. London: Universal Editions, 1958.
Hovhaness, Alan. *Fantasy on Japanese Wood Prints*. New York: C. F. Peters, 1965.
———. *October Mountain*. New York: C. F. Peters, 1957.
Humphrey, Doris. *Dance Rhythms*. San Francisco: New Music Editions, 1936.
Ishii, Maki. *Marimbastück*. Tokyo: Zen-On Music, 1983.
Johnston, Ben. *Knocking Piece*. Sharon, VT: Smith Publications, 1962.
Jolivet, André. *Ceremonial*. Paris: Billaudot, 1970.
Kagel, Mauricio. *Dressur*. Frankfurt: Henry Litolff's Verlag, 1983.
———. *Match*. London: Universal Edition, 1967.
———. *Rrrrrr . . . : 6 Schlagzeug Duos*. Frankfurt: Henry Litolff's Verlag, 1985.
Kraft, William. *Concerto for Timpani and Orchestra*. King of Prussia, PA: Presser, 1983.
———. *Suite for Percussion*. New York: Mills Music, 1963.
Kurka, Robert. *Concerto for Marimba and Orchestra, Op. 34*. New York: Weintraub Music Co., 1960.
Macmillan, James. *Veni, Veni, Emmanuel*. London: Boosey & Hawkes, 1994.
Miki, Minoru. *Marimba Spiritual*. Tokyo: Ongaku No Tomo Sha Corp., 1985.
Milhaud, Darius. *Concerto pour marimba (et vibraphone) et orchestre*. Paris: Enoch et Cie, 1954.

———. *La Création du monde, Opus 81a*. Paris: Éditions Max Eschig, 1929.
Miyoshi, Akira. *Torse III in Modern Japanese Marimba Pieces 1*. Tokyo: Ongaku No Tomo Sha Corp., 1989.
Nørgård, Per. *Waves*. Copenhagen: Edition Wilhelm Hansen, 1969.
Ohana, Maurice. *Etudes chorégraphiques*. Mainz: B. Schott's Söhne, 1969.
Partch, Harry. *U.S. Highball*. Manuscript, 1955. Sousa Archives and Center for American Music, University of Illinois, Urbana–Champaign.
Ptaszynska, Marta. *Siderals*. King of Prussia, PA: Presser, 1977.
———. *Space Model*. King of Prussia, PA: Presser, 1975.
Reich, Steve. *Drumming*. New York: Hendon Music, 1971.
———. *Piano Phase*. London: Universal Edition, 1980.
Roldan, Amadeo. *Ritmicas*. New York: Southern Music Pub., 1967.
Rouse, Christopher. *Der gerettete Alberich*. New York: Hendon Music, 1997.
Russell, William. *Fugue*. San Francisco: New Music, 1933.
———. *Three Dance Movements*. San Francisco: New Music, 1936.
Schäffer, Boguslaw. *Constructions for Vibraphone Solo*. Kraków: PWM Edition, 1974.
Serocki, Kazimierz. *Continuum*. Kraków: PWM Edition, 1968.
Shostakovich, Dimitri. *The Nose*. Vienna: Universal Edition, 1970.
Smith, Stuart Saunders. *Links*. Sharon, VT: Smith Publications, 1974.
Stockhausen, Karlheinz. *Mikrophonie I*. London: Universal Edition, 1964.
———. *Musik im Bauch*. Kürten, Germany: Stockhausen Verlag, 1975.
———. *Nr. 12. Kontakte*. London: Universal Edition, 1966.
———. *Refrain*. London: Universal Edition, 1961.
———. *Zyklus*. London: Universal Edition, 1961.
Strang, Gerald. *Percussion Music*. San Francisco: New Music, 1936.
Stravinsky, Igor. *Histoire du soldat*. London: Chester Music, 1987, 1992.
———. *Le Sacre du printemps*. London: Boosey & Hawkes, 1912, 1921.
Takemitsu, Toru. *Rain Tree*. Tokyo: Schott Japan, 1981.
Tcherepnin, Alexander. *"Percussion Movement"* from *Symphony No. 1*. Bryn Mawr, PA: Presser, 1973.
Tenney, James. *Having Never Written a Note for Percussion*. Baltimore: Smith Publications, 1997.
———. *Three Pieces for Drum Quartet*. Toronto: Caveat Music Pub., 1982.
Thärichen, Werner. *Konzert für Pauken und Orchester*. Berlin: Bote & Bock, 1954.
Tomasi, Henri. *Concert Asiatique*. Paris: Alphonse Leduc, 1953.
Udow, Michael. *The Shattered Mirror*. Longmont, CO: Equilibrium Press, 1998.
———. *Understanding*. Chicago: Media Press, 1970.
Varèse, Edgard. *Amériques*. Milan: Ricordi, 1997.
———. *Arcana*. New York: Franco Colombo, 1964.
———. *Déserts*. New York: Ricordi, 1959.
———. *Hyperprism*. Milan: Ricordi, 1986.
———. *Intégrales*. Milan: Ricordi, 1980.

———. *Ionisation*. New York: Colfranc Music, 1934.
Wuorinen, Charles. *Invention for Percussion Quintet*. New York: Music for Percussion, 1962.
———. *Janissary Music*. New York: C. F. Peters, 1967.
———. *Prelude and Fugue for 4 Percussionists*. New York: Music for Percussion, 1956.
Xenakis, Iannis. *Persephassa*. New York: Éditions Salabert, 1970.
———. *Psappha*. New York: Éditions Salabert, 1976.
———. *Rebonds*. New York: Éditions Salabert, 1991.

INDEX

Page numbers in italic refer to figures.

THOMAS SIWE is a professor emeritus of music at the University of Illinois at Urbana-Champaign. He is the author of *Percussion: A Course of Study for the Future Band and Orchestra Director* and *Ten Hall of Fame Snare Drum Solos,* and a member of the Percussive Arts Society's Hall of Fame.

Music in American Life

Only a Miner: Studies in Recorded Coal-Mining Songs *Archie Green*
Great Day Coming: Folk Music and the American Left *R. Serge Denisoff*
John Philip Sousa: A Descriptive Catalog of His Works *Paul E. Bierley*
The Hell-Bound Train: A Cowboy Songbook *Glenn Ohrlin*
Oh, Didn't He Ramble: The Life Story of Lee Collins, as Told to Mary Collins *Edited by Frank J. Gillis and John W. Miner*
American Labor Songs of the Nineteenth Century *Philip S. Foner*
Stars of Country Music: Uncle Dave Macon to Johnny Rodriguez *Edited by Bill C. Malone and Judith McCulloh*
Git Along, Little Dogies: Songs and Songmakers of the American West *John I. White*
A Texas-Mexican *Cancionero*: Folksongs of the Lower Border *Américo Paredes*
San Antonio Rose: The Life and Music of Bob Wills *Charles R. Townsend*
Early Downhome Blues: A Musical and Cultural Analysis *Jeff Todd Titon*
An Ives Celebration: Papers and Panels of the Charles Ives Centennial Festival-Conference *Edited by H. Wiley Hitchcock and Vivian Perlis*
Sinful Tunes and Spirituals: Black Folk Music to the Civil War *Dena J. Epstein*
Joe Scott, the Woodsman-Songmaker *Edward D. Ives*
Jimmie Rodgers: The Life and Times of America's Blue Yodeler *Nolan Porterfield*
Early American Music Engraving and Printing: A History of Music Publishing in America from 1787 to 1825, with Commentary on Earlier and Later Practices *Richard J. Wolfe*
Sing a Sad Song: The Life of Hank Williams *Roger M. Williams*
Long Steel Rail: The Railroad in American Folksong *Norm Cohen*
Resources of American Music History: A Directory of Source Materials from Colonial Times to World War II *D. W. Krummel, Jean Geil, Doris J. Dyen, and Deane L. Root*
Tenement Songs: The Popular Music of the Jewish Immigrants *Mark Slobin*
Ozark Folksongs *Vance Randolph; edited and abridged by Norm Cohen*
Oscar Sonneck and American Music *Edited by William Lichtenwanger*
Bluegrass Breakdown: The Making of the Old Southern Sound *Robert Cantwell*
Bluegrass: A History *Neil V. Rosenberg*
Music at the White House: A History of the American Spirit *Elise K. Kirk*
Red River Blues: The Blues Tradition in the Southeast *Bruce Bastin*
Good Friends and Bad Enemies: Robert Winslow Gordon and the Study of American Folksong *Debora Kodish*
Fiddlin' Georgia Crazy: Fiddlin' John Carson, His Real World, and the World of His Songs *Gene Wiggins*
America's Music: From the Pilgrims to the Present (rev. 3d ed.) *Gilbert Chase*
Secular Music in Colonial Annapolis: The Tuesday Club, 1745–56 *John Barry Talley*
Bibliographical Handbook of American Music *D. W. Krummel*
Goin' to Kansas City *Nathan W. Pearson Jr.*
"Susanna," "Jeanie," and "The Old Folks at Home": The Songs of Stephen C. Foster from His Time to Ours (2d ed.) *William W. Austin*

Songprints: The Musical Experience of Five Shoshone Women *Judith Vander*
"Happy in the Service of the Lord": Afro-American Gospel Quartets in Memphis *Kip Lornell*
Paul Hindemith in the United States *Luther Noss*
"My Song Is My Weapon": People's Songs, American Communism, and the Politics of Culture, 1930–50 *Robbie Lieberman*
Chosen Voices: The Story of the American Cantorate *Mark Slobin*
Theodore Thomas: America's Conductor and Builder of Orchestras, 1835–1905 *Ezra Schabas*
"The Whorehouse Bells Were Ringing" and Other Songs Cowboys Sing *Collected and edited by Guy Logsdon*
Crazeology: The Autobiography of a Chicago Jazzman *Bud Freeman, as Told to Robert Wolf*
Discoursing Sweet Music: Brass Bands and Community Life in Turn-of-the-Century Pennsylvania *Kenneth Kreitner*
Mormonism and Music: A History *Michael Hicks*
Voices of the Jazz Age: Profiles of Eight Vintage Jazzmen *Chip Deffaa*
Pickin' on Peachtree: A History of Country Music in Atlanta, Georgia *Wayne W. Daniel*
Bitter Music: Collected Journals, Essays, Introductions, and Librettos *Harry Partch; edited by Thomas McGeary*
Ethnic Music on Records: A Discography of Ethnic Recordings Produced in the United States, 1893 to 1942 *Richard K. Spottswood*
Downhome Blues Lyrics: An Anthology from the Post–World War II Era *Jeff Todd Titon*
Ellington: The Early Years *Mark Tucker*
Chicago Soul *Robert Pruter*
That Half-Barbaric Twang: The Banjo in American Popular Culture *Karen Linn*
Hot Man: The Life of Art Hodes *Art Hodes and Chadwick Hansen*
The Erotic Muse: American Bawdy Songs (2d ed.) *Ed Cray*
Barrio Rhythm: Mexican American Music in Los Angeles *Steven Loza*
The Creation of Jazz: Music, Race, and Culture in Urban America *Burton W. Peretti*
Charles Martin Loeffler: A Life Apart in Music *Ellen Knight*
Club Date Musicians: Playing the New York Party Circuit *Bruce A. MacLeod*
Opera on the Road: Traveling Opera Troupes in the United States, 1825–60 *Katherine K. Preston*
The Stonemans: An Appalachian Family and the Music That Shaped Their Lives *Ivan M. Tribe*
Transforming Tradition: Folk Music Revivals Examined *Edited by Neil V. Rosenberg*
The Crooked Stovepipe: Athapaskan Fiddle Music and Square Dancing in Northeast Alaska and Northwest Canada *Craig Mishler*
Traveling the High Way Home: Ralph Stanley and the World of Traditional Bluegrass Music *John Wright*
Carl Ruggles: Composer, Painter, and Storyteller *Marilyn Ziffrin*
Never without a Song: The Years and Songs of Jennie Devlin, 1865–1952 *Katharine D. Newman*

The Hank Snow Story *Hank Snow, with Jack Ownbey and Bob Burris*
Milton Brown and the Founding of Western Swing *Cary Ginell, with special assistance from Roy Lee Brown*
Santiago de Murcia's "Códice Saldívar No. 4": A Treasury of Secular Guitar Music from Baroque Mexico *Craig H. Russell*
The Sound of the Dove: Singing in Appalachian Primitive Baptist Churches *Beverly Bush Patterson*
Heartland Excursions: Ethnomusicological Reflections on Schools of Music *Bruno Nettl*
Doowop: The Chicago Scene *Robert Pruter*
Blue Rhythms: Six Lives in Rhythm and Blues *Chip Deffaa*
Shoshone Ghost Dance Religion: Poetry Songs and Great Basin Context *Judith Vander*
Go Cat Go! Rockabilly Music and Its Makers *Craig Morrison*
'Twas Only an Irishman's Dream: The Image of Ireland and the Irish in American Popular Song Lyrics, 1800–1920 *William H. A. Williams*
Democracy at the Opera: Music, Theater, and Culture in New York City, 1815–60 *Karen Ahlquist*
Fred Waring and the Pennsylvanians *Virginia Waring*
Woody, Cisco, and Me: Seamen Three in the Merchant Marine *Jim Longhi*
Behind the Burnt Cork Mask: Early Blackface Minstrelsy and Antebellum American Popular Culture *William J. Mahar*
Going to Cincinnati: A History of the Blues in the Queen City *Steven C. Tracy*
Pistol Packin' Mama: Aunt Molly Jackson and the Politics of Folksong *Shelly Romalis*
Sixties Rock: Garage, Psychedelic, and Other Satisfactions *Michael Hicks*
The Late Great Johnny Ace and the Transition from R&B to Rock 'n' Roll *James M. Salem*
Tito Puente and the Making of Latin Music *Steven Loza*
Juilliard: A History *Andrea Olmstead*
Understanding Charles Seeger, Pioneer in American Musicology *Edited by Bell Yung and Helen Rees*
Mountains of Music: West Virginia Traditional Music from *Goldenseal* *Edited by John Lilly*
Alice Tully: An Intimate Portrait *Albert Fuller*
A Blues Life *Henry Townsend, as told to Bill Greensmith*
Long Steel Rail: The Railroad in American Folksong (2d ed.) *Norm Cohen*
The Golden Age of Gospel *Text by Horace Clarence Boyer; photography by Lloyd Yearwood*
Aaron Copland: The Life and Work of an Uncommon Man *Howard Pollack*
Louis Moreau Gottschalk *S. Frederick Starr*
Race, Rock, and Elvis *Michael T. Bertrand*
Theremin: Ether Music and Espionage *Albert Glinsky*
Poetry and Violence: The Ballad Tradition of Mexico's Costa Chica *John H. McDowell*
The Bill Monroe Reader *Edited by Tom Ewing*
Music in Lubavitcher Life *Ellen Koskoff*
Zarzuela: Spanish Operetta, American Stage *Janet L. Sturman*
Bluegrass Odyssey: A Documentary in Pictures and Words, 1966–86 *Carl Fleischhauer and Neil V. Rosenberg*
That Old-Time Rock & Roll: A Chronicle of an Era, 1954–63 *Richard Aquila*

Labor's Troubadour *Joe Glazer*
American Opera *Elise K. Kirk*
Don't Get above Your Raisin': Country Music and the Southern Working Class *Bill C. Malone*
John Alden Carpenter: A Chicago Composer *Howard Pollack*
Heartbeat of the People: Music and Dance of the Northern Pow-wow *Tara Browner*
My Lord, What a Morning: An Autobiography *Marian Anderson*
Marian Anderson: A Singer's Journey *Allan Keiler*
Charles Ives Remembered: An Oral History *Vivian Perlis*
Henry Cowell, Bohemian *Michael Hicks*
Rap Music and Street Consciousness *Cheryl L. Keyes*
Louis Prima *Garry Boulard*
Marian McPartland's Jazz World: All in Good Time *Marian McPartland*
Robert Johnson: Lost and Found *Barry Lee Pearson and Bill McCulloch*
Bound for America: Three British Composers *Nicholas Temperley*
Lost Sounds: Blacks and the Birth of the Recording Industry, 1890–1919 *Tim Brooks*
Burn, Baby! BURN! The Autobiography of Magnificent Montague *Magnificent Montague with Bob Baker*
Way Up North in Dixie: A Black Family's Claim to the Confederate Anthem *Howard L. Sacks and Judith Rose Sacks*
The Bluegrass Reader *Edited by Thomas Goldsmith*
Colin McPhee: Composer in Two Worlds *Carol J. Oja*
Robert Johnson, Mythmaking, and Contemporary American Culture *Patricia R. Schroeder*
Composing a World: Lou Harrison, Musical Wayfarer *Leta E. Miller and Fredric Lieberman*
Fritz Reiner, Maestro and Martinet *Kenneth Morgan*
That Toddlin' Town: Chicago's White Dance Bands and Orchestras, 1900–1950 *Charles A. Sengstock Jr.*
Dewey and Elvis: The Life and Times of a Rock 'n' Roll Deejay *Louis Cantor*
Come Hither to Go Yonder: Playing Bluegrass with Bill Monroe *Bob Black*
Chicago Blues: Portraits and Stories *David Whiteis*
The Incredible Band of John Philip Sousa *Paul E. Bierley*
"Maximum Clarity" and Other Writings on Music *Ben Johnston; edited by Bob Gilmore*
Staging Tradition: John Lair and Sarah Gertrude Knott *Michael Ann Williams*
Homegrown Music: Discovering Bluegrass *Stephanie P. Ledgin*
Tales of a Theatrical Guru *Danny Newman*
The Music of Bill Monroe *Neil V. Rosenberg and Charles K. Wolfe*
Pressing On: The Roni Stoneman Story *Roni Stoneman, as told to Ellen Wright*
Together Let Us Sweetly Live *Jonathan C. David, with photographs by Richard Holloway*
Live Fast, Love Hard: The Faron Young Story *Diane Diekman*
Air Castle of the South: WSM Radio and the Making of Music City *Craig P. Havighurst*
Traveling Home: Sacred Harp Singing and American Pluralism *Kiri Miller*
Where Did Our Love Go? The Rise and Fall of the Motown Sound *Nelson George*

Lonesome Cowgirls and Honky-Tonk Angels: The Women of Barn Dance Radio *Kristine M. McCusker*

California Polyphony: Ethnic Voices, Musical Crossroads *Mina Yang*

The Never-Ending Revival: Rounder Records and the Folk Alliance *Michael F. Scully*

Sing It Pretty: A Memoir *Bess Lomax Hawes*

Working Girl Blues: The Life and Music of Hazel Dickens *Hazel Dickens and Bill C. Malone*

Charles Ives Reconsidered *Gayle Sherwood Magee*

The Hayloft Gang: The Story of the National Barn Dance *Edited by Chad Berry*

Country Music Humorists and Comedians *Loyal Jones*

Record Makers and Breakers: Voices of the Independent Rock 'n' Roll Pioneers *John Broven*

Music of the First Nations: Tradition and Innovation in Native North America *Edited by Tara Browner*

Cafe Society: The Wrong Place for the Right People *Barney Josephson, with Terry Trilling-Josephson*

George Gershwin: An Intimate Portrait *Walter Rimler*

Life Flows On in Endless Song: Folk Songs and American History *Robert V. Wells*

I Feel a Song Coming On: The Life of Jimmy McHugh *Alyn Shipton*

King of the Queen City: The Story of King Records *Jon Hartley Fox*

Long Lost Blues: Popular Blues in America, 1850–1920 *Peter C. Muir*

Hard Luck Blues: Roots Music Photographs from the Great Depression *Rich Remsberg*

Restless Giant: The Life and Times of Jean Aberbach and Hill and Range Songs *Bar Biszick-Lockwood*

Champagne Charlie and Pretty Jemima: Variety Theater in the Nineteenth Century *Gillian M. Rodger*

Sacred Steel: Inside an African American Steel Guitar Tradition *Robert L. Stone*

Gone to the Country: The New Lost City Ramblers and the Folk Music Revival *Ray Allen*

The Makers of the Sacred Harp *David Warren Steel with Richard H. Hulan*

Woody Guthrie, American Radical *Will Kaufman*

George Szell: A Life of Music *Michael Charry*

Bean Blossom: The Brown County Jamboree and Bill Monroe's Bluegrass Festivals *Thomas A. Adler*

Crowe on the Banjo: The Music Life of J. D. Crowe *Marty Godbey*

Twentieth Century Drifter: The Life of Marty Robbins *Diane Diekman*

Henry Mancini: Reinventing Film Music *John Caps*

The Beautiful Music All Around Us: Field Recordings and the American Experience *Stephen Wade*

Then Sings My Soul: The Culture of Southern Gospel Music *Douglas Harrison*

The Accordion in the Americas: Klezmer, Polka, Tango, Zydeco, and More! *Edited by Helena Simonett*

Bluegrass Bluesman: A Memoir *Josh Graves; edited by Fred Bartenstein*

One Woman in a Hundred: Edna Phillips and the Philadelphia Orchestra *Mary Sue Welsh*

The Great Orchestrator: Arthur Judson and American Arts Management *James M. Doering*
Charles Ives in the Mirror: American Histories of an Iconic Composer *David C. Paul*
Southern Soul-Blues *David Whiteis*
Sweet Air: Modernism, Regionalism, and American Popular Song *Edward P. Comentale*
Pretty Good for a Girl: Women in Bluegrass *Murphy Hicks Henry*
Sweet Dreams: The World of Patsy Cline *Warren R. Hofstra*
William Sidney Mount and the Creolization of American Culture *Christopher J. Smith*
Bird: The Life and Music of Charlie Parker *Chuck Haddix*
Making the March King: John Philip Sousa's Washington Years, 1854–1893 *Patrick Warfield*
In It for the Long Run *Jim Rooney*
Pioneers of the Blues Revival *Steve Cushing*
Roots of the Revival: American and British Folk Music in the 1950s *Ronald D. Cohen and Rachel Clare Donaldson*
Blues All Day Long: The Jimmy Rogers Story *Wayne Everett Goins*
Yankee Twang: Country and Western Music in New England *Clifford R. Murphy*
The Music of the Stanley Brothers *Gary B. Reid*
Hawaiian Music in Motion: Mariners, Missionaries, and Minstrels *James Revell Carr*
Sounds of the New Deal: The Federal Music Project in the West *Peter Gough*
The Mormon Tabernacle Choir: A Biography *Michael Hicks*
The Man That Got Away: The Life and Songs of Harold Arlen *Walter Rimler*
A City Called Heaven: Chicago and the Birth of Gospel Music *Robert M. Marovich*
Blues Unlimited: Essential Interviews from the Original *Blues* Magazine *Edited by Bill Greensmith, Mike Rowe, and Mark Camarigg*
Hoedowns, Reels, and Frolics: Roots and Branches of Southern Appalachian Dance *Phil Jamison*
Fannie Bloomfield-Zeisler: The Life and Times of a Piano Virtuoso *Beth Abelson Macleod*
Cybersonic Arts: Adventures in American New Music *Gordon Mumma; edited with commentary by Michelle Fillion*
The Magic of Beverly Sills *Nancy Guy*
Waiting for Buddy Guy *Alan Harper*
Harry T. Burleigh: From the Spiritual to the Harlem Renaissance *Jean E. Snyder*
Music in the Age of Anxiety: American Music in the Fifties *James Wierzbicki*
Jazzing: New York City's Unseen Scene *Thomas H. Greenland*
A Cole Porter Companion *Edited by Don M. Randel, Matthew Shaftel, and Susan Forscher Weiss*
Foggy Mountain Troubadour: The Life and Music of Curly Seckler *Penny Parsons*
Blue Rhythm Fantasy: Big Band Jazz Arranging in the Swing Era *John Wriggle*
Bill Clifton: America's Bluegrass Ambassador to the World *Bill C. Malone*
Chinatown Opera Theater in North America *Nancy Yunhwa Rao*
The Elocutionists: Women, Music, and the Spoken Word *Marian Wilson Kimber*
May Irwin: Singing, Shouting, and the Shadow of Minstrelsy *Sharon Ammen*
Peggy Seeger: A Life of Music, Love, and Politics *Jean R. Freedman*

Charles Ives's *Concord*: Essays after a Sonata *Kyle Gann*
Don't Give Your Heart to a Rambler: My Life with Jimmy Martin, the King of Bluegrass *Barbara Martin Stephens*
Libby Larsen: Composing an American Life *Denise Von Glahn*
George Szell's Reign: Behind the Scenes with the Cleveland Orchestra *Marcia Hansen Kraus*
Just One of the Boys: Female-to-Male Cross-Dressing on the American Variety Stage *Gillian M. Rodger*
Spirituals and the Birth of a Black Entertainment Industry *Sandra Jean Graham*
Right to the Juke Joint: A Personal History of American Music *Patrick B. Mullen*
Bluegrass Generation: A Memoir *Neil V. Rosenberg*
Pioneers of the Blues Revival, Expanded Second Edition *Steve Cushing*
Banjo Roots and Branches *Edited by Robert Winans*
Bill Monroe: The Life and Music of the Blue Grass Man *Tom Ewing*
Dixie Dewdrop: The Uncle Dave Macon Story *Michael D. Doubler*
Los Romeros: Royal Family of the Spanish Guitar *Walter Aaron Clark*
Transforming Women's Education: Liberal Arts and Music in Female Seminaries *Jewel A. Smith*
Rethinking American Music *Edited by Tara Browner and Thomas L. Riis*
Leonard Bernstein and the Language of Jazz *Katherine Baber*
Dancing Revolution: Bodies, Space, and Sound in American Cultural History *Christopher J. Smith*
Peggy Glanville-Hicks: Composer and Critic *Suzanne Robinson*
Mormons, Musical Theater, and Belonging in America *Jake Johnson*
Blues Legacy: Tradition and Innovation in Chicago *David Whiteis*
Blues Before Sunrise 2: Interviews from the Chicago Scene *Steve Cushing*
The Cashaway Psalmody: Transatlantic Religion and Music in Colonial Carolina *Stephen A. Marini*
Earl Scruggs and Foggy Mountain Breakdown: The Making of an American Classic *Thomas Goldsmith*
A Guru's Journey: Pandit Chitresh Das and Indian Classical Dance in Diaspora *Sarah Morelli*
Unsettled Scores: Politics, Hollywood, and the Film Music of Aaron Copland and Hanns Eisler *Sally Bick*
Hillbilly Maidens, Okies, and Cowgirls: Women's Country Music, 1930–1960 *Stephanie Vander Wel*
Always the Queen: The Denise LaSalle Story *Denise LaSalle with David Whiteis*
Artful Noise: Percussion Literature in the Twentieth Century *Thomas Siwe*

The University of Illinois Press
is a founding member of the
Association of University Presses.

University of Illinois Press
1325 South Oak Street
Champaign, IL 61820-6903
www.press.uillinois.edu